The
Etablissements
de Saint Louis

The Etablissements de Saint Louis

Thirteenth-Century Law Texts from Tours, Orléans, and Paris

Translated and with an Introduction by
F. R. P. AKEHURST

PENN

University of Pennsylvania Press

Philadelphia

The Etablissements de Saint Louis : thirteenth-century law texts from Tours,
Orléans, and Paris / translated and with an introduction by F. R. P. Akehurst.
    p.   cm. — (Middle Ages series)
  Includes bibliographical references and index.
  ISBN 0-8122-3350-6 (alk. paper)
  1. Etablissements de Saint Louis. 2. Law—France—History. 3. Customary
law—France—History. 4. Law, Medieval. I. Akehurst, F. R. P. II. Series.
KJV263.E86 1996
340.3'0944—dc20   96-20334
CIP

For my children
Mary and Colin

Contents

Abbreviations   xvii

Introduction   xxi

The Laws of Saint Louis   1

Prologue   3

BOOK I
THE RULES OF PROCEDURE IN THE CHÂTELET   7

1. The first rubric of the first case is: The duties of the
   provost.   7
2. On forcing witnesses to give testimony in the provost's
   court.   10
3. On forbidding judicial battles and producing valid proof.   10
4. On informing the plaintiff about the penalty and on
   contesting witnesses.   11
5. These are the cases of high justice of barons.   12
6. On appealing against a man for serfdom in the secular
   court.   13
7. On reversing a judgment in the king's court.   13
8. On appealing against your lord for default of judgment.   14
9. On punishing false witnesses.   14

THE CUSTOMS OF TOURAINE AND ANJOU   15

10. On gifts by a gentleman to his children, and how they
    should distribute the estate if the father dies without
    making provisions.   15

11. On making partitions.   16
12. On distributions made among sisters after the father's
        death.   17
13. On the marriage gift given at the church door and
        keeping it for life after the heir has cried or yelled.   17
14. On promiscuous gentlewomen.   18
15. On having a partition as the oldest son.   18
16. On purchased or otherwise acquired real property.   18
17. On [a gentlewoman] paying her husband's debts.   18
18. On the rights of gentlewomen and on keeping their
        dower in good condition.   19
19. On keeping custodianship lands in good condition until
        the heir comes of age.   19
20. Suits on land.   20
21. On gifts to a [new] knight [or] as a marriage gift.   20
22. On distributing property descended from grandfathers
        and grandmothers.   20
23. On lateral inheritance from brothers.   21
24. On relief paid for land held in coholdership.   21
25. On marrying a commoner.   21
26. On distributing a barony.   22
27. On high justice in a barony; on murder, rape, and
        homicide of pregnant women [ancis].   22
28. On summoning and banishing an offender and coming
        and destroying property after the banishment.   23
29. On suspicion and summonses by a judge in the secular
        court.   24
30. On fights.   24
31. On requesting a guaranteed peace [asseürement] in the
        secular court, and on broken truces.   25
32. On stealing an animal or a horse, and loss of limb for
        the offense.   26
33. On high justice in the matter of treachery by a
        household member.   26
34. On the jurisdiction of a [lower] vassal [vavassor].   26
35. On women who consort with thieves or murderers.   26
36. On going along with murderers and thieves.   27
37. On accomplices of murderers.   27
38. On punishing suspicious persons on the initiative of the
        provost.   27
39. On women's misadventure and a repeat thereof.   28
40. On the intention of homicide without more.   28

41. On threats and refusing to give a guaranteed peace
    before the judge, and on requesting [a guaranteed
    peace] from the sovereign, maintaining the rights
    [*droit faisant*] of the parties.   28
42. On the power of [lower] vassals to administer justice.   29
43. On releasing thieves and clearing oneself of suspicion. 30
44. On requesting jurisdiction and cognizance, according to
    correct procedure, and leading off by the hand a
    man under one's jurisdiction, to one's court,
    honestly.   30
45. On arresting and pursuing [*suite*] murderers and thieves. 31
46. On coholders [of fiefs].   32
47. On holding [fiefs] as coholders.   32
48. On demonstrating your kinship to your lord, and on
    holding as a coholder without giving a service horse
    [*roncin de service*].   33
49. How a man should behave toward his lord when [the
    lord] threatens him with losing his land.   33
50. On showing your fief to your liege lord.   34
51. On cutting wood in a forest.   35
52. On [a gentleman's] laying hands on his lord with evil
    intent, and on lawfully defending his lineage against
    his rightful liege lord without losing his fief.   36
53. On summoning your vassal to make war on the king.   36
54. On resisting arrest by your lord, giving false measure,
    and fishing in [his private] fish pond, and hunting
    and catching rabbits in [his] game preserve, and
    lying with [his wife or daughter] by force.   37
55. On deflowering by force a woman who is in
    custodianship or guardianship.   37
56. On [a lord's] refusing a hearing and the judgment of his
    court to his liegeman and others.   38
57. On standing an honest watch at your liege lord's castle. 38
58. On gentlemen's personal property when they lose it
    [*perdent leur propre*].   38
59. On a complaint made in the king's court against your
    lord, without paying a fine to your lord.   39
60. On inspections made by a judge.   39
61. On the king's law [*Du droit au prince*].   40
62. On thieves or murderers.   40
63. The tax-free status [*franchise*] of a gentleman.   41
64. The tax-free status of officers [*sergant*].   41

65. On summoning vassals to serve in the king's army.   41
66. On taking the fruits of the land from a lord as his relief
        [*rachat*], and a woman's relief when she marries.   43
67. On giving security to your liege lord because of the
        possibility of marriage [of your daughter], and on
        [the family's] doing the best and most honorable
        thing for the young lady.   43
68. On keeping fiefs without detriment, and on the gift of a
        gentleman.   44
69. On novel disseisin and keeping things safely while
        maintaining the rights of the parties, and on
        awarding costs and damages.   45
70. On a default after a court inspection.   46
71. On assigning of court dates by a judge.   47
72. On summoning your vassal and entering your lord's
        faith without default.   48
73. On a decision given in a judgment.   49
74. On repaying damages.   50
75. On wrongs and default of judgment.   51
76. On the right of a baron to be judged by his peers.   51
77. On the privilege of a knight.   51
78. On the age when a child need not answer when in the
        care of a custodian, and on proving your age.   52
79. On calculating [*conter*] your kinship and demonstrating
        it to your lord.   53
80. On service as a coholder.   53
81. On holding in coholdership without giving any service
        to a lord.   54
82. On holding a custodianship on the proper terms [*en
        bonne estance*] without doing homage to the lord.   54
83. On [appeal for] false judgment or accepting the
        judgment as good and valid.   55
84. On seeking a hearing from the king.   55
85. How to request amendment of a judgment, and on
        requesting it on the same day.   56
86. On appealing against your lord for false judgment.   57
87. On a [judicial] battle between a knight and a
        commoner.   58
88. On breaking out of prison.   58
89. On jurisdiction over clerks, and on handing over
        crusaders to Holy Church.   58
90. On punishing heretics and unbelievers.   59

91. On punishing usurers. 59

92. On foreigners and suicides. 60

93. On persons who die unconfessed. 60

94. On finding [buried] treasure [*fortune*]. 60

95. On vouching your warrantor [*garent*] for something
    stolen. 61

96. On reimbursement of costs and expenses for a res
    judicata. 62

97. On breach of seisin and on refusing [to swear] an oath. 63

98. On seizing and holding a commoner's lodging. 64

99. On land on which a gentleman must pay a tax [*heritage
    taillable*]. 64

100. On foreigners. 65

101. On how a bastard's estate passes. 65

102. On the sale of land by a bastard. 65

103. On bastards and *terrage* lands [*terres a terrage*]. 66

104. On measuring lands held for quitrent [*censives*]. 66

105. On failure to pay service dues, and on seizure for lack
     of a vassal. 67

106. On legal excuses [*essoine*] because of sickness, and on
     appointing your son as your attorney. 68

107. On a plaintiff who offends while awaiting the court
     date. 69

108. On appealing against a man for murder or treachery
     [*traïson*], without release and without bail, and on
     detention [under identical conditions]. 70

109. On various offenses and various suits. 71

110. On requesting a judicial partition by making a
     judgment [*droit faisant*]. 71

111. On millers and mills. 72

112. How you should treat the coholder of a mill. 73

113. On the vassal's rights and the baron's rights. 74

114. On milling at the lord's mill. 74

115. On the general jurisdiction of barons over the fiefs
     within their castellanies, and on doing homage and
     obeissance for fiefs. 75

116. On the king's rights to a debt admitted or proved to be
     owed to him. 75

117. On the king's gift "to him and to his heirs born of a
     legal marriage." 76

118. On gifts between a man and his wife. 77

119. On marriage gifts. 77

120. On the gift to your brother of an homage [*foi*] as a
     coholdership, and on doing two homages for one
     fief.   78
121. On the custodianship of a fief, and on [not] giving the
     custodianship of a child to a suspicious person for
     fear of the dangers that could arise.   79
122. How you should discharge [*nantir*] your surety, and
     on suing your principal debtor before having
     recourse to the surety.   80
123. On appealing against a person for a default, and on
     losing seisin after an inspection.   82
124. On a legal excuse [*essoigne*] of sickness, and being
     summoned to the sovereign's court.   82
125. How you make reimbursement for damage caused by
     your animal and pay a fine [*droit faisant*].   83
126. On a suit against the father which devolves to the heir,
     and on proving your debts.   84
127. On forcing an excommunicated person to make
     amends, and on subsequent punishment.   84
128. On contracts in contemplation of marriage.   85
129. On gifts to the church.   86
130. On warranting as coholders, and on doing service to
     your lord.   86
131. On running water.   87
132. On a complaint in the baron's court by a king's man.   87
133. On Jews.   88
134. On knighthood.   88
135. How you should give a service horse [*roncin de servise*]
     to your lord.   88
136. On dividing among brothers what is inherited from
     [their] father and mother.   89
137. On holding dower property in good condition, and
     suing on it.   91
138. On partitions where boundaries are marked by a judge,
     and on being your own judge.   91
139. On distribution among children.   92
140. On [lateral] inheritances with no heir.   92
141. On the custodian of a commoner.   93
142. On appealing for false judgment.   93
143. On a marriage between a poor woman and a rich man.   94
144. On prodigal [*fous*] children.   94
145. On making improvements on another's land without
     reimbursement.   95

146. On the coming of age of commoners.   95
147. On giving faith as a commoner [*De foi en vilenage*].   96
148. On avoiding tolls.   96
149. On avoiding the toll and being arrested outside the
     boundaries.   96
150. On a merchant traveling by water.   97
151. On false measures and false cloth [measure].   97
152. On a judgment for false dealing in cloth.   97
153. On married women merchants, and on answering
     married women merchants [in court].   97
154. On calling a man dishonest [*desloial*], or the same
     [slander] for a woman.   98
155. On having your witness [*garant*] at a hearing.   98
156. On striking your lord with evil intent.   99
157. On striking a judge or a provost or an officer.   99
158. On breaking the lord's seisin [trespassing] and fishing
     in his ponds.   99
159. On seizure [*saisine*].   100
160. On sales taxes [*ventes*].   100
161. On redemption by the family, and on challenging sales
     [*ventes*] within a year and a day.   100
162. On offering money for a redemption before a judge,
     and on improvements made after the offer.   101
163. On recovering your proven costs at a redemption.   102
164. On redemption by the lord in the absence of family.   102
165. On redeeming your land without paying sales tax.   103
166. On swearing to honest costs and expenses in a
     redemption.   103
167. On postponement of sales tax by a judge.   104
168. On redemption among brothers and sisters.   104
169. On paying your dues on a day certain.   105
170. On taking *terrage* lands for cultivation by the lord.   105
171. On appealing against a man for murder or treachery
     [*traïson*].   105
172. On lost bees, and following them without losing sight
     of them, on your oath.   106
173. On a woman's dower rights; on enforcing the
     ecclesiastical judge's orders; and on things done out
     of fear of your husband and by coercion.   107
174. On a [judicial] battle between brothers.   108
175. On having a judicial battle fought by champions in a
     murder case, on account of an obvious infirmity [of
     a party].   108

BOOK 2
THE CUSTOMS OF THE ORLÉANS DISTRICT   113

1. Prologue.   113
2. On arresting offenders in the execution of the crime, and
     proving the same.   115
3. On the king's jurisdiction of some dispute between
     parties who have to make a complaint against the
     king [*marchir au roi*].   116
4. On requesting seisin as the nearest relative of the heir,
     and on making an objection and reserving rights
     according to the practice in the baron's court.   116
5. On requesting a reclamation [*recreance*].   118
6. On refusing a reclamation according to the custom in the
     district.   118
7. On requesting seisin without pleading when not in
     possession [*despoilliés*].   119
8. On cases of high justice, without giving property back or
     allowing bail, and on summoning parties without
     delay.   119
9. On the duties of the attorney; on continuance for a legal
     excuse [*contremant de essoigne*]; and on decertifying
     an attorney and on appointing an attorney.   120
10. On confirming a bail by a judgment.   122
11. On appealing against a man for default after the
     inspection day.   123
12. On appealing against a man for murder or treachery. 124
13. On appealing against a man for larceny, and on naming
     the stolen object [*larrecin*].   125
14. On being summoned by the king and declaring that you
     are in the jurisdiction of another lord, and on
     proving your assertion to the judge.   126
15. On the duties of the advocate, and how you should give
     a judgment; and on appealing to the sovereign's
     court for false judgment and default of judgment. 129
16. On judging honestly your men's cases; on petitioning in
     the king's court; and on appealing immediately
     without delay.   130
17. On bad reputation, and the duties of the judge, and on
     punishing offenders.   134
18. On claiming something that has been stolen, and on
     doing business wisely and without suspicion.   135

19. How you should seek your lord and enter into his faith
    [*foi*], without delay, and give him your obedience
    [*obeïssance*] as liege.   137
20. How you should ask for bail for your vassals, and on an
    inquest when the case is under the king's
    jurisdiction.   139
21. On appealing against a man for murder or treachery
    [*traïson*]; on giving an immediate answer; and on
    making a reservation to proceed in the baron's
    court, without defaulting.   141
22. On the king's rights; on holding a man in prison for his
    admitted and proven debt; on abandoning your
    property, according to the custom of the Orléans
    district; and on authorizing a sale for your debt.   142
23. On the king's commands.   143
24. On fines in the court of high justice for spilling blood
    or causing bruises.   144
25. On fines for words where no blows are struck.   145
26. On gifts by man and wife.   145
27. On being in default and resisting an officer.   146
28. On being a judge in your own suit.   146
29. On giving a guaranteed peace [*asseürement*].   147
30. On seizing your fief for default of a vassal, and on
    disavowing your lord.   147
31. On bastards and strangers; on appealing against a man
    as your serf; on forbidding persons to change the
    lord they claim to hold from; and on being free.   148
32. On asking to have a case sent down when it concerns
    those in your jurisdiction, in court [*droit faisant*]; on
    enforcing the sovereign's rulings [*fait*]; and on
    runaway serfs.   152
33. On the jurisdiction of a vassal without recall from
    memory [*recort*].   154
34. On a sentence given in mercy, and on executing a
    judgment.   156
35. On appealing against a man for treachery [*traïson*] or a
    broken truce, and on stating your legal reasons [for
    having a hired champion].   157
36. On the jurisdiction of all judges, and on cases of high
    justice.   158
37. On executing judgment in cases where fault is admitted
    and judged, and on abandoning one's possessions.   160

38. On a mounted expedition under arms made on
      another's property; and on disavowing your lord.   161

Bibliography   163
List of Topics   167
Index   171

Abbreviations

The following works are cited in the notes by the short form indicated:

Beaumanoir.   Philippe de Beaumanoir. *Coutumes de Beauvaisis*, ed. Am[édée] Salmon. 2 vols. 1899–1900. Paris: Picard, 1970. May also be consulted in: *The* Coutumes de Beauvaisis *of Philippe de Beaumanoir*, trans. F. R. P. Akehurst (Philadelphia: University of Pennsylvania Press, 1992).

In the *Corpus iuris canonici* the various books are cited as follows:

   Decr. Greg. IX.   Decretales Gregorii P. IX, ed. Emil Ludwig Richter and Emil Friedberg. Graz: Akademische Druck- und Verlagsanstalt, 1959. This is a reprint of the 1879 edition. Gregory IX's chaplain, Raymond of Peñafort, collected the decretals of Gregory IX and added them to a selection of decretals taken from five earlier compilations. The new collection was sent to the universities of Paris and Bologna in 1234. The *Decretals of Gregory IX* forms the second part of the *Corpus iuris canonici*. (I cite the page numbers from the edition as, e.g., Richter 400.)

   Decretum.   Decretum Magistri Gratiani, ed. Emil Ludwig Richter and Emil Friedberg. Graz: Akademische Druck- und Verlagsanstalt, 1959. This is a reprint of the 1879 edition. (I cite the page numbers from the edition as, e.g., Richter 400.)

In the *Corpus iuris civilis*, the various books are cited as follows:

   Cod.   Caesar Flavius Justinianus. *Codex Iustinianus*, ed. Paul Krueger. Berlin: Weidmann, 1906. (Citations in notes giving the reference to this edition will be accompanied by a page number with the name of the editor, e.g., Krueger 345.)

   Dig.   Caesar Flavius Justinianus. *The Digest of Justinian*, ed. Alan Watson (English text), and Theodor Mommsen and Paul Krueger (Latin text). 4 vols. Philadelphia: University of Pennsylvania Press, 1985. (Although the pages in this translation are continuous throughout the four volumes, I shall give

a volume number and page number in each reference, e.g.,
Watson 1:23.)

Inst.   Caesar Flavius Justinianus. *Justinian's Institutes*, ed. Paul
Krueger, trans. with an introduction by Peter Birks and Grant
McLeod. London: Duckworth, 1987. (Birks gives Krueger's
page numbers, but he also numbers consecutively throughout his own translation and the facing page Latin text. I shall
therefore give two page numbers—the first is Krueger's and
the second Birks's—separated by an equals sign, e.g., Birks
1=37.)

Coutumes de Lorris.   *Coutumes de Lorris*, ed. Ad. Tardif. Recueil de textes
pour servir à l'enseignement de l'histoire du droit. Paris: Picard,
1885.

de Laurière.   Notes by Eusèbe de Laurière in his edition of the *Etablissements de Saint Louis*, which is printed in his *Ordonnances des rois de
France de la troisième race*, vol. 1. Paris: Imprimerie Nationale, 1723.

Du Cange.   Notes by Du Cange to his edition of the *Etablissements de
Saint Louis*, which is printed in his edition of the *Histoire de S. Louis
par Jean, Sire de Joinville*. Paris: Sébastien Mabre-Cramoisy, 1668.

Etablissements.   *Les Etablissements de Saint Louis*, ed. Paul Viollet. 4 vols.
Société de l'Histoire de France. Paris: Renouard, 1881–1886.

Fontaines.   *Le conseil de Pierre de Fontaines, ou traité de l'ancienne jurisprudence française*, ed. M. A. J. Marnier. Paris: Durand, libraire and
Joubert, libraire, 1846.

Glanvill.   Ranulf de Glanvil(le). *The Treatise on the Laws and Customs
of the Realm of England Commonly called Glanvill*, ed. and trans.
G. D. G. Hall. Medieval Texts. London: Nelson, 1965.

Gruchy.   *L'ancienne coutume de Normandie*, ed. William Laurence de
Gruchy. St. Helier, Jersey, British Channel Islands: Charles le
Feuvre, 1881.

Jostice et plet.   *Li livres de Jostice et de Plet*, ed. [Pierre-Nicolas] Rapetti,
glossary by P. Chabaille. Collection de documents inédits sur
l'histoire de France publié par les soins du Ministre de l'Instruction
publique. Première série, Histoire politique, 81. Paris: Firmin
Didot, 1850.

Saint Martin.   Notes by the editor in Saint Martin, abbé de, *Les Etablissements de Saint Louis, roi de France, suivant le texte original et
rendus dans le langage actuel avec des notes*. Paris: Nyon l'aîné, 1786.

Viollet.   Textual notes, introduction, and commentary by the editor
Paul Viollet in the four-volume edition of the *Etablissements de
Saint Louis*. See *Etablissements*, above.

Textual Notations

The following notations (see Introduction) are used in the translated text:

[ ]   Enclose the Old French word found in the *Etablissements* immediately after its translation; also used by the translator to enclose explanatory words or where nouns are used to replace pronouns.

{ }   Indicates passages from the *Coutume de Touraine-Anjou* not found in any of the manuscripts of the *Etablissements*, or, accompanied by a note, Viollet's reconstructions.

⟨ ⟩   Encloses those passages Viollet has identified as being added to the text of Book 1 of the *Etablissements* by the Compiler (i.e., not original to the manuscripts of the *Coutume de Touraine-Anjou*) or which Viollet believes were added by the Compiler to Book 2 of the *Etablissements*, the *Usage d'Orlenois*. In Book 2 the identification of such passages is purely conjectural.

Introduction

IN HIS MONUMENTAL WORK on the *Spirit of the Laws*, Montesquieu asks: "Qu'est-ce donc que cette compilation que nous avons sous le nom d'*Etablissements* de Saint Louis? Qu'est-ce que ce code obscur, confus et ambigu, où l'on mêle sans cesse la jurisprudence françoise avec la loi romaine; où l'on parle comme un législateur, et où l'on voit un jurisconsulte; où l'on trouve un corps entier de jurisprudence sur tous les cas, sur tous les points du droit civil?"[1] Montesquieu had consulted the edition of Ducange and rightly found that the work called *Etablissements de Saint Louis* was not all of a piece. But he thought it was a book *on* the *Etablissements*, and not the *Etablissements* themselves.[2] As for the work being obscure, confused, and ambiguous, the reader will have to judge whether that is true. I hope that my translation has not aggravated these deficiencies, but I know that it has not done away with all of them. What is more certain is that, in spite of Montesquieu, the *Etablissements* do not contain a complete body of law.

The *Etablissements de Saint Louis*, of which this is the first English translation, were compiled soon after the middle of the thirteenth century by an unknown hand.[3] The work consists of two

1. "What is this compilation which we have under the name of the *Laws* of Saint Louis? What is this obscure, confused, and ambiguous code, where French legal material is always being mixed up with Roman law; where the text speaks like a legislator, and where we discern the work of a legal consultant; where you find a complete body of law on all kinds of cases, on all the points of civil law?" Charles-Louis de Secondat, baron de Montesquieu, *Oeuvres complètes*, 2 vols., Bibliothèque de la Pléiade (Paris: Gallimard, 1951) 2:852. (My translation.)

2. Montesquieu, 2:852.

3. Viollet points out that manuscript *D* (Montpellier, Faculty of Medicine Ms. 395) is dated June 19, 1273, which establishes the latest date by which the compiler must have finished his work (Viollet 1:2).

books. Book 1 contains one hundred and seventy-five chapters, some of them extremely short, of which the first nine are an outline of procedure as used in the Châtelet, the principal law court in Paris, and the rest a customary compilation from the Touraine-Anjou region of France, southwest of Paris. Book 2 contains only thirty-eight chapters, of which some are very long, and is a customary compilation from the region of Orléans, closer to Paris. Orléans, Tours, and Angers are all towns on the Loire river.

This patched-together book of customs never enjoyed official status, although it was copied many times and the copies found their way to many regions of France.[4] The customs of Touraine, Anjou, and the Orléanais as contained in this book probably go back decades before the *Etablissements* were compiled; some of the provisions of the Châtelet rules were quite new and changed the system of criminal justice at this time (especially the prohibition of the judicial battle). These rules were not promulgated only by means of the *Etablissements*. In spite of their unofficial status (some customary compilations *were* accepted officially), the *Etablissements de Saint Louis* are often cited by scholars as evidence of customs from the thirteenth century. As such, they find their place among other compilations such as the *Coutumes de Beauvaisis* of Philippe de Beaumanoir, the *Conseil* of Pierre de Fontaines, and the compilations that bear the name of a particular province (Brittany, Champagne, Normandy).[5]

It would not be too much to claim that the *Etablissements*, like most customaries, leave a great deal unsaid. To help the reader to understand the text, and place these customs in their context, this introduction will first give a brief sketch of the state of French law in the middle of the thirteenth century and then discuss the status of the two compilations and the nineteenth-century French edition from which the translation was made. The reader will also find at the end of the volume a list of topics by chapter and an index.

4. Viollet 1:280–394.
5. See Bibliography.

Medieval Law

Like modern law, medieval law can be divided into two broad categories: procedural and substantive.

Procedural law deals with the way the law is to be administered: it provides the rules that govern the conduct of a trial, the roles of the judge and other officers of the court, the parties (plaintiffs, defendants, and appellants), advocates, attorneys, and witnesses; it provides rules about how each phase of the trial is to proceed, what delays can be properly taken, and when a default has occurred. It also deals with proofs, punishments, and appeals.

Substantive law deals with the rules that govern people's status. A basic distinction was that between serfs and free persons. Substantive law also deals with people's conduct toward one another. It gives the rules concerning what is permitted and not permitted (crimes, contracts, private disputes, agency, etc.) and the rules that concern property, its ownership, and how it is passed from one person to another. Real property ("immovable" property, or that which produces revenue, such as land, mills, or markets) is distinguished from personal property ("movable" objects such as horses, agricultural products, or money). The procedural law and substantive law of thirteenth-century France will now each be outlined briefly in turn.

Procedural Law

It is important to understand the phases of the thirteenth-century French trial, which differed from modern procedure in certain very important ways. There was less difference in the thirteenth century than today between criminal and civil trials, since a criminal accusation required an injured plaintiff, or person with standing as we say today, and was rarely brought by the authorities. Thus, for example, if a man was murdered, an accusation had to be made by a relative or the dead man's lord or vassal.

The first step was to summon the accused or defendant. This was done by means of officers who could later testify in court that they had informed the person that he[6] must appear before the judge. The offense or subject of the trial was not necessarily announced to this person until he was actually in court. When the plaintiff and the person summoned were before the judge, the plaintiff made known his complaint. At this point, the defendant was entitled to all sorts of defenses, such as that the court had no jurisdiction over him, or that the matter had already been litigated and settled in another court, or that he wanted the judge changed because the current judge and he were in a feud, or that he was a minor and wanted a delay until he came of age. All these delaying defenses were called "dilatory" because they served only to delay the trial, not to end it (see Beaumanoir §236). There were two other kinds of delays granted: a continuance [*contremand*], for which no particular reason was needed but which lasted only a set time (say two weeks) and an adjournment [*essoine*], which had to be justified by a good reason, such as sickness or absence on the king's business, but which was for an unlimited time (*Etablissements* 1:124). These delays would probably be requested by an attorney, who would be sent to the court in place of his "client" (*Etablissements* 2:9 and see Beaumanoir, chapter 3).

When all these matters had been settled, either by intermediate judgments by the court or by the passage of time, the plaintiff and the defendant might once again (or indeed for the first time) find themselves in front of the judge. If the person was complaining or appealing against the defendant in a case of serious crime, then both would be detained without bail (*Etablissements* 1:108 and 2:8), and the appellant would be warned by the judge that if his appeal were unsuccessful he would receive the punishment he was seeking for the defendant (*Etablissements* 1:4). The plain-

6. Since the person called before a court is in the overwhelming majority of cases a man, either as a party or on behalf of his wife, I have chosen to use masculine pronouns throughout. The reader should be aware that this pronoun sometimes includes the feminine. In some jurisdictions women were able to sue and be sued in person only if the suit concerned their business. A woman might, of course, be the subject of a criminal accusation; see Beaumanoir §1159.

tiff could state his complaint (for example, according to the form in *Etablissements* 2:12), and the defendant would have to answer the complaint. His answer could, of course, be an admission of its truth, whereupon the judge would merely pronounce judgment. Execution of judgment followed very quickly unless the loser appealed (Beaumanoir §246). Usually the answer would take the form of a denial or other defense (such as self-defense in criminal cases). The judge would try to make sense of the claims and denials. Both the dilatory and the other defenses were sometimes called "exceptions." Those that were not merely dilatory went to the substance of the accusation and might lead to an end of the litigation. Once the parties were satisfied that the judge understood their positions, they would declare themselves "ready for judgment," which meant that their role in the trial was over (*Etablissements* 2:16).

If the plaintiff had to make proof of his claims, he could do so by various methods: he could produce a writing or witnesses, or even offer to fight a judicial battle with the defendant (*Etablissements* 1:175). In the *Etablissements*, much is made of the fact that Louis IX had attempted to do away with judicial battles and had banned them as a method of proof in his own domains (*Etablissements* 1:4). But outside the king's domain, the use of the judicial battle as a proof was still quite common, and all the customaries mention it (see, for example, Beaumanoir §1148 and chapters 61, 63, 64). In an area where the judicial battle was not permitted, the defendant might produce witnesses to prove his argument if he had made a positive defense, such as self-defense (*Etablissements* 1:30), or if he had an alibi.

Witnesses could be challenged by the party against whom they were called to testify. They might be excluded for various reasons: women and serfs could not testify, nor could churchmen in certain kinds of cases. Persons who could be shown to be potentially biased, such as the other party's close relatives, were excluded. Those witnesses not thus excluded were interrogated by special officers, who asked them questions prepared by the two parties and wrote down and sealed their answers in a report to the court. The testimony of the witnesses was reported to the parties, who had an opportunity to contest it but not to cross-examine the actual witnesses (*Etablissements* 1:1).[7] Two witnesses whose testimony was materially the same were needed.[8] The proof of the facts, which in modern American courts is submitted to a jury, was thus mechanical: if two unexcluded witnesses testified to the same facts, they were counted as proved without further ado. The examination of witnesses is not fully discussed in the *Etablissements* as it is, for example, in Beaumanoir.

The judge then either gave a judgment (*Etablissements* 1:4) or sent the case to the jury (*Etablissements* 1:42 and 2:4, 2:16). The jury consisted of a number of jurors, sometimes as few as two. Their job was to consider the pleadings and proofs and to identify the law that applied in the case. The jury must often have appeared more like a panel of judges than a jury in the modern sense. When they had reached a decision, the judge summoned the parties to hear the judgment. If the loser did not appeal immediately (*Etablissements* 1:85, 2:16), then the judgment was taken as final and executed without delay (Beaumanoir §§ 246, 1915). Of course, if the proof had been established by means of a judicial battle, the loser might already be dead.

Appeals could be made to a higher court. The normal appeal by a loser was for false judgment; such an appeal might also involve him in a judicial battle against his lord (*Etablissements* 1:86). Another kind of appeal was for default of judgment, which meant that some plaintiff had been refused a hearing by the lord with jurisdiction (*Etablissements* 1:8). For the person appealed against to lose either of these appeals was very serious and could cause him to lose his life, his property, or his power to administer justice. This last was more grave than it appears, since the person who

7. In Beauvais, the testimony of witnesses not excluded for bias could not be challenged, and was not reported to the adverse party, except where the witnesses could be challenged by a wager of battle (Beaumanoir §§1221–1222).

8. *Etablissements* 1:4 is clear on the number of witnesses needed; *Etablissements* 1:26 implies two, but *Etablissements* 1:119 suggests three or four, whereas Beaumanoir is quite explicit that only two are needed; see Beaumanoir, chapter 39, especially §1149.

administered justice also collected the fines, which were an important source of revenue. Criminal trials were also a kind of appeal, but perhaps in name only: the injured plaintiff who accused a defendant of some crime did so in an action called an appeal, even though the case was being heard for the first time.

An obvious need was a way to determine whether something had been done or what the details of some transaction had been. In modern societies, this is accomplished by writings of various degrees of trustworthiness (for example, holograph wills, signed receipts and contracts, notarized antenuptial agreements). In a society that rarely used writing, another method was necessary: it relied on the memory of various persons and their assertion that something had occurred. If a person was accused of theft of some object, the accused could "vouch a warrantor," that is, call into court the person who could testify that he or she had actually sold or given the accused the object in question. Warrantors could then vouch their own warrantors to explain their own possession of the object before the accused had it, and so on (*Etablissements* 1:95 and 2:18). If it was a question of proving what had happened in a court, then some of those who had been present at the original event could be brought to some new court to recall from memory [*recorder*] what they had seen done. An officer who had served a summons on a party could be called on to testify to that service (*Etablissements* 1:71). If it was a question of the ownership of land, a panel of local residents (who could be expected to know who owned what) might be assembled to inquire into the matter and testify. Their testimony might be dispositive even against the king (*Etablissements* 1:84).

Much of this procedure is outlined in the *Etablissements*. The topic appears already in *Etablissements* 1:1, where the procedure used in the Châtelet in Paris is outlined. It appears again in dozens of chapters in the *Coutume de Touraine-Anjou*. In the *Usage d'Orlenois* (Book 2) every chapter but one addresses one or more issues of procedural law.

Substantive Law

The Law of Persons

The law of persons deals with the status of persons. The law treated men and women differently, but it also treated freemen and serfs differently. Not much is said about serfs in the *Etablissements*, aside from details on how to sue for the return of a runaway serf (*Etablissements* 1:6, 2:31). Gentlemen and commoners were both free, but they differed in many ways: gentlemen tended to own fiefs, whereas commoners were more likely to pay rent or quitrent for their land; there were often very different penalties for the same crime committed by a gentleman as opposed to a commoner (*Etablissements* 1:52 and 1:156). There were also special ways of dealing with the king's men, merchants, barons, vassals, strangers, bastards, officers, provosts, baillis, widows, crusaders, clerks, Jews, and of deciding who had power (lordship) and jurisdiction over them. These issues are dealt with in the *Etablissements*, but other issues of status are not dealt with there: the rules dealing with lepers, conspirators, and city dwellers are not mentioned in the *Etablissements*, although they are in some customaries (Beaumanoir §§1617–1623, §§883–885, and chapter 50, respectively).

Another part of the law of persons might be defined as the way people deal with one another. This would include such issues as crimes, contract, agency, and the feudal ties between members of society. Nevertheless, not all interpersonal issues were dealt with by the customaries, because some came under the jurisdiction of the church: marriage, divorce, heresy, and other purely religious matters were under the jurisdiction of the church's own courts. These matters were generally governed by canon law, as set out in the *Corpus iuris canonici*.

One of the differences between a gentleman and a commoner was that gentlemen were permitted to engage in private war, although various monarchs tried to prevent it (see *Etablissements* 2:38 note). A gentleman who had been injured in a way that could have led to his appeal against the aggressor in a court of law could in effect use self-help to pursue his enemy. This was a private war, and the *Etablissements* show that when a man's close relative was at war, he could join in even if the campaign was against his own lord (*Etablissements* 1:52). There was a remedy, however, for the weaker person: he could ask a judge for a guaranteed peace [*asseürement*], which would be arranged and sanctioned by a court of high justice (*Etablissements* 1:31, 2:29). Any breach of this peace was considered a serious crime and could lead to the death penalty (*Etablissements* 1:31, 41; 2:29, 35). The many mentions of the guaranteed peace in the customaries indicate that protection from one's powerful neighbors was often needed (Beaumanoir, chapter 60).

The fidelity a man owed his lord might be the subject of a lawsuit. If a lord claimed that a certain fief was held from him, but the vassal occupying the fief claimed that it was held from a different lord, the first lord would have to sue on the matter in the court of the second lord. It may seem that a man would certainly know who his lord was, and from whom he held his fief; but the number of times that the situation (known as "disavowing") occurs in customaries suggests that such problems did arise. Of course, if the lower lord had in fact avowed the wrong lord, and this was shown in court, then he would lose his fief.

In the modern world, many transactions are made firm and many obligations are created by a person's signature. In the thirteenth century, such obligations and transactions were made binding by an oral ceremony to which two or more persons were invited as witnesses; the witnesses could then later testify in court, if need be, that they had seen the business done. Such persons were best chosen from those who had a good reputation and would not be excluded from a trial for bias. Likewise, to make an obligation firmer, and to act as an insurance against loss, a man might require a surety (Old French *pleige*) from a person promising or contracting something. A surety is a person who can be sued if the original party to an agreement fails to fulfill his obligations. In present-day banking, similarly, a bank will make a loan to a person with a poor or no credit record only if another person with a better credit rating acts as a cosigner. Each time an individual endorses a check, the bank is assured that if the maker of the check (who signs on the front) cannot cover the check, the bank can recover its money from the endorser. The endorser is a kind of surety. In the time of Saint Louis, sureties were used for such operations but also to warrant that a person released by a court pending trial would in fact come back to stand trial. A person posting bail for another is thus a kind of surety. In some kinds of suits, a person even had to provide sureties to a court as a guarantee that he or she would pursue a suit (not fail to prosecute). This was the case in the suit called "Novel Disseisin" (*Etablissements* 1:69).

Various classes of persons were of course given special protection by the customs of the time. The king could imprison those who owed him money, but no one else could do so (*Etablissements* 2:22 and Beaumanoir §1538). Crimes against gentlemen, and especially against one's own lord, were more severely punished than those against commoners. The lord's dignity extended to his officers and judges, so that an offense against them was as if it was against the lord (*Etablissements* 1:157). Obviously then, as now, a particularly well-protected class of persons were creditors.

Included in the law of persons is crime. A lord who held the high justice in his jurisdiction presided over trials for certain crimes for which the punishment was death or disfigurement—murder, homicide, rape, and treachery [*traïson*] being the principal high crimes (Beaumanoir §824; *Etablissements* 1:27, 2:8); but a man could also be hanged for counterfeiting and arson. Murder is defined as a homicide where the act was committed without warning or by stealth, such as in an ambush. Homicide was a killing that resulted from the escalation of a fight, often in situations where honor was involved. Treachery included not only lèse-majesté but any serious infraction against a person to whom you had sworn an oath, and more generally crimes of stealth (Beaumanoir §§826–827).[9] Treachery was also considered to be an element of murder (Beaumanoir §826 and *Justice et plet*, chapter 19, 6, §1). When a

9. For *traïson* see my "Murder by Stealth: *Traïson* in Old French Literature," *Studies in Honor of Hans-Erich Keller*, ed. Rupert T. Pickens, Medieval Institute Publications (Kalamazoo: Western Michigan University, 1993), pp. 459–473.

man was hanged for a crime, his property was forfeited to the lord or ruined by ravaging (*Etablissements* 1:28), leaving his family destitute. In trials for high crimes, there could be a proof by judicial combat (also called wager of battle). Even in a trial for a low justice crime, a wager might occur, and the battle itself would have to be fought in a court having high justice (Beaumanoir §§233–234). For an account of a battle see *Etablissements* 1:95.

The jurisdiction of other crimes, where the punishment was generally a fine, belonged to low justice [*vaarie*]. An anomaly was theft, which was a low justice crime, but for which the penalty was death. Crimes against property were treated in various ways. Some hints in the customaries suggest that petty theft was not a hanging matter; crimes against a lord or his agents and servants were severely punished. Fines and penalties were assessed differently for gentlemen and for commoners, the latter often paying only a small fraction of the gentleman's fine for the same offense. Fines were crudely assigned, a small fine of five sous [10] or a large fine of sixty sous being the only alternative. In some cases, the fine could be at the lord's discretion up to complete confiscation. Beaumanoir reports a fine of forty thousand livres levied on some burghers of Ghent (Beaumanoir §1779) and of five hundred livres in a case involving knights (Beaumanoir §1100).

Thus a man (or a woman) might play many roles in thirteenth-century society, and the law of persons was well developed. It was constructed for a society where writing was rare, yet where commercial transactions were becoming more common. It recognized that some system was necessary for dealing with strangers—for example, merchants, who were not known and trusted neighbors but who needed assurances that they would not be delayed by suits brought against them. Of course, the law also ensured the effectiveness and dignity of the courts themselves and the power and prestige of the nobility and the wealthy.

---

10. This small fine is referred to in *Etablissements* 1:51 and elsewhere as the "wager of law."

The Law of Property and the Exchange of Property

The most important kind of property was land, also called real property. All customary compilations devote a good deal of space to a discussion of how land is assessed, measured and taxed, inherited (directly or indirectly), bought and sold, and given away. Land might pass from one person to another by action of law (a man could leave only a fifth of his land in a will, the rest passed by law to his heirs), or by the action of the person owning it. Just as there were two essential kinds of personal status, free and serf, so there were two kinds of land. Free fiefs were held in exchange for the homage of a nobleman; nonfree land (called villeinage or quitrent land) was held for a money payment like a rent. There were different rules for how the different kinds of land could be inherited, bought, and protected by the law.

In medieval France, each free piece of land was generally held by some gentleman (nobleman) from some other gentleman (his lord) as a fief. Gentlewomen could also hold land. The king was the only lord who did not have a lord. In return for the grant of land from the king or some intermediary lord, each gentleman owed homage to his immediate superior. The homage generally took the form of military service, and the usual term of service was forty days a year (*Etablissements* 1:65). Some gentlemen owed another form of homage, that of guarding their lord's castle (*Etablissements* 1:57). The fief-holders acquired their land in three ways: direct and indirect (lateral) inheritance, gift, and purchase.

On the death of a lord, his direct heir or heirs inherited his fief. This was so normal a way of acquiring land that the very name for land in Old French is *eritage*. In many districts the oldest son took two-thirds of the fief and the other sons (and daughters) shared the remaining one-third (*Etablissements* 1:10). If only daughters survived their father, then they shared the fief equally between them (*Etablissements* 1:12). In both these cases, however, the oldest heir would also take the principal dwelling (or castle, if there was one) before the division was made (*Etablissements* 1:10, 12). Another way of acquiring a fief was by lateral inheritance: a piece of land might be inherited from a more distant relative not in the direct line, such as a childless uncle or brother (*Etablissements* 1:22, 23).

To a son or daughter who married, a father might give the portion of his fief that they would have inherited when he died (*Etablissements* 1:10). This wedding gift was then normally all the child received. If the portion was smaller or larger than the child's fair share would have been on the parent's death, that child or the others might insist that it be brought back on the death of the father, and a new division made of the whole (but see *Etablissements* 2:26). In modern legal terms this estate, which includes the portions brought back by various persons who had been given them during the lifetime of the decedent, is called the "hotchpot" (*Etablissements* 1:136). Acquiring land by gift is like an anticipation of the distribution of a decedent's estate after his or her death.

A third way of acquiring land was, of course, by purchase. Medieval French law did not favor the purchase or sale of land, and many obstacles were placed in the way of the would-be buyer and seller. If a man sold his land for a certain sum of money, his relatives were permitted to buy back or "redeem" the land from the buyer if he was a stranger, or even if he was a less closely related person than themselves (*Etablissements* 1:168). They merely gave the buyer the same amount of money he had given for the land (*Etablissements* 1:162). In most places, the relatives had a year and a day to make up their minds and make their offer. When they did so, they had to have the purchase money in full, or they lost their opportunity. If none of the relatives wanted to redeem, then the overlord, the man from whom the land was held, also had the opportunity to redeem from the stranger (*Etablissements* 1:164). These rules concerning redemption applied to lands held by commoners as well as gentlemen. Redemption tended to keep fiefs in the same family, and to keep them together as a parcel, while the laws governing inheritance by children tended to split the fiefs into ever smaller portions. These two countertendencies seem to have been in a kind of equilibrium.

Various laws and cases demonstrate the difficulties of the inheritance laws. How is the oldest son compensated when there

is no dwelling on the fief? Can a son be *forced* to bring back to
the hotchpot, or can he opt out of the distribution of his parent's
estate? Supposing he is forced back in but he has built a house on
the parcel? Can a more distantly related male redeem rather than
a more closely related female? If two persons equally distantly related to the seller want to redeem, who gets the first chance? Must
the actual redemption and payment be made before the year is up,
or does the person wishing to redeem need only to begin the process within that time? Some or all of these questions, and many
like them, may find an answer in a given compilation of customary laws. This area of the law was clearly one that needed a lot of
regulation and generated a lot of law.

In some areas, when a fief was divided after the parent's
death, each of the heirs took an actual parcel of the fief and did
homage for it to their ancestor's lord or to their oldest sibling
(Beaumanoir §465). In other areas, including the Touraine-Anjou
area, the oldest son alone did homage to his father's lord, and the
other siblings assumed a somewhat dubious status as "coholders"
of the remainder. They did no homage but seem to have been joint
holders of the land, which may have been left whole and not partitioned among them unless they requested it (*Etablissements* 1:10).

Another complication was that children inherited from their
mother as well as from their father. The holdings of any man were
carefully classified according to whether they came to him from
his father's side of the family or his mother's. If he died without
heirs, only the relatives on the side from which a certain piece of
land derived could inherit it laterally. If he sold a fief, only relatives on the side from which it descended could offer to redeem it.

Still another complication was created by the law of dower:
a married noble woman received after her husband's death a portion, usually a half, of all the land he owned during the marriage,
and she held it as a life interest until she died. A noble widow
took only a third of her husband's real property in the Touraine-
Anjou region, however (*Etablissements* 1:16).[11] A son inheriting

---

11. A commoner widow, however, took a half of her husband's lands (*Etablissements* 1:137).

land from his father might have to wait to occupy such dower land until his mother had also died. In some areas, the children of a predeceased first wife inherited her dower rights, so that a second wife, widowed by her husband's death, might receive only a quarter of his lands in dower, with a half going as a life interest to her stepchildren (the first wife's children), who might also still be minors (Beaumanoir §430).

When minor children inherited land, they were given a custodian or guardian to look after them until they came of age. In the customs outlined in this book, that guardian could not be the person who stood to inherit the land if the children died (*Etablissements* 1:121). Presumably it was felt that such a person would have no interest in seeing the children survive! In other areas, however, the heir to the land after the children *could* be the custodian, and in any case a surviving parent always had the right to be the children's guardian (*Etablissements* 1:19).

Quitrent land, or villeinage, was generally held by commoners for an annual payment, generally in money but sometimes in goods such as grain, or even gloves or capons (*Etablissements* 1:170). When the owner died, all the children inherited equal shares (*Etablissements* 1:136). While it was generally true that gentlemen held fiefs but commoners held quitrent land, there was a certain amount of holding across those lines, so that the definition blurred at the edges.

All property not classified as real property was called personal property [*mueble*]. The rule for personal property was that the oldest son inherited it all if his mother was already dead, but she inherited half of it if her husband predeceased her. In any case, whoever inherited the personal property had to pay the decedent's debts out of it (*Etablissements* 1:10, 17). Any person with the right to inherit personal property also had the right to refuse it and thus escape paying the debts.[12] While there were many offenses for which a person might be obliged to pay as a fine all his

12. The legality of this custom was upheld by the Parlement of Paris. See *Les Olim ou registre des arrêts rendus par la cour du roi, sous les règnes de Saint Louis, de Philippe le Hardi, de Philippe le Bel, de Louis le Hutin et de Philippe le Long*, ed. le comte Beugnot, 4 vols. (Paris: Imprimerie Royale, 1839–44), volume 1, p. 240.

personal property (*Etablissements* 1:51, 54), some types of property were exempt even from this forfeiture (*Etablissements* 1:58), just as in today's law certain kinds of property are protected in a bankruptcy. In most areas of France, if a person was convicted of a capital crime and executed, *all* his property was forfeited to the lord. This rule is not discussed in the *Coutume de Touraine-Anjou*. But in the chapter on highway robbery, not the most serious offense, it is said that those convicted were hanged and their real property could be ravaged: the houses burned, the meadows ploughed up, and the trees destroyed (*Etablissements* 1:28). This was probably what happened in the Touraine-Anjou when someone was executed for any capital crime.

The *Etablissements* deal with many of these customary laws, both substantive and procedural. However, the customary compilations often seem to leave the obvious unsaid: the customs deal with the interesting exceptions rather than the mainstream law. Everybody knew about the laws or customs that governed common or everyday situations, so it was not necessary to write them down. Only the more easily forgotten because less frequently applied rules needed to be carefully preserved. Jean-Marie Carbasse remarks in his study of the criminal law in southern France in the Middle Ages: "Ajoutons qu'ils [sc. les textes coutumiers] sont fort lacunaires: le but poursuivi par leurs rédacteurs étant de fixer les points obscurs ou contestés, toutes les règles bien établies ou évidentes sont restées orales" (p. 251).[13] These remarks are to some extent applicable also to the northern customaries. Thus, for example, in *Etablissements*, Book 2, the service horse is mentioned only once, in passing. It is never defined, nor are the rules for how to ask for it, offer it, accept it, test it, give it back, demand another, avoid having to give another, and so on, such as they are in *Etablissements* 1:135 and Beaumanoir, chapter 28. By reading the *Usage d'Orlenois* one would not know how to deal with the service horse. As another example, when the writer of the *Coutume*

---

13. "We should add that customary texts contain many gaps: since the goal of their writers was to fix obscure or disputed matters, all the well-established or obvious rules remained oral [were not written down]."

de Touraine-Anjou enumerates the serious crimes in chapter 27, he does not mention that the punishment for each of these crimes is death. The reader must wait until chapter 36 to discover that murderers are hanged, and until chapter 55 to discover that rapists are hanged. The reader must read *Etablissements* 2:36, almost the last chapter in the work, to discover that the real *and* personal property of those hanged for capital crimes is forfeited to the lord. Thus, the sets of customs are not complete or comprehensive or even very coherent. This is what makes them so difficult to understand on first reading.

Every judicial system is grounded on some fundamental guarantee of justice. In modern American law, that guarantee is provided by the Bill of Rights and the adversarial system of arguing before an impartial judge or jury. While lip service is given to this guarantee (no trial lawyer *really* wants an impartial jury, for example), it must be obvious that in fact a determined liar can often arouse "reasonable doubt." In a system where a judicial battle or an ordeal was permitted, it was believed that God would not permit the wrong side to win. By the thirteenth century, the "irrational" proofs were in decline: the ordeal gradually fell out of use after 1215,[14] and the judicial battle was becoming less favored as a method of proof. Instead, the preferred methods of proof were the "inquest," usually a trial with witnesses, and the exculpatory oath. In both of these kinds of proof, the person testifying had to swear to tell the truth. The oath of truthfulness itself depended on a religious fear of hell, for the swearing was done with a hand on the sacred relics, implying the seriousness and truthfulness of the swearer. By the thirteenth century, however, it was clear that a witness could not necessarily be trusted to tell the truth, even after a solemn oath. The exculpatory oaths were permitted only in minor matters, and in some situations a nobleman was allowed to swear an exculpatory oath even when an officer, probably a commoner, had sworn the opposite (*Etablissements* 1:71). The lan-

---

14. After a decision of the Fourth Lateran Council of 1215, priests were not permitted to participate in ordeals. See John W. Baldwin, "The Intellectual Preparation for the Canon of 1215 Against Ordeals," *Speculum* 36 (1961): 613–636.

guage is revealing here: the person either "dares to swear," or "dare not swear," implying that to swear falsely is a risky undertaking. Would a man imperil his immortal soul by making a false oath or a false declaration under oath? The law of the *Etablissements* seemed to think he might. A new method of proof was soon to become more and more widely used: the production of written documents. This development had not made a measurable impact by the time the *Etablissements* were written down, although Beaumanoir, writing only a few years later, devotes a whole chapter to written contracts (chapter 35).

The Text of the *Etablissements* and This Translation

This translation has been made from an edition of the *Etablissements* published in 1881–1886 by Paul Viollet. In his introduction, Viollet shows that the *Etablissements* as they are today consist of three parts, put together by a person whom I shall call the Compiler, following Viollet who calls him the *compilateur* (*Etablissements* 1:81).[15] Book 1 contains (1) some procedural rules from the Châtelet or principal court in Paris, which also announce the abolition of the judicial combat or duel in the king's domain (1:1–9), followed by (2) an annotated[16] copy of the *Coutume de Touraine-Anjou* (1:10–175); Book 2 contains (3) an annotated copy of the *Usage d'Orlenois* (2:1–38). Thus, the name of the collection is shown to be misleading. The *Etablissements* are for the most part not *établissements* (pronouncements or ordinances by the king, having the force of law) but customary laws, and none of them was written by Saint Louis, although the wording of the first nine

---

15. Montesquieu had already understood the role of the compiler, "quelque bailli." See Charles-Marie de Secondat, Baron de Montesquieu, *Oeuvres complètes*, ed. Roger Caillois, 2 vols. Bibliothèque de la Pléiade (Paris: Gallimard, 1951), vol. 2, p. 853.

16. The annotations are chiefly references to Roman law as found in the *Corpus iuris civilis* and the *Corpus iuris canonici*. I have left these references in Latin where they are cited in Latin by the Compiler; I have translated into English citations given in Old French, with the original Latin indicated in notes.

chapters may have been approved by him. Since the only part of the book that might justify the title is the group formed by the first nine chapters, it seems that this prestigious but very small part gave its name to the book as a whole.

There are other manuscript copies of the procedural rules of the Châtelet (*Etablissements* 1:1–9). Viollet enumerates these manuscripts in his volume 1 (pp. 422–425). They include Rome Reine Christine MS 773 (α), the *Livre de Jostice et de Plet* in Paris Bibliothèque Nationale MS fr. 2844 (β) and Bibliothèque Nationale MS fr. 20,048 (λ). Viollet provides an edition of these manuscripts at the end of his volume 1 (pp. 483–493).

Not counting the various manuscripts of the *Etablissements*, two copies of the *Coutume de Touraine-Anjou*, which is the basis of chapters 10–175 of the first book of the *Etablissements*, have survived. They are Paris Arsenal MS 2465 (ε) and Paris Bibliothèque Nationale MS fr. 5359 (ζ). In these manuscripts, the *coutume* is given the name *Coutume d'Anjou et Maine*, but Viollet denies that the law contained therein is from the province of Maine (Viollet 1:23). The references to it in the *Etablissements* itself always call it the *Usage de Touraine et d'Anjou*. Viollet prints a copy of this coutume in his volume 3 (pp. 1–104). Since these two independent manuscripts of the original *Coutume de Touraine-Anjou* agree largely between themselves but differ from the version given in manuscripts of the *Etablissements*, it is possible to separate out the additions of the Compiler. In the edition of the *Etablissements* in his volume 2, Viollet prints the portions copied directly from the *Coutume de Touraine-Anjou* in roman type, and the additions of the Compiler in italic. I have followed this division by indicating the compiler's additions in angle brackets thus ⟨ . . . ⟩.[17]

Many of these additions are references to Roman and Canon law. Since the medieval system of citation is different from our

17. I have made one systematic exception to this practice. The chapter headings are all supplied by the Compiler and do not appear in the separate manuscripts of the *Coutume de Touraine-Anjou*. In order to avoid clutter, I have not used angle brackets around every title. Let the reader be aware that the chapter headings were not part of the original *Coutume* but were added by the Compiler of the *Etablissements*.

own, I have given in footnotes the references to modern editions of the *Corpus iuris cvilis* and the *Corpus iuris canonici*. The *Etablissements* were compiled in the thirteenth century, hence they contain references to the *Decretals of Gregory IX* (promulgated 1234) but not to later collections (see Bibliography). Sometimes a few words that are found in the manuscripts of the *Coutume de Touraine-Anjou* are omitted by all the manuscripts of the *Etablissements*. In such cases, Viollet prints them with a note to explain their origin. I have systematically indicated these additions by the use of curly brackets { . . . }. It must be stressed that these additions are to be found nowhere in the surviving manuscripts of the *Etablissements*. Finally, Viollet sometimes simply supplies by conjecture one or more missing words needed to complete the sense. I have followed his conjectures in most cases, while using the curly brackets and notes, and where I disagree I have said so in a note. I have also used single square brackets [. . .] to provide the italicized Old French word when I have felt doubtful of my translation, and ordinary parentheses to enclose parenthetical expressions that made the sentence clearer. Square brackets also enclose my own clarifying additions or substitutions, often when I have substituted a noun for an ambiguous pronoun.

In editing the *Usage d'Orlenois*, which forms Book 2 of the *Etablissements*, Viollet had no manuscripts of the original compilation to consult, for none has survived separately from the *Etablissements*. He believed that the references to Roman and Canon law in this portion of the *Etablissements* were also the work of the Compiler, and therefore, he indicated by italics what he believed to be additions. His indications are, of course, conjectural. In the translation of Book 2, I have nevertheless shown, by the use of angle brackets as in Book 1, those portions that may be the work of the Compiler. By subtracting the "additions," Viollet was able to reconstruct what the original *Usage d'Orlenois* probably looked like, and he printed this at the end of his volume 1 (pp. 494–520). It must be stressed that this is purely Viollet's reconstruction and has no manuscript authority. Another source for verification of Orléans law in the *Usage d'Orlenois* is a book called *Li livres de jostice et de plet*, which was edited by Pierre-Nicolas Rapetti in 1853 and which is being reedited (in 1996) by a doctoral student in Finland. The *Jostice et plet*, as it is usually called, contains what are probably a student's notes from study at the Orléans law school in the middle of the thirteenth century, and which reflect Orléans law at that period.

Viollet's four-volume edition of the *Etablissements* is made up as follows:

1. Volume 1 contains an introduction dealing with the sources of the *Etablissements*, the law contained in it, the influence of the compilation, and the manuscripts in which it is preserved. At the end, Viollet prints an edition of the *Regulations for the Procedure at the Châtelet*, according to sources other than the *Etablissements*,[18] and his reconstruction of the *Usage d'Orlenois*.

2. Volume 2 contains the text of the *Etablissements* proper[19] and, in an appendix, the prologue found only in manuscripts *Q*, *R*, and *S*, followed by the table of contents found in manuscripts *G*, *I*, *K*, and *U*.[20]

3. Volume 3 contains the text of the *Coutume de Touraine-Anjou*[21] and editions of various other texts derived from or similar to the *Etablissements*, followed by the beginning of the notes on the text. The notes contain some lengthy quotations of notes by earlier editors (du Cange, de Laurière, and the Abbé de Saint Martin) as well as some notes by Viollet himself, who does not always agree with his predecessors.

4. Volume 4 contains the rest of the notes and a glossary.

The present volume contains, apart from this introduction, my English translation of the text of Viollet's edition of the *Etablissements* as contained in his volume 2, with notes, some of which

---

18. Five manuscripts as listed in Viollet 1:422–425.
19. Using manuscript *B* (Paris Bibliothèque Nationale MS fr. 5278) as a base.
20. Viollet lists these manuscripts in 1:396–422.
21. From two manuscripts listed in Viollet 1:425–427.

refer to Viollet's notes (and to the notes of his predecessors), and a list of topics. I have added an index.

As translator, I have not presumed to be an editor. The translation is made directly from Viollet's printed text, with various parentheses and brackets and notes to indicate the status of that text (whether from the *Etablissements* manuscripts, the Compiler's sources, or reconstructed by Viollet). A reader who wants to follow the Old French version and the translation will find no difficulty in doing so, as the sentences of the translation correspond to the sentences of Viollet's edition.

Language and Style

One of the difficulties in translating a text now seven hundred years old is that a word used only once or twice may not reveal its meaning by its context. The translator must then have recourse to the dictionaries and to other works of the period where the word may be used in a more revealing way. Another difficulty is that the same word in Old French may be translated by several different words in Modern English, according to the context. Thus, for example, *recreance* is translated "reclamation" when applied to things, and "bail" when applied to people. A troublesome word of this kind is one of the most basic of the legal vocabulary: *droit*. It should and does mean "law," but even in Modern French it has the meanings of "straight" and "right." It is associated with other words: *faire droit* can mean "to give a hearing" and also "to pay a fine." Sometimes the word seems very close to the meaning of "right" as in the modern "civil right" or "human right." Associated with a present participle, it becomes *droit faisant*, a puzzling expression that appears several times in the *Etablissements* in different contexts. Also found frequently is the expression *par droit*, which I have often translated as "in a judgment." I was sometimes tempted to translate it as "by rights" but did not feel able to justify this free a rendering.

Many words used in legal contexts have undergone a kind of metonymic shift. A metonymy is a figure of speech in which one word is used in place of another because the things to which the words refer (the referents) are found in close proximity in the real world. Thus "Bordeaux" stands for "the wine of Bordeaux" (region for product of the region) and "the sword" stands for military might (instrument for user of the instrument). In the same way, *justice* has come to mean "judge" (agent for abstract principle), as in English, and *essoine* meaning "postponement of procedure because of a proper excuse, such as sickness," has come to mean "sickness." Some words also change their meaning by synecdoche, in which the part is used to mean the whole, or vice versa. An example of this is *jugement*, which has come to mean "trial" and not just its part, the judgment as such. It is through these metonymic and synecdochical shifts that *droit* has come to have so many meanings.

The styles of the two customaries that make up the greater part of the *Etablissements* are somewhat different, and each also differs from the style of Beaumanoir's treatise on the laws of Beauvais. The *Coutume de Touraine-Anjou* seems preoccupied with daily problems, such as inheritance, multiple ownership of land, even the swarming of bees. On the other hand, the *Usage d'Orlenois* is very concerned with court procedure and especially with jurisdictional matters. Beaumanoir deals with both of these things and frankly addresses his treatise to those who have been summoned to go to court and who need some guidance about procedure. The *Usage d'Orlenois*, however, seems to be addressed rather to the administrators of the courts. The *Etablissements* contain very few warnings of danger such as permeate the *Coutumes de Beauvaisis* (although for an example see *Etablissements* 1:123, the last sentence). Whereas in Beaumanoir there is clearly a man behind the book, who sometimes says "I" to the reader and who reveals his character and tastes, the two customaries of the *Etablissements* are anonymous and faceless. It is possible to conjecture that the writer of the *Usage d'Orlenois* was a royal employee, possibly a judge; but his personality is not evident from what he says.

Both the *Coutume de Touraine-Anjou* and the *Usage d'Orlenois* are somewhat repetitive, as if the writer had not read over what he wrote and purged the text of material used a second or third time. Of course, many topics are covered in both customaries. I have made many cross-references in the footnotes. Furthermore, the Compiler also makes cross-references of his own within the same customary, from one customary to another, and from either to the beginning of Book 1, the Châtelet rules. By the use of these cross-references and the notes, I have attempted to make the *Etablissements de Saint Louis* less obscure, confused, and ambiguous than Montesquieu found them.

It remains only for me to thank those who have helped me to prepare this translation. In particular, I would like to acknowledge the generosity of the College of Liberal Arts, University of Minnesota, for granting me a single quarter leave in winter quarter, 1993; and of the National Endowment for the Humanities, for the award of a Translation Grant for the period of spring quarter and part of the summer of 1993. My consultant for the project was Professor William C. Calin, University of Florida, Gainesville, to whom go my special thanks. I would also like to thank my editor, Mindy Brown, of the University of Pennsylvania Press.

The Laws of Saint Louis

Prologue

IN THE YEAR OF GRACE 1270 good king Louis of France made and imposed these laws, before he went to Tunis, in all the secular courts of the kingdom and in the jurisdiction [*poosté*] of France. And these laws show how all judges in secular courts should hear cases and judge them, and bring to an end all the disputes brought before them, and concerning all the practices of the whole kingdom and Anjou, and in the barons' courts, and the entitlements [*redevances*] that the king and the barons have over knights and gentlemen who hold their lands from them. And these laws were made after great consultation of wise men and good clerks,[1] through the concordance of laws and canons[2] and decretals,[3] to confirm the good practices and ancient customs, which are adhered to in the kingdom of France, in all disputes and all cases that have arisen there, and that still arise every day. And by this law the plaintiff must be taught how to make his complaint, and the defendant to defend himself. And it begins as follows:

"Louis, king of France by the grace of God, to all good Christians living in the realm and lordship [*segnorie*] of France, and to all those others who are there now and in time to come, greetings in Our Lord.

"Because evil and deception have grown so much among the human race that some men often do other men wrong and harm,

This prologue appears only in manuscripts *Q*, *R*, and *S*. Viollet prints it in 2:473–474.

1. The "wise men" probably represent the secular courts and the "clerks" the ecclesiastical courts.

2. Canons are ecclesiastical laws, such as those found in Gratian's *Decretum* (collected about 1140), which forms the first part of the *Corpus iuris canonici*.

3. Decretals are laws made by church courts or the pope, such as those found in the *Decretals of Gregory IX* (promulgated in 1234), which forms the second part of the *Corpus iuris canonici*, often quoted in the *Etablissements*.

and commit crimes against them against the will and commandments of God, and many have no fear nor dread of the severe judgment of Jesus Christ, and because we wish the people beneath us
to be able to live honestly and in peace, and so that one will refrain
from doing harm to another through fear of bodily punishment
or the confiscation of property, and in order to punish and con-
trol offenders by means of law and rigorous justice, we call upon
the help of God, who is a just judge above all others, [and] we
have set out these laws which we want to be put into practice in
the secular courts in the whole kingdom and lordship of France."

BOOK 1

The Rules of Procedure
in the Châtelet

HERE BEGIN THE Laws of the King of France which the Provost of Paris and [the provosts] of the kingdom observe in their suits and use everywhere.

1. The first rubric of the first case is: The duties of the provost.[1]

The provost of Paris will[2] use the following procedure in his cases:

If someone brings before him a complaint against another person, on the issue of a bargain that he made, or if he is suing for real property, the provost will summon the person against whom the complaint is being made; and when the parties appear at the appointed time, the plaintiff will make his complaint: and the person against whom the complaint is lodged will answer, on the very same day, if the suit concerns his actions; and if it concerns someone else's actions, he may have one more court date to answer, if he asks for it; and on that day he must answer. If the person being complained against admits what is said against him, the provost will enforce and have executed what was admitted, according to

---

The title *The Rules of Procedure in the Châtelet* does not appear in the manuscripts of the *Etablissements*.

1. The words "The first rubric in the first case is" were probably a note from the scribe to the rubricator, rather than the words of the title. They were copied by mistake and have remained. The provost is the chief judicial officer of Paris. Elsewhere the chief judicial officer is generally called a *bailli* or seneschal.

2. The use of the future here and throughout the chapter is equivalent to a statement of command.

the custom, ⟨and according to written law[3] in the *Code*, De transactionibus, l. Si causa cognita in fine,[4] and in the *Digest*, De re judicata, l. A divo Pio,⟩[5] unless the person being complained against
raises some issue that should be valid in his defense. And if it happened that the person complained about denied what was in the
complaint, or if the plaintiff denied the issues raised by the defendant in his defense against the plaintiff, the parties would swear an
oath concerning the suit; and the form of the oath will be as follows: the plaintiff will swear that he believes he has a proper complaint and that he will reply the plain truth to what is asked him
according to his belief, and that he will give nothing (and promise
nothing) to the judge for the suit, nor to the witnesses except for
their expenses, nor will he obstruct his adversary's proofs, nor say
anything against the witnesses called against him except what he
believes to be the truth, and that he will not use false methods of
proof. The defendant will swear he believes he is right to defend
himself and will swear the other things mentioned above. After
these oaths, the provost will ask the parties [to declare] the truth of
what is said before him, and if the defendant denies the complaint
made against him, if the plaintiff has his witnesses ready the provost will accept them immediately. If not, the plaintiff may have
two days,[6] if he likes, and no more, to make a proof, after a short
or a long interval, according to whether the witnesses are near or
far away, and as the provost sees fit. And it should be known that
when the witnesses are present, the provost will ask whether the
person against whom they are called wants to challenge them; and
he must reply. If he says no, from that time forward he will not be
able to challenge them; and if he says yes, he must say what [his

3. References are explained in the Abbreviations section.
4. *Cod.* 2.4.32 (Krueger 96).
5. *Dig.* 42.1.15pr for the general rule, and *Dig.* 42.1.15.9 for admissions (Watson 4:537–538).
6. The person calling witnesses in support of his contentions could bring
them to court on two separate days. In some places, three days were granted (L.
Tanon, *L'ordre du procès civil au XIVe siècle au Châtelet de Paris* [Paris: Larose et Forcel, 1886], p. 43 n. 3). Beaumanoir states that until this ordinance of Louis IX, all
the witnesses had to be brought on the first day, and there was no second opportunity (Beaumanoir §1165).

objection is]; and if he says something valid, he will be given a court date to prove what he says against the witnesses, in a single day. And the provost will accept the plaintiff's witnesses; and each will swear an oath separately; and he should hear their testimony in secret, and then make their testimony known [*les puepleera*]; and the defendant can raise valid issues against the testimony of the witnesses.[7] And if it happens, when the witnesses are called, that the defendant says under oath that he does not know the witnesses, he will be given a court date to speak against the witnesses, one day to speak and one to make proof, if he asks for it, and if he raises some valid point; nevertheless, the plaintiff's witnesses will be accepted and their testimony made public in the manner set forth above. And if witnesses were called against the plaintiff's witnesses, the plaintiff would be asked, as explained above, if he wanted to raise some issue against the witnesses called to discredit his own witnesses; and he would have to answer according to what is said above. And the form set out above would be followed in everything; and further witnesses will not be accepted from that point to discredit other witnesses. And the provost would give a judgment on the whole proceedings if the issue was clear. And there is no appeal from his judgment, ⟨according to written law in the *Code*, De precibus imperatori offerendis l. ult,[8] and l. Si quis,[9] cum autentica ibi signata, Quae supplicatio gloriosis;⟩[10] but you can request that the king review the judgment, and reverse it if it is against the law; ⟨according to written law in the *Code*, De sententiis praefectorum praetorio, l. unica,[11] where this subject is discussed⟩.

---

7. The party against whom the witness is called has an opportunity to challenge the *validity* of the witness (and can exclude the witness for bias, because he/she is a serf or a woman, etc.), and also to challenge *the testimony itself* (as false, hearsay, etc.).

8. *Cod*. 1.19.8 (Krueger 75).

9. *Cod*. 1.19.5 (Krueger 75).

10. The Authentics were laws made after the 533 publication of the *Codex*. They are also referred to as *Novels*, of which this one is 119 c.5, referred to in *Cod*. 1.19.5 (Krueger 510). The *Novels* form a fourth book of the *Corpus iuris civilis*.

11. *Cod*. 7.42.l (Krueger 314).

2. On forcing witnesses to give testimony in the
provost's court.

This same order of proof will be adhered to if there is a suit
on real property or deriving from real property. Again, if the defendant raises a valid defense, the order described above will be
followed in making proof. And it should be known that false witnesses will be punished as the provost sees fit. And witnesses will
be forced to give testimony in suits in the provost's court.[12]

3. On forbidding judicial battles and producing valid proof.

We forbid judicial battles in our whole domain in all suits,[13]
but we do not do away with the complaints, the answers, the continuances,[14] nor any other procedures that have been customary
in secular courts until now, according to the practice of different areas, except that we abolish judicial battles; and in place of
battles, we put proof by witnesses or writings; ⟨and this is written
in the *Code*, De pactis l. Pactum quod bona fide interpositum[15]
and in the *Code*, De transactionibus, l. Cum te transegisse.⟩[16] And
we do not abolish the other good and valid proofs that have been
customary in secular courts until now.

12. The only kind of suit mentioned in this chapter is civil. In such a suit, the
witnesses could not be challenged to a judicial battle, and thus their lives were not
in danger. In a criminal suit, a witness might be subject to a challenge to a judicial
battle, and to force such a person to be a witness might be to put his life in danger. Beaumanoir outlines an elaborate system of guarantees for witnesses, which
allows them to avoid any risk of a dangerous challenge; he states that where they
are subject to such a challenge, they cannot be forced to give testimony (Beaumanoir §1766).

13. This is the ordinance many times referred to which forbids judicial battles
in the king's domain. Lords in other jurisdictions could, however, permit judicial
battles. See Beaumanoir §1722.

14. A continuance [*contremand*] is a delay taken by a party for a limited
period of time, so that a court date is set for the suit to resume. Typically such a
delay is fifteen days. No special reason need be given for taking the continuance,
but only a limited number, usually three, may be taken. An adjournment [*essoine*]
is a delay taken or granted because of circumstances such as illness, where no date
for the resumption of proceedings is set. See Beaumanoir, chapter 3.

15. *Cod.* 2.3.17 (Krueger 93).
16. *Cod.* 2.4.5 (Krueger 95).

4. On informing the plaintiff about the penalty and on contesting witnesses.

We command that if any man wants to appeal against another for murder, he must be heard,[17] and when he is about to make his complaint, he must be told: "If you want to appeal for murder, you will be heard, but you must bind yourself[18] to suffer the same punishment as your opponent would do, if he were found guilty," ⟨according to written law in the *New Digest*, De privatis delictis, l. finali, libro nono.⟩[19] "And be assured that you will not be granted a judicial battle; but you must make proof by sworn witnesses; and you must have at least two valid [*bons*] ones; and bring as many witnesses as you like to make proof, and as many as you think will help you; and whatever is valid [as a proof] will be valid for you; for we abolish no proof that has been accepted in secular courts until now except the judicial battle; and you should know that your opponent can challenge your witnesses." And if the person wishing to make the complaint, when he has been told this, no longer wishes to pursue his suit, he can abandon it without penalty and without danger; and if he wants to go on with his complaint, he will make his complaint as he should according to the custom of the area and the district; and he will have his postponements [*respiz*] and his continuances.[20] And the defendant will have his defenses and his continuances according to the practice of the district. And when they reach the point where the

17. In criminal cases, the accusation had to be made by a plaintiff who had suffered loss as a result of the accused's action, and who thus became a party to the suit. In a murder case, this was typically a lord, vassal, or relative of the deceased. It was not usual for a criminal charge to be brought against a person without such a party-accuser.

18. That is, if you lose the suit.

19. *Dig.* 47.1.3 (Watson 4:737). This citation does not seem apposite. The *New Digest* is the third volume of the *Digest*, starting at Book 39.

20. Trial procedure included provision for various delays, postponements and interruptions, either at the request of the parties, the judge, or the jurors, or because of excusable failure to appear. Inexcusable absence counted as a default. Many customals contain lengthy discussions of these different kinds of postponements and delays. (Glanvill 1:10–29, pp. 7–17; Beaumanoir, chapter 3, *Etablissements* 1:124).

battle used to take place, the party who would have made proof
by battle if there had been a battle must make his proof by witnesses. And the judge will compel the presence of the witnesses
at the cost of the person calling them, if they are within his jurisdiction. And if the person against whom the witnesses are called
wishes to say anything against the witnesses called against him,
because of which they should not be accepted, he will be heard.
And if the reason is good and manifest and commonly known,
the witnesses will not be accepted. And if the reason is not commonly known, and the other party denies it, the witnesses will be
questioned, on both sides; and the testimony of the witnesses will
be communicated to the parties.[21] And if it happened that after
this communication the person against whom the witnesses were
called wanted to say something reasonable against the testimony
of the witnesses, he would be heard, ⟨according to written law
in the *Decretals*, De testibus, capitulo Praesentium statuimus,[22]
where this subject is written about and discussed⟩. And afterward
the judge will give his judgment.

5. These are the cases of high justice[23] of barons.

Suits on treachery [*traïson*], rape, arson, larceny, and all serious crimes where the penalty may include loss of life or limb,[24]

21. See note 6 above.

22. *Decr. Greg. IX* 2.20.31 (Richter p. 326).

23. High justice is jurisdiction over suits for which the punishment might be
death or dismemberment. Although larceny was punishable this way, it nevertheless belonged to low justice. In some districts, certain kinds of cases were reserved
for the count's court. Beaumanoir enumerates ten such kinds of suits (Beaumanoir,
chapter 10).

24. The *Etablissements de St. Louis* provide definitions of some of these crimes
in *Etablissements* 1:27. See also Beaumanoir, chapter 30. Most capital crimes were
against the person and often included violence. Larceny, or theft, which is a crime
against property, was nevertheless a capital crime. Other crimes of this kind included counterfeiting and robbery. Loss of life could mean execution by hanging
(for men) or burning or being buried alive (for women). See *Etablissements* 1:39.
Loss of limb could include loss of an eye, a hand, or a foot (*Etablissements* 1:32).
In some jurisdictions, counterfeiters were boiled as well as hanged (Beaumanoir
§835). A lower kind of jurisdiction is called *voierie* or *vaarie* in the *Etablissements*.
See *Etablissements* 1:33, 1:42, etc.

where there used to be a battle, will use these procedures. And in all these cases mentioned above, if somebody is accused in some *bailli*'s court, the *bailli* will hear the case up to the proof; and then he will alert us; and we will send somebody to hear the proofs; and those whom we send will call to hear the proofs some of those who will be giving the judgment.[25]

6. On appealing against a man for serfdom[26] in the secular court.

In a suit on serfdom, the person asking for a man as his serf will make his complaint and prosecute his suit according to the former practice until the moment of the battle; and instead of a battle, the person who would have made his proof by battle will prove what he would have proved by the battle by means of witnesses, or by a writing, or by other good and valid proofs that have been customary in secular courts until now, so that if the plaintiff makes his proof, the defendant will remain his serf; and if he does not make his proof, his fine will be at the will of the lord.[27]

7. On reversing a judgment in the king's court.

If somebody is trying to reverse a judgment in an area where judgments may be reversed, there will be no battle, but the complaint and the answer and the other proceedings will be brought to our court; and according to the proceedings the judgment will be affirmed or reversed. And the person found to be in the wrong will pay a fine according to the custom of the district.

25. Those who give the judgment are the *jugeors* rather than the judge, who merely runs the proceedings.

26. Such a suit would involve a runaway serf, who was being pursued by his or her master.

27. A fine at the lord's will might include all of a person's personal property, with a few exceptions; see *Etablissements* 1:58. In practice, it seems to have been much less; see Beaumanoir §848.

8. On appealing against your lord for default of judgment.[28]

If someone wants to appeal against his lord for default of judgment, the default must be proved by witnesses and not by a battle; so that if the default is not proved, the person appealing against his lord for default will have to pay the proper penalty, according to the custom of the area; and if the default is proved, the lord appellee must lose what is proper by the custom of ⟨the area and⟩ the district. And it should be known that the testimony of witnesses called in a case on serfdom, or in a suit where a lord is appealed against for default of judgment, will be made public, as was said above. And if the person against whom the witnesses were called wants to say something reasonable against the witnesses called against him, he will be heard.

9. On punishing false witnesses.

If somebody is found guilty or caught in false testimony in the above suits, he will be at the lord's discretion ⟨as to his fine⟩. And we abolish judicial battles in our whole domain forever: and we want the other procedures to be followed in our domain, as is explained above, in such a way that [*en tel maniere que*][29] we can add to them or take something away from them, or alter them whenever we want, if we see that it is right.[30]

28. Default of judgment is a refusal to give someone a hearing. The lord in whose court someone is seeking justice may take various delays, but when they are exhausted he must give the person a hearing. Failure to do so may be appealed to the next higher court, and if the lord is found guilty he may lose his jurisdiction over cases in his district. This was a serious situation because he would then also lose the revenue coming from the fines.

29. The expression *en tel maniere que* may here have the sense of "with the proviso that."

30. With Chapter 9 ends the portion of the *Etablissements* that gives rules of procedure in the courts of the Provost of Paris (see beginning of Chapter 1). Starting in Chapter 10 now appears the *Coutume de Touraine-Anjou*, which continues to Chapter 175, the last of Book 1, where the titles of these customals are given. Viollet prints an edition of the *Coutume de Touraine-Anjou* in volume 3, pp. 3–104 of his edition. The original is in two Paris manuscripts.

The Customs of Touraine and Anjou

10. On gifts by a gentleman to his children, and how they should distribute the estate if the father dies without making provisions.

A gentleman cannot give his younger children more than a third of his inherited real property;[1] but he can give his purchased or otherwise acquired real property [*ses achaz et ses conquestes*] to whichever of his children he wants: and so he could to a person outside the family if he wanted. But if he had purchased some properties that were part of his fief, and gave them to someone other than his oldest son, the latter could redeem[2] them [from the donee] by paying the [same] price his father had paid for them.

And if it happened that the gentleman died ⟨and went from life to death,⟩ without making a partition among his children, and

---

The title *The Customs of Touraine and Anjou* does not appear in the manuscripts of the *Etablissements*.

1. In Modern French called *propres*, "inherited real property" is that land, etc., which came to a person by descent from his or her ancestors. A man might also buy property, in which case in Old French it is called *acquets* if he buys it alone and *conquestes* if he buys it with a partner, such as his wife. The terminology is confused in Old French: Beaumanoir uses the term *conquès* (§365) and *aqueste* (§505). The *Etablissements* generally use *conquestes* as here, but also *aquestes* in 1:16, where the title of the chapter includes the word *conquestes*. I have generally translated *acquets* and *conquestes* as "purchased real property." A person's right to sell inherited real property is limited; but a person can freely dispose of purchased real property, either in a will or inter vivos, as this chapter shows.

2. If real property was sold outside the family, then a member of the family had the right to purchase the property from the buyer for the same price (*Etablissements* 1:161). This is called *retrait*, in Modern French *retrait lignager*, for which I have used the word "redemption." If no one in the family wanted to redeem, the lord could do so (*Etablissements* 1:164). The redemption typically had to be completed within a year and a day of the original gift or sale.

he had no wife, all the personal property would go to the oldest son, but he would pay his father's debts and charitable gifts.³ And if the younger children asked for a partition, he would by law give them their share of a third of his [father's] real property. And if the property [in that third] consisted of a single fief, the oldest need only warrant the others in coholdership [*parage*].⁴ And if he did not happen to give them a complete fief, he would warrant them in coholdership. And if the oldest son was contentious [*rioteus*] and he had made their one-third too small, the younger siblings need not take it unless they wished, but it would remain the oldest son's, and the younger sons would divide the larger part into two halves, and the oldest son would take the half he wanted. Thus the oldest son gets two-thirds, and in addition he takes the dwelling.⁵

11. On making partitions.

A gentleman can give his daughter, when she marries, a greater gift than is fair. And if her father married her [off] giving less than was fair, she could not come back to the distribution among the siblings [*fraresche*].

If a gentleman marries [off] his sister and gives her a small marriage gift, the husband cannot ask for more. But when her husband [*li sires*] dies,⁶ she can ask for a fair distribution if it seems

---

3. If the wife was still alive, she could elect to take half of the personal property and pay half the debts; see *Etablissements* 1:17.

4. The system of *parage* here referenced is created when a fief formerly held for homage by one man is divided after his death between two or more heirs. It is only the principal heir (typically the oldest son) who has to continue to do the homage. The other siblings hold in *parage*, which means that although they hold their land freely as a fief, they do not do homage for it to anyone. This system also obtained in Normandy (Gruchy, pp. 110–111). In Champagne all the brothers received an equal share in their father's land, but the oldest brother occupied the château and administered justice and also did homage to the overlord while his brothers did homage to him. This system was called *frérage* and is described in Beaumanoir §465 and in the *Ancien coutumier de Champagne*, chapter 1 (and see also Portejoie's introduction, pp. 47–48).

5. The dwelling is the principal dwelling on the fief, along with a small surrounding area of land. The calculation of the two-thirds of the property did not take account of this residential property.

6. Once the husband has accepted the marriage gift, he cannot sue on it.

to her that the brother gave her very little so as to keep more for himself; and her children [can also sue] if their mother has died.[7]

12. On distributions made among sisters after the father's death.[8]

If a gentleman has only daughters, each one will take as much as the other; but the oldest daughter will take the dwelling in addition and a one-*chesé* plot around it if there is one,[9] and if there is none then she will take five sous in annual income and warrant the others in coholdership.[10]

13. On the marriage gift given at the church door and keeping it for life after the heir has cried or yelled.[11]

After the death of his wife, a gentleman keeps, as a life interest, what he was given at the door of the church as a marriage gift, even though he has no heir, provided that he had one who cried and yelled, and that his wife was given to him as a virgin; for if she was a widow or had not been given to him as a virgin, he would keep nothing.

However, once he dies, his widow, the donor's sister, can sue, as can her children if she dies before her brother.

7. My emendation makes the somewhat obscure original express the law as explained by de Laurière in a note to this chapter in his edition. Viollet adds a note saying that the law is the same in Orléans.

8. Similar customs are found in Beaumanoir §§464, 1479, and in the *Ancien Coutumier de Champagne*, p. 145 and ibid., n. 2.

9. In the *Coutumes de Lorris*, this portion of land is defined thus: ". . . le vol d'un chapon estimé a ung arpent de terre allentour dudict manoir . . ." 'The flight of a chicken estimated as one *arpent* of land around the said dwelling' (p. 7).

10. Special rights for the oldest sister differ from district to district. In Anjou, as this chapter shows, the oldest sister inherits the dwelling and an equal share of the rest of the property. There is no special right in Lorris, where the sisters all inherit the same amount (*Coutumes de Lorris* §25). In Beauvais, the oldest daughter takes the dwelling before the rest is divided and also receives the homage of her sisters for their shares in the inheritance (Beaumanoir §§ 472–473).

11. The crying or yelling refers to the proof of the birth of a live child.

14. On promiscuous gentlewomen.

If a gentlewoman has a child before she is married, or if she loses her virginity, she loses her legal right to inherit when it is proved against her.[12]

15. On having a partition as the oldest son.

If a gentlewoman is the heir to some land, and her husband is dead, and she has given birth to his heir, and she wants to take her dower from her husband's land, which is one-third, her oldest son will take a third of *her* land.

16. On purchased or otherwise acquired real property.

A gentlewoman receives in dower only a third of her husband's land; but her husband may leave her his purchased or otherwise-acquired real property in his will; and if the husband had purchased part of his fief, the oldest son could redeem [from his mother] that purchased portion by paying the [same] price his father had paid.

17. On [a gentlewoman] paying her husband's debts.

A gentlewoman[13] does not contribute to her husband's bequests[14] [at his death]. And she may take a half of his personal property, if she wants, but she must pay half his debts; and if she does not want to take any of the personal property, she need pay none of the debts. And in this matter she can make her choice.[15]

---

12. In Normandy, (loss of) virginity was proved by a jury of seven widows and married women (Gruchy, p. 156).

13. The rights of commoner women were identical; see *Etablissements* 1:137.

14. In spite of the name, *aumone* in this context means a bequest to any person. Any bequest in a will used language such as "for the good of my soul." See Beaumanoir §426.

15. This choice was widespread with regard to personal property. See Beaumanoir §440, and the *Ancien coutumier de Champagne*, chapter 11. Those who inherited a deceased person's personal property were obligated to pay his or her

18. On the rights of gentlewomen and on keeping their dower in good condition.

A gentlewoman should have the dwelling of her husband after his death, until the person who has the remainder[16] [*le retour*] of the land has provided her with an appropriate dwelling. And she should keep it in good condition; and if she did not, the remainderman could take it away from her in a judgment [*par droit*], provided it was by her negligence that the dwelling had deteriorated: and she would also be required to make good the damages, and if she could not, he could take away the land in a judgment and retain it in his own keeping; for she would have forfeited [*meffet*] the dower, and she should lose it in a judgment [*par droit*]. And in the same way she should keep up vines and fruit-bearing trees, if she had them in her dower lands, without cutting them down or ill-treating them.

19. On keeping custodianship lands in good condition until the heir comes of age.

If it happened that a gentlewoman had a minor child and her husband died, she would keep the guardianship of the male heir until he was twenty-one, and the guardianship of her daughter until she was fifteen, provided there was no male heir; and she must keep everything in good order. And if there was a wood or a pond that her husband had previously sold, she could sell it.[17] And her [second] husband could do the same if she had one. And if she and her [second] husband allowed the house to deteriorate or fall down, of if they sold wood or a pond that had not been pre-

---

debts; see *Coutumes de Lorris* §265. Guardians could also take their wards' ancestors' personal property if they paid the debts; and they also could refuse it (Beaumanoir §§509, 518).

16. Since the widow only has a life interest, there is another heir who will come into the land on her death. This person is said to have the "remainder" or to be a "remainderman"; see *Etablissements* 1:121 and note.

17. The author means that she could sell the timber cut in the wood or the fish raised in the pond.

viously sold, the remainderman of the land could ask to be given the guardianship by a judgment.

20. Suits on land.

A woman can make her complaint concerning her dower in the king's court, or in the court of the castellany where it is situated, or in the ecclesiastical court; and the choice is hers. And a gentleman can do the same concerning his marriage gift that was given him at the church door.[18]

21. On gifts to a [new] knight [or] as a marriage gift.

If a gentleman marries [off] his son,[19] he should give him a third of his land, and also when he is [made] a knight; but he does not partition with him what has been given [to the father] as a marriage gift at the church door, {unless his wife is the heir to some land}, [but if she is] he will give him a third of his mother's land.[20]

22. On distributing property descended from grandfathers and grandmothers.

If it happened that a gentleman had a grandfather and grandmother, and a father and mother [all living], and he took a wife and he died before his wife, and they had no issue, then when the father and mother and the grandfather and the grandmother died, she would have dower rights in his inherited property.[21] And in all other [lateral] inheritances, whether from sisters and brothers,

---

18. For the life interest of a gentleman in the marriage gift, see §13.

19. This must mean his oldest son.

20. The last part of this paragraph is somewhat confused in the manuscripts; Viollet expresses his doubts and supplies a few words from the *Coutume de Touraine-Anjou*. Nevertheless, the translation is not incompatible with the textual lessons or with common sense. In Chapter 15 supra may be found the explanation: if the mother has inherited some land, her oldest son will receive a third of it when she becomes a widow.

21. That is, in the property the husband would have inherited if he had lived.

uncles or nephews, or some other relative, she would take noth-ing, if they occurred after her husband married her. And if they had passed laterally [to him] before [the marriage], then she would take dower in them.

23. On lateral inheritance from brothers.

All [lateral] inheritances that come to brothers go to the oldest,[22] after the death of the father, but not those [inheritances] coming from the mother, or from a grandfather or grandmother; for these are called direct inheritances [*escheoites droites avenues*].

24. On relief[23] paid for land held in coholdership.

No gentleman pays relief for anything that he takes as an in-heritance unless it passes laterally from further away than his first cousin, and no one can ask anyone for a distribution among rela-tives, unless he is a first cousin or closer [in kinship]. And for things that a gentleman takes on behalf of his wife, provided that she swears fidelity to her lord,[24] he pays relief of one year['s profits] of the land; and if she holds in coholdership, he pays no relief.[25]

25. On marrying a commoner.

If a gentlewoman marries a commoner [*vilain costumier*], their issue will take equal shares in their mother's fief, if there is no homage; and if there is an homage, the oldest will do the homage and will have in addition [to his share] the dwelling and also a *chesé* of land, if there is one;[26] and if there is no dwelling or not enough land, he will take an appropriate portion of the fief [as recom-

22. In some districts, lateral inheritances are shared among brothers without any special rights for the oldest (Beaumanoir §469).
23. Relief is a payment by the new holder of land to the lord from whom the land is held.
24. That is, if she is the principal holder of a fief.
25. That is, if she is only a minor holder of a fief, and not the principal holder.
26. For *chesé*, see note 9 above.

pense] for doing homage to the lord and for warranting the others [in coholdership]. And the fief will always be distributed this way until it descends the third time; and then it will ever afterward be distributed in the manner of gentlemen's fiefs [*gentilment*].

26. On distributing a barony.[27]

A barony is not divided between brothers, if their father has not partitioned it among them, but the oldest brother must give a fair gift [*bienfait*] to the younger ones and should marry the daughters. A baron has all the jurisdiction in his lands, and the king cannot issue proclamations [*metre ban*][28] in a baron's land without his consent, nor can the baron issue orders in a vassal's land without the consent of the vassal.

27. On high justice in a barony; on murder, rape, and homicide of pregnant women [*ancis*].[29]

A baron has [jurisdiction] in his land over murder, rape, and homicide of pregnant women, even if there was [a baron] who had not had this jurisdiction in the past. Rape is forcing women. *Ancis* is a woman who is pregnant when you hit her, and she dies with the child [*de l'enfant*]. Murder concerns a man ⟨or a woman⟩, when someone kills [either of] them in their bed, or in some manner provided it is not in a fight: a person could murder a man on his way somewhere, if he struck him so that he died, without quarreling with him or defying him.

27. A barony is usually a fief held directly from the king; see *Etablissements* 2:33.

28. Such orders might include conscription for military service, or the collection of taxes.

29. Du Cange thinks that *ancis* is derived from *incisio* since on the death of a pregnant woman an incision might be made for a cesarean section. Cited by Viollet 3:288.

28. On summoning and banishing an offender and coming and destroying property after the banishment.

When something is taken away from a person, on the road or in the forest, whether by day or by night, this is called robbery [*escharpelerie*]; and all those who commit this offense must be hanged and drawn,[30] and all their personal property is [forfeited] to the baron; and if they have lands, or houses on the baron's lands, the baron should burn them and plough the meadows, and tear up the vines, and ring [*cerner*] the trees.[31] And if any such offender fled and could not be found, the baron should have him summoned in the place where he was from ⟨according to written law in the *Code*, De foro competenti, l. Juris ordinem[32] and in the *Decretals* De dolo et contumacia, capitulo Causam quae[33] where this matter is discussed⟩, and in the church of the parish where he lived, [saying] he should come to court [*a droit*] within seven days and seven nights, to admit or to defend himself; and [the baron] would have him summoned in the marketplace. And if he did not appear within seven days and seven nights, he should be summoned again by a judicial order [*par jugement*] to appear within fifteen days and fifteen nights; and if he did not appear within fifteen days and nights, he would be summoned again to appear within forty days and forty nights; and if he did not appear within the forty days and nights, he would be banished [by an announcement] in the marketplace; and if he appeared later, and could not demonstrate a valid legal excuse [such as] that he had been on a pilgrimage or in some other reasonable place, where he did not hear the banishment, nor the summonses, the baron would have his lands ravaged [*revagier*] and the personal property would go to the baron.

30. Drawn probably means dragged through the streets, perhaps tied behind a horse, perhaps tied to a hurdle. It represented a kind of ignominy and, if done violently, could cause the death of the condemned prisoner.

31. A way to kill a tree without much effort is to cut off a strip of bark all round the tree, which will then die.

32. *Cod.* 3.13.2. (Krueger 128). The title of this book in Krueger is *De iurisdictione omnium judicum et de foro competenti.*

33. *Decr. Greg. IX* 2.14.3 (Richter 292).

29. On suspicion and summonses by a judge in the
secular court.

And if someone was suspected of such a crime, or of another,
similar one for which the penalty was death, and he had fled the
district and did not appear before the seven days and seven nights,
and the fifteen days and fifteen nights, and the forty days and forty
nights, had passed, and he appeared before the judge and said that
as soon as he heard that he had been summoned to court he had
appeared to make his defense, then the judge should take his oath
that he was telling the truth; and with that he would be permitted
to make a defense, if anyone wanted to appeal against him.[34] And
if there was no one who appealed, the judge could hold him on
suspicion; ⟨for suspicion should be far from all honest men [*prudes
homes*], according to written law in the *Code*, De furtis, Incivilem
rem et l. Civile),[35] for seven days and seven nights and fifteen days
and fifteen nights and forty days and forty nights, and would have
the deceased's family [*lignage*] summoned, if he had any, to find
out if they would appeal against him, and he would have [the
matter] announced in the church and in the marketplace; and if
nobody stepped forward to appeal against him, the judge should
release him after he presented sureties;[36] and if he could not obtain any, he should be made to promise and swear that he would
not run away for a year, nor would he hide, and that he would
come to court, if anyone wanted to appeal against him.[37]

30. On fights.

A man who kills another in a fight and can show a wound
which the other inflicted on him before he killed him will not be

34. An injured accuser is needed to commence a criminal trial. The court
rarely proceeded on its own initiative in criminal cases.
    35. *Cod.* 6.2.2,5 (Krueger 238).
    36. Sureties are like bail bondsmen, who guarantee that a released person
will return to court if summoned.
    37. In Beauvais, a person thus held could be released by a judgment after a
year, and would be thenceforth immune from accusations (Beaumanoir §917).

hanged by a judgment, except in one instance, which is that if a member of the dead man's family [*lignage*] appealed against him for the death of the person and accused him of having killed the person without having been struck or wounded by him, and he claimed that the dead man had commanded him and appointed him to prove it and argue it,[38] the other man could say that he did not believe that the dead man had given him the command and the appointment; and at that point a battle could be ordered by a judgment. And if either man was sixty years old, he could have another replace him [in the battle], but he would have to swear he was that old. And the person defeated in the battle would be hanged.

31. On requesting a guaranteed peace [*asseürement*] in the secular court, and on broken truces.[39]

If it happened that a man was on his guard against another[40] and he appeared before the judge to obtain a guaranteed peace, the judge should obtain the guaranteed peace for him, since he is asking for it; and he must make the person he is complaining of promise or swear that neither he nor his family [*li sien*] will do any harm to him or his family.[41] And if after this he did him some harm, and it could be proved against him, he would be hanged; for this is called a broken truce, which is one of the greatest treacheries there is. And the baron has jurisdiction of this matter.

And if he did not want to give a guaranteed peace, and the judge admonished him and said to him: "I forbid you to go away until you have given him this guaranteed peace"; and if he went away after the judge had forbidden it, and someone burned down one of the other person's houses, or spoiled his vines or killed him, he would be as guilty as if he had committed the action.

38. One must presume that before the injured man died, he was able to make these arrangements.

39. The contents of this chapter are much the same as those of *Etablissements* 1:41.

40. That is, he was afraid of him or in a private war with him.

41. In a private war or feud the relatives of the principal combatants are also involved because of their kinship (Beaumanoir §§1684–1686).

32. On stealing an animal or a horse, and loss of limb for the offense.

A thief is to be hanged who steals a horse or mare. And a person who burns down a house by night loses his eyes. A person stealing something from a church, or making false coinage, or who steals a plowshare, or steals other things, clothing or money, or other little things, should lose his ear for the first offense, and for the next theft he loses a foot, and at the third theft he is to be hanged; for you do not go from the large limb to the small one, but from the small one to the large one.

33. On high justice in the matter of treachery by a household member.

A man who steals from his lord, when he is fed at his lord's expense, is to be hanged; for this is a kind of treachery [*traïson*]; and the person against whom he offends can hang him, if he has the low justice [*la voierie*] in his lands.

34. On the jurisdiction of a [lower] vassal [*vavassor*].⁴²

No [lower] vassal can banish anyone, nor make anyone leave his castellany, without the assent of the baron in whose castellany he is. And if he does so, he loses his power to administer justice [*sa joutise*]; for a vassal has no such jurisdiction.

35. On women who consort with thieves or murderers.

Women who consort with murderers and consent to [their crimes] are to be burned. {And if they steal horses or donkeys, they are to be burned, but not otherwise.}⁴³ And if somebody was

---

42. A *vavassor* is a gentleman of lower rank than a baron.
43. The sentence in curly brackets does not appear in the manuscripts of the *Etablissements* but is borrowed by Viollet from the *Coutume de Touraine-Anjou*. The last part of the sentence, *ne autres choses*, could mean "or other things"; but Viollet proposes an amendment, "*non autrement*," which is what I translate here.

present [at the theft] and went along with it, and did not [them-selves] steal anything, they would have as great a punishment as if they had committed a theft.

36. On going along with murderers and thieves.

And if the murderers who kill people carry off something that belonged to those whom they murdered, and take it to some man's house, and the man knows they are thieves and suchlike malefactors [*menestrel*],⁴⁴ and he conceals [*recete*] them, he is to be hanged just like the murderers, ⟨according to written law in the *Code*, De sacrosanctis ecclesiis, l. Jubemus, §Iconomus⁴⁵ and in the *Decretals*, De officio delegati, c. Quia quaesitum;⁴⁶ for those who go along are punished like perpetrators⟩.

37. On accomplices of murderers.

If some thief or murderer says that some person is his accom-plice [*conpainz*], he is not thereby proved to be such; but the judge should arrest him to see if he can make him admit anything.

38. On punishing suspicious persons on the initiative of the provost.

If there is a man who has nothing, and who lives in the town without earning anything, and he likes to go to the tavern, the judge should arrest him and ask what he lives on. And if he under-stands him to be lying, and that he is debauched [*de mauvaise vie*], he should throw him out of the town; ⟨for it is part of the pro-vost's duties to weed bad men and women out of his jurisdiction and his province, according to written law in the *Digest*, De offi-cio praesidis, l. Congruit⟩.⁴⁷

44. In one of the manuscripts of the *Etablissements*, a marginal note in a sixteenth-century hand glosses the word *menestrel* as "murtriers."
45. *Cod.* 1.2.14.5 (Krueger 13). This section, *Cod.* 1.2.14.5, was formerly num-bered 1.2.14.2, and in Krueger commences *Oeconomus*.
46. *Decr. Greg. IX* 1.29.1 (Richter 158).
47. *Dig.* 1.18.13 (Watson 1:36). Cf. *Etablissements* 2:17 and also Beaumanoir:

39. On women's misadventure and a repeat thereof.

If by misadventure a woman kills her child, or strangles it, by day or night, she will not be burned the first time; but she should be handed over to Holy Church; but if she killed another, she would be burned, for it would be a habitual offense [*acoustumance*], ⟨according to written law in the *Code*, De episcopali audientia, l. Nemo, in fine,[48] cum suis concordanciis⟩.

40. On the intention of homicide without more.

If some persons had undertaken to go and kill a man or a woman, and they were arrested en route, by day or night, and taken before a judge, and the judge asked them what they were intending to do, and they said they were going to kill a man or a woman, and they had committed no more of an offense than that, they would not lose life or limb for that reason.

41. On threats and refusing to give a guaranteed peace before the judge, and on requesting [a guaranteed peace] from the sovereign, maintaining the rights [*droit faisant*] of the parties.[49]

If in the presence of a judge a man threatened to do another man harm, to his person or his property, and the latter requested a guaranteed peace, and the other replied: "I will take counsel," and the judge said to him: "Do not go away until you have given him a guaranteed peace"; and he went away, when this had been said and the prohibition stated, without giving a guaranteed peace; and the

---

"Ne nus plus grans biens, uns pour un, ne puet estre a baillif que d'essarter les mauvès hors des bons par radeur de justice" 'And a *bailli* can do no greater good (all things considered) (§14) than to weed out evil men from among the good by strictness of justice' (§14).

48. *Cod.* 1.4.3.4 (Krueger 39).

49. The contents of this chapter are much the same as those of *Etablissements* 1:31.

second man's house was burned; and the man who did not want
to give him a guaranteed peace had not yet done so, he would be
proved guilty and found guilty just as if he had truly done it. Or
if somebody killed the person who was seeking the guaranteed
peace, and the other was accused in court, who had refused to give
the guaranteed peace in the court of the king, or in a baron's court,
or that of any other man who had the power to administer justice
in his lands, then he would be as guilty as if he had performed the
act; and he could be arrested by law [*par droit*], even if he had
done nothing; and he would have deserved to be punished. For
this reason no one should refuse a safe truce before a judge. ⟨And
if somebody is in fear, he should come before a judge and request
a guaranteed peace, according to written law in the *Code*, De hiis
qui ad Ecclesiam confugiunt, l. Denunciamus, in fine.⟩[50]

42. On the power of [lower] vassals to administer justice.

All gentlemen who have low justice [*vaarie*] in their lands
hang thieves, whatever larceny they have committed on their
lands; but in some castellanies they are taken to be judged before
their lord; and when the lord has judged them, they are sent back
[to the lower] lord and he executes the sentence [*font la joutise*].

Lower lords have even more [power to administer justice]
when they administer battles for all matters except for the serious
crimes we have named above. And they have their standard measures in their lands and they take them and put them in the court-
yards of their castles and give them to their men [*homes*];[51] and
then if they find their men in possession of false measures, they
have jurisdiction; and they can exact a fine of sixty sous. And if the
sovereign discovers this before the lower vassal, he has jurisdiction. And if it can be proved that the vassal issued a false measure,
he will lose his personal property; and if he is willing to swear he

50. *Cod.* 1.12.5 (Krueger 66).
51. From the last sentence in this chapter, it appears that the word *homes* here
does not mean "noblemen."

did not issue a false measure, his oath would be sufficient to excuse him. And the man [*li vilains*] would pay a fine of sixty sous.

43. On releasing thieves and clearing oneself of suspicion.

No lower lord can release men or women thieves without his overlord's agreement or order; and if he does release one, and it can be proved and found against him, he loses his administration of justice [*sa joutise*].[52] And if he wanted to say he did not release the thief, but he escaped, and that he guarded him as well as he could, and added: "I will do whatever is needful in this matter,"[53] then the lord could give a judgment requiring an oath; and if he dared to swear the oath, he would be cleared.[54]

44. On requesting jurisdiction and cognizance, according to correct procedure, and leading off by the hand a man under one's jurisdiction, to one's court, honestly.

Whatever the crime of which an overlord has accused a man of one of his vassals,[55] the vassal can have the jurisdiction of the case, if he appears [in court] to request it, leading his man by the hand, unless it is a case of high justice;[56] for if any man makes a

---

52. Loss of power to administer justice would also mean loss of revenue from the fines.

53. This formula implies that the person saying it is willing to make a proof as required by the court, such as swearing an oath that what he claims is true.

54. In minor matters, where there is no way to prove or disprove a contention, a person may be required to swear (if he dares) an oath that what he says is true. The implication is that a person will not dare to swear a false oath for fear of damnation. Once the oath is sworn, the matter is considered closed.

55. In the circumstances described here, there are three men, all gentlemen, involved: first, the overlord [*baron*] who holds his fief directly from the king; second, the overlord's vassal; and third the man (or vassal of the vassal), whom the overlord is accusing, or who is accused in the overlord's court. The middle vassal, the man's immediate superior, has the right to try his own man for most offenses, if he requests to have the case sent down [*ravoir sa court*]. He must present himself when his man is summoned in the overlord's court, holding his man by the hand, to request that the case be sent down.

56. High justice concerns crimes for which the punishment is death or dismemberment, but not usually including larceny, for which the punishment is

complaint in the overlord's court against the man of a vassal, the vassal can have the case sent down to his own court, unless it is a case of failing to pay a toll [*chemin brisé*] or an offense in the marketplace. He cannot have these [former] cases sent down, unless he appears leading the man by the hand. Nor would he obtain jurisdiction of a case of default [of judgment], if the other party was appealing for that reason, or of res judicata, if the other person says that he has obtained a judgment in the sovereign's court, nor for offenses admitted [there], even if he admitted them [again] later [*tout les avoast-il emprès*];[57] for the sovereign and his judges should not make a recall from memory[58] in a vassal's court of any case tried before them.[59]

45. On arresting and pursuing [*suite*] murderers and thieves.

If a thief or a murderer commits a larceny or a murder in one castellany and flees into another, [and] if the baron in whose castellany the crime was committed sends someone to get him back, he can have him back by law, on payment of two sous and a half for each thief to the baron who has arrested them. And if the larceny had been committed in the lands of some lower vassal, provided the vassal had low justice [*vaarie*] in his lands, his lord should give [the vassal] back [the accused] on payment of the two sous and a half the lord had given the [other] baron.

---

nevertheless hanging. Larceny and all other crimes belong to low justice. See *Etablissements* 2:33.

57. The higher court does not give evidence in a lower court about its own judgments or about the admissions made there; so when either of these things has occurred, the case remains where the judgment or admission was made and is not sent down.

58. In an oral culture, memory was used instead of written records. A person who had heard or seen something could be called to court to repeat it or recall it from memory; thus the meaning of *recorder* 'to recall from memory' and *recort* 'a recall from memory'. Cf. the Italian *ricordarsi* 'to remember'. Only some courts were considered competent to produce decisions that could later be recalled; see *Etablissements* 2:11, 33. Persons making a recall from memory were immune to appeal.

59. A higher judge is not obliged to give account of his judgments to a lower court, which could not in any case overturn them.

46. On coholders [of fiefs].

If the baron is requesting an aid[60] from his vassals, he should summon them before him. And if a vassal has any coholders[61] who should contribute to the aid, the baron should assign him [the vassal] a day on which he can have his coholders present; and the vassal should tell the coholders to appear on that day to see the aid given; and if the coholders do not appear, {the coholder will still have to contribute to the aid and}[62] they will not thereby avoid contributing, since they have been summoned. And if someone pays his aid without summoning his coholders, they need not contribute unless they want [to do so].

47. On holding [fiefs] as coholders.

No man who holds as a coholder owes an aid to his coholder [*aparageor*],[63] unless the latter is giving an aid to his overlord. And if there is someone who has coholders who hold from him as coholders, he cannot by law summon them outside the fief.

A man who holds as a coholder holds freely and in the condition of a gentleman just like the person from whom he holds; and as a coholder he shares equally in the jurisdiction.

60. An aid is a payment made by fiefholders to their lord on certain occasions, such as to pay his ransom or on the marriage of his oldest daughter.
61. Where an older son does homage for his younger brothers for a fief they have inherited, they may be all responsible for paying an aid. The relationship between them is called *parage*, and they are *parageors*, here translated "coholders."
62. The words in curly brackets do not appear in the manuscripts of the *Etablissements*, but are taken by the editor Viollet from the *Coutume de Touraine-Anjou* where they appear at this point.
63. The *aparageor* is the person from whom a coholder holds his fief, usually his brother. This relationship is expressed as a paraphrase in *Etablissements* 1:81.

48. On demonstrating your kinship to your lord and on holding as a coholder without giving a service horse [*roncin de service*].[64]

When someone has held as a coholder for a long time, and the person from whom he holds wants him to do homage,[65] or if not that then what he should, then the former must show that there is between them such a degree of kinship that their children may not marry.[66] And if he cannot prove this kinship, he must by law do homage; and the lord cannot require of him more than one service horse[67] because the fief is no longer held in coholdership.

49. How a man should behave toward his lord when [the lord] threatens him with losing his land.

If the baron asks his vassal for land that the vassal holds from him, the vassal does not plead against him in the baron's own court unless he wants to do so; for the baron is like the taker, and for this reason he is not obliged to plead before him; instead, he will plead in the court of the lord from whom the baron holds; and if a judicial battle is judged between the lord and his vassal, the man need not fight in the lord's court, for the court would

---

64. The material in this chapter is repeated in *Etablissements* 1:79.

65. When land was held in coholdership (typically by younger siblings who inherited only one-third of a fief among them) the coholders did not do homage (*Etablissements* 1:81). After the third generation of coholders, however, the land reverted to being a fief that did homage (*Etablissements* 1:25). In the present chapter, the lord thinks he may be entitled to this homage and demands that the landholder show in court the status of the holding.

66. Under canon law after 1215, a person could not marry another person descended from the same great-great-grandfather or great-great-grandmother. The person making the proof here would have to show that he and the person challenging him had a common great-grandfather (or great-grandmother). The children of the marriage would thus have a common great-great-grandfather or great-great-grandmother and would not be outside the forbidden degrees of kinship for marriage. For degrees of kinship, see Beaumanoir, chapter 19 and §1686; *Decr. Greg. IX* 4.14.8; and the Tree of Consanguinity on pp. 1425–1426 of the first volume of the *Corpus iuris canonici* in Friedberg's edition.

67. A service horse [*roncin de service*] was part of the service given for a fief. See *Etablissements* 1:80.

not be impartial [*igauz*], for there would be an appearance that the lord had more power than the man. If the lord is a baron, he should name the king's court, or the courts of two other barons, and the man can take whichever of the three he wishes; and if the greater lord is a vassal, the battle will be in the court of the baron from whom he holds, unless he can prove that his lord has done him harm [*fait grief*].

50. On showing your fief to your liege lord.

If the baron summons his man to show him his fief, he should give him a court date fifteen days and fifteen nights later; and the vassal should show him all he knows about. And if the man had a vassal or a man who did not want to appear, the overlord should help him to pursue him and force him to appear. And afterward, when the lord has been shown his fief, he should ask his man: "I ask you if you have any more held from me." The man should answer and say: "Sir, I ask for time to have an inquiry [*anqueste*], as I should, for I am not fully informed." And the lord should give him forty days and nights to inquire in a hearing [*par droit*] and ask questions. And afterward, if the man says to his lord, "Sir, I cannot discover that I hold any more from you," the lord should ask him if he is ready for judgment. And when the man has shown him that the inquiry revealed nothing else, the lord can declare in a judgment that he can hold nothing more from him. And if the lord knew some things and he spoke to the vassal in this manner: "I want you to lose the fief you hold from me, because this is part of my own fief"—and he should show [the vassal] what [he is talking about]—"and you did not show it to me"; and if the man says: "Sir, I was not aware of it, and I will do whatever I must for it",[68] it can be decided that he will swear with his right hand on the saints that he knew nothing of it on the day he reported the results of the inquiry; and the baron will keep possession of however much

68. This is a formula meaning that the man is ready to do whatever the court's judgment says he must do.

land he found.[69] And if the man does not dare swear the oath, he loses his fief; for it is apparent that he wanted to steal it from [the baron]. And it would be the same for all lords who had sworn vassals [*hommes de foi*], who held fiefs from them, if such a case arose.

51. On cutting wood in a forest.[70]

For a gentleman there are only three kinds of penalties [*droiz*]:[71] a wager of law,[72] or [loss of] his fief or his personal property; except in the case of established penalties, that is to say: if he appeals against a man or woman in reckless folly [*de folie desloial*], or if he cuts wood in the forest, the penalties for which are sixty sous {or if he fails to pay a toll [*tranche chemin*], or if he had oxen herded in a forbidden area [*defois*], or if he committed some other offense for which the penalty is sixty sous}. The wager of law is five sous in the king's court and in several castellanies.

69. It appears that the portion not shown by the vassal reverts to the baron (overlord). If the vassal is prepared to swear he knew nothing about it, he may keep the rest of his fief. If he dares not swear, he loses the whole fief.

70. This chapter heading seems inadequate. Some manuscripts have a different heading: "On the Penalties of Gentlemen."

71. My reading of this chapter is that it enumerates the penalties (fines) to which a gentleman may be subjected. De Laurière, while admitting that the chapter is difficult, reads it as enumerating the fines a gentleman can impose in his court.

72. As is clear from the last sentence of the chapter, a wager of law is five sous in most districts. The term is said by Viollet (1:245–250) to refer to a fine that may differ according to the law under whose jurisdiction a man is. That situation goes back to the time of personality of law, when the occupying Franks were subject to their law and the occupied, romanized Gauls were subject to theirs, even if they all lived in the same place. In another use of a similar term, *gager sa loi* is, according to Raguau and de Laurière's *Glossary* (p. 260), a term of Norman law meaning an oath of denial permitted in minor matters [*simple action personnelle*], taken by a defendant, with an undertaking to come to court for trial. The Norman procedure was also called a *desresne*. The trial itself might take the form of another oath. See Gruchy, chapters 84–85, pp. 191–194. It may be observed that five sous is the fine for minor matters.

52. On [a gentleman's] laying hands on his lord with evil
intent, and on lawfully defending his lineage against his
rightful liege lord without losing his fief.

If a gentleman lays hands on his lord with evil intent before
his lord has laid hands on him, he loses his fief as a penalty. And if
he attacks his lord in a private war or an armed cavalcade with persons who are not his relatives, he loses his fief.[73] And if any liege
man hears his lord who is his liege lord accused of treachery [*trai-
son*][74] and does not offer to defend him, he loses his fief.

53. On summoning your vassal to make war on the king.

If a baron has a liegeman and he says to him: "Come away
with me, for I want to make war on my lord the king who has refused me a hearing in his court," the man should answer his lord
this way: "Sir, I will be glad to go find out from the king if it is the
way you tell me." Then he should go to the king and say to him:
"Sir, my lord has told me that you refused him a hearing in your
court; for this reason I have come to you to find out the truth; for
my lord has summoned me to go to war against you." And if the
king says: "I will never give your lord a hearing in my court," the
man should immediately return to his lord; and the lord should
reimburse his expenses. And if he would not go away with him
[to war], he would lose his fief as a penalty [*par droit*]. And if the
king had answered: "I will willingly give your lord a hearing in
my court," the man should come back to his lord and say: "Sir, the
king told me that he will willingly give you a hearing in his court";
and if the lord says: "I will never enter his court, but come away

73. These words imply that a gentleman could attack his own lord if he did so
as a family participant in a private war. The title of the chapter supports this view.
74. *Traïson* seems to mean "stealth," doing something without warning. The
crime of *occire en traïson* or "killing by stealth" is often shortened to the single
word *traïson*. Thus the word *traïson* by itself is often a way to say "homicide." See
Beaumanoir §826, and my "Murder by Stealth: *Traïson* in Old French Literature,"
*Studies in Honor of Hans-Erich Keller: Medieval French and Occitan Literature and
Romance Linguistics*, ed. Rupert T. Pickens (Kalamazoo: Western Michigan University, 1993), pp. 459–473.

with me as I summoned you," then the man could say: "I will not go." He would not lose any part of his fief as a penalty [*par droit*].

54. On resisting arrest by your lord, giving false measure, and fishing in [his] [private] fish pond, and hunting and catching rabbits in [his] game preserve, and lying with [his wife or daughter] by force.

A man who resists arrest by his lord loses his personal property; or if he lays hands on his certain representative with evil intent, or if he resists him, the same penalty; or if with evil intent he accuses him of lying; or if he has issued a false measure in his lands; or if he continually avoids[75] his lord with evil intent; or if he has fished in his ponds without his knowing; or if he has stolen his rabbits in his game preserves; or if he lies with his wife, or his daughter (provided she is a virgin), he loses his fief, provided it is proved.[76] ⟨And law and custom are in agreement.⟩

55. On deflowering by force a woman who is in custodianship or guardianship.

If a gentleman gave a virgin in guardianship to another gentleman who was his vassal, whether of his own lineage or another, [and] if he deflowered her and it could be proved, he would lose his fief, even though it was the wish of the virgin. And if it was by force, he would be hanged, if it could be proved. ⟨And so he should be punished according to written law in the *Code*, De raptoribus, l. prima et per totum titulum.⟩[77]

75. The different manuscripts read "pursues" or "deceives" or "avoids" at this point.

76. The penalty of losing personal property is clearly imposed for the first offense mentioned in this chapter: resisting arrest. Deflowering the lord's daughter, the last offense mentioned, is clearly punished by the loss of the fief. The offenses in between are all joined by the word "or," and it is therefore difficult to tell which of the intermediate offenses belongs to which punishment.

77. *Cod.* 9.13.1 (Krueger 378). The heading cited by the author is an error. In the *Code*, 9.13 begins *De raptu*, and its law 1 begins *Raptores*. The heading *De raptoribus* belongs to Constitution 35 of the Emperor Leo.

56. On [a lord's] refusing a hearing and the judgment of his court to his liegeman and others.

When a lord refuses the judgment of his court to his man, and it can be proved, the man will never more hold anything from him, but from his lord's overlord. And so it would be if a lord lay with his vassal's wife or his daughter (if she was a virgin); or if one of the man's female relatives was a virgin, and he gave her into the custodianship of his lord, and the lord deflowered her, he would never hold anything from him again.

57. On standing an honest watch at your liege lord's castle.

If the lord summons his men who owe him their watch,[78] a man who owes the watch should be there with his wife, if he owes it with his wife; and if he owes it without his wife, he and his officers must be there; and he must sleep there every night; and if he did not perform as we have said, he would lose his personal property. He who owes a liege watch must be there with his wife and his officer, and with most of his household; but he need not neglect going about his own business as needed; and if he had left the liege watch, and the lord accused him and said that he had left in neglect of his liege watch, the lord could demand him to swear an oath that he had not left in neglect of his liege watch. And if he did not dare swear the oath, he would lose his personal property.

58. On gentlemen's personal property when they lose it [*perdent leur propre*].

If a gentleman loses his personal property [as a penalty], he must swear to his lord, when he loses it, that he will conceal nothing, but bring it all forward. If he is not a man who bears arms,

78. The "watch" means the duty of standing guard at the lord's castle, which is part of feudal duty.

he will keep his palfrey, and his squire's horse [*roncin*], and two saddles for him and his squire if he is rich, and his packhorse that draws him around his land, and his bed, {and his everyday garment [*robe*]}, and his ceremonial garment [*robe a cointoier*], if he has two, and a ceremonial belt, and a brooch and a ring, if he has one, and his wife's bed, and the lady's ceremonial dress, and a belt, and a ring and a purse, and a brooch and her wimple; and everything else goes to the lord who has been awarded [*a gueaignié*] the personal property. And if he bears arms, he will keep his horse and all his arms; and otherwise as we have said above. And if the lord does not believe his man has told the truth about his personal property, he can do no more than make him swear an oath.

59. On a complaint made in the king's court against your lord, without paying a fine to your lord.

If any man complains against his lord in the king's court, the man will never pay a penalty nor a fine to his lord. If the king's judge found out that the lord was accusing his man over this, he would have the suit stopped and the lord would pay a penalty to the king for having started the suit.

60. On inspections made by a judge.

If a man complains in the king's court that some other man is wronging him with respect to some land or houses, and the baron in whose lands they are asks to have the case sent down to him, and the plaintiff says: "I do not wish to leave this court until there has been an inspection," then they should give him an inspection day; and the king's judge and the baron's judge must attend. And the plaintiff must show the two judges what he is demanding from the other party. And after the inspection, the baron should have jurisdiction of the case, if it concerns his fief; and if they complain, he must assign a day for a hearing before him. And if the other party asks again to have an inspection of what was inspected by the judgment of the king's court, he will have no right to it; for all inspections made in the court of the highest lord are firm and fixed by law.

61. On the king's law [*Du droit au prince*].

A baron does not have a case concerning his vassal sent down from the king's court in cases on default [of judgment] [*de defautes*]; but when accusations are admitted [to be true], the case is sent down for him to do what he wants with, and to deal with [*enteriner*] the issues admitted before the king's judge.[79] But if the baron did not do this, and there were follow-up complaints in the king's court because of the baron's default, and it could be proved and he asked to have the case sent down, he would not get it; instead, the king would, by his own hand, deal with everything that had been done before him.

62. On thieves or murderers.

If a thief or a murderer had been arrested in the king's court, when the crime had been committed in a baron's castellany, the baron would take custody of [him], and would not pay the two sous and a half;[80] for no man pays this to his lord, and no lord pays it to his own man. But [the baron] pays the reasonable costs that were incurred before [the criminals] were asked for. {This is what a lord should do for his man. And if [criminals] had been asked for and [the lord] kept them,}[81] none of the costs from then on would be reimbursed.

79. The author means that the penalties for the admitted actions should be executed by the lower lord.

80. See *Etablissements* 1:45.

81. The words in curly brackets are taken by Viollet from the *Coutume de Touraine-Anjou*. They appear in a very attenuated or garbled form in some of the manuscripts of the *Etablissements*.

63. The tax-free status [*franchise*] of a gentleman.

No gentleman pays any customary dues or tolls [*paages*][82] for anything he buys or sells, unless he is buying to resell; and if he had bought some animals and kept them a year and a day in his house or under his care, he would pay no sales tax [*vantes*].

64. The tax-free status of officers [*sergant*].

Gentlemen exempt their officers from sales taxes and tolls [*de vantes et de paages*] for their animals and the food they grow in their castellanies, and the wine and wheat that grow in their castellanies.

Each vassal can exempt one officer, provided he is his provost and collects his customary dues for him. And [gentlemen] exempt them from being called up for the army or for mounted expeditions.

65. On summoning vassals to serve in the king's army.

If the baron has his men summoned for them to bring their commoners for service in the king's army, the provost should bring one from each house to the lord's command, in the castle courtyard; and when they have brought these men to the lord's command, the provosts should go back home. No commoner woman owes any service in the army or on a mounted expedition; nor do the bakehouse keepers or the millers who take care of the bakehouses and the mills. And if any who were summoned failed to come, and the baron could discover it, they would pay a fine of sixty sous. And the baron's provost should bring them to

82. *Paages* usually means "tolls" yet de Laurière, quoted by Viollet, argues that this word is here derived from *pacare* 'pay' rather than from *pedaticum* 'toll,' so that it should be translated as "sales tax". However, in a similar rule in Beauvais, the gentleman is subject to *travers* and *chauciees*, as well as to *toutes manieres de paages*, and the proximity of these words suggests that the word *paage* in the *Etablissements* does indeed mean "tolls" and not "sales tax" (Beaumanoir §892).

the king's provost at the castle in whose jurisdiction they are; and then he should return home.

Commoners in the castellanies owe to their baron service in a mounted expedition; and the vassal's provost should lead them to the castle courtyard to the baron's command. And the baron should not lead them to a place from which they cannot come home in the evening; and whoever stayed behind would pay a fine of sixty sous. And if the baron tried to lead them so far away that they could not come home in the evening, they would not have to go, unless they wanted to, and they would have to pay no penalty or fine.

The barons and the king's vassals must serve in his army, when he summons them; and they must serve at their own expense, forty days and forty nights, with as many knights as each one is responsible for. And they owe him this service if he summons them and there is a need for it. And if the king wanted to detain them longer than the forty days and forty nights at their own expense, they need not stay unless they wanted to; and if the king wanted to keep them there at his own expense to defend the kingdom, they should remain by law; but if the king wanted to lead them out of the kingdom, they would not have to go unless they wanted to, once they had served their forty days and forty nights.

And no lady owes service in the army or on a mounted expedition in person; but if she is the king's vassal, she must send as many knights as her fief owes; and then the king cannot lay any blame on her [*ochoisoner*]. And if the king's men found in the castellanies any commoners who had stayed away from service in the king's army, besides those who were supposed to remain behind, the king could fine each one sixty sous by law, and the baron could do nothing to protect them. And commoners are supposed to serve only forty days and forty nights in the king's army; and if they left before the forty days and forty nights were up, and it were proved, the king's judge could fine them sixty sous by law [*par droit*].

66. On taking the fruits of the land from a lord as his relief [*rachat*], and a woman's relief when she marries.

No woman pays relief,[83] unless she marries;[84] but if she marries, her husband must pay relief to the lord whose woman she is. And if the lord is not happy with what he offers, he can take [instead] only the fruits of his fief for one year. And if there were timber which the woman had begun to sell and which she and her husband had formerly sold, and she was entitled to sell it the other time,[85] [then] by law and because of the relief the lord could sell it at the same price at which it had begun to be sold, but he could not make a better deal than they had made earlier.

67. On giving security to your liege lord because of the possibility of marriage [of your daughter], and on [the family's] doing the best and most honorable thing for the young lady.

When a lady is left a widow and she has a daughter, and the lady gets sick, and the lord who is her liege lord comes to her and makes this request: "Lady, I want you to give me security that you will not marry off your daughter without my advice, nor the advice of her father's family; for she is the daughter of my liege man, and for this reason I do not want her to be deprived of our counsel [*forsconsoilliée*]": then the lady must by law give him security. And when the young lady is of marriageable age, if the lady finds a man who is asking for her [in marriage], she should come to the lord and the young lady's father's family, and speak to them in this way: "Lords, I have been asked for my daughter in marriage, and I do not want to give her without your advice, nor should I; now give me good and honest advice; for such-and-such a man is ask-

83. Relief is a payment made to the overlord of a fief when the fief changes hands because of the death of the former holder. It is like an inheritance tax.

84. The various manuscript variants make it clear that this means "remarries."

85. Perhaps this means that the timber has grown up again. Timber of less than seven years' growth could not normally be cut (Beaumanoir §437). But it could easily be seven years or more since the woman and her first husband had first sold timber.

ing for her"—and she should name the man. And if the lord says: "I don't want this man to have her, for such-and-such a man is asking me for her, who is a much richer and nobler man than the one you are speaking about, and he will gladly take her [in marriage]"—and he should name him—and if the father's family says: "We know of a richer and nobler man than either of those you have named"—and they should say his name—then they should determine [*regarder*] the best of the three and the most beneficial to the young lady. And the person who decides [*qui dit*] which is the best of the three must be given credence [*crëus*], for by law no one should pretend to be deaf [*faire lou seurdois*]. And if the lady married off [her daughter] without the advice of her lord and the father's family, after she had been forbidden to do so, she would lose her personal property. And if it was necessary, her lord could compel her [to make disclosure] before she left her fief or her fealty; and she would have to swear to tell the truth concerning her personal property, as soon as she lost them by a judgment; and when she had brought all of them [to court], she would keep her everyday dress and her ceremonial dress, and appropriate jewels if she had any, and her bed and her cart, and her horse which would be enough for her to go about on business, provided she had no husband, and her palfrey if she had one.

68. On keeping fiefs without detriment, and on the gift of a gentleman.

A lady is only the custodian of her land once she has a male heir, and she cannot give it away or exchange it for anything else to the detriment of the heir, except for her memorial services [*aniversaire*], and she cannot give even a third or a quarter or a fifth, according to the custom of the secular court. A gentleman can give a third of his land, whether he has a child or not; but he cannot give a greater gift that would be enforceable [*estable*] by law.

69. On novel disseisin[86] and keeping things safely while maintaining the rights of the parties, and on awarding costs and damages.

If some man, whether a gentleman or a commoner, appears before his lord (provided the latter has the low justice in his lands) and says: "Sir, such-and-such a man has recently [*de novel*] come to me and disseised me of a house, or of meadows, or of a vineyard, or of land, or of quitrents [*cens*],[87] or of some other thing which I have enjoyed the benefits of [*esploitié*] this year and last year and the year before, and for which I was doing service to the lord, right up till now when he has disseised me wrongfully and by force; for which reason I request you to take the matter into your hands," the lord should answer: "And I will, if you give sureties [*pleges*] to prosecute the claim that this man has disseised you wrongfully and by force, as you have said"; and if he does not give him good sureties, the lord does not have to disseise the other man. And if he says: "I will be glad to give you good sureties," he should take the sureties, good ones and of sufficient wealth [*soufisans*][88] according to the magnitude of the suit. And when he has taken the sureties, he should send a sure messenger to summon the other party, and he should say to him: "Such-and-such a man has given good sureties that he will provide evidence [*prouver*] that you [*il*] have disseised him wrongfully and by force of such-and-such a thing"—and he must name it—"and in novel disseisin; I want to know if you will give sureties as a defendant"; and if he says: "I will not give sureties," then the other person must be given seisin because he did give sureties; and if the [other] man says: "I will give good sureties for my defense that there is nothing [in the claim] and that I am within my rights," the judge should assign a court date to both parties and take the property into his hands

86. That is, a recent deprivation of someone of possession and use, by occupying, usurping, or otherwise illegally seizing the property. See D. W. Sutherland, *The Assize of Novel Disseisin* (Oxford: Oxford University Press, 1973).

87. Quitrents could be usurped by being collected by a person who was not entitled to them. The right to collect rents is considered as real property.

88. *Soufisans* has the meaning of "solvent," or "able to pay."

until one or other of them has won seisin by a judgment [*par droit*]. ⟨And it is written in the *Code*, De ordine cognitionum, l. Si autem negotium, circa medium legis.[89] [The defendant]⟩ comes to the lord and should say to him: "Sir, this man made you think that I had disseised him by force, and gave sureties he would make his proof, and had me disseised wrongfully; and I have won my rights [*droiture*][90] by the judgment of your court;[91] for which reason I request you as my lord to have me reimbursed my costs and the expenses I paid during this suit"; for it is right that if someone has another person disseised and accuses him of disseising him wrongfully and by force, and then loses the suit, then that person losing the suit should reimburse the other for his costs and damages and expenses because he had him disseised; and this is the reason why sureties are required; and he must be made to reimburse the costs and damages and expenses the other person suffered during the suit; {but he should swear how much he spent} on hiring advocates and the other things belonging to the suit; and upon that he will get [his reimbursement] ⟨on the estimate of the judge, according to written law in the *Code*, De judiciis, l. Properandum et l. Sancimus omnes judices[92] etc., and in the *Digest*, de judiciis, l. Eum quem[93] etc., and in the *Decretals*, De dolo et contumacia, c. Finem litibus,[94] where this issue is discussed⟩.

70. On a default after a court inspection.

Everything in the hands of a judge is as if it had been shown in court; and when two parties have a court date concerning something in the hands of the judge and one of them defaults, the de-

---

89. *Cod.* 7.19.7 (Krueger 304). In Krueger this law commences *Si quando negotium*.

90. *Droiture* here probably means "fundamental ownership" as opposed to seisin.

91. This scenario assumes that the defendant prevails in the suit.

92. *Cod.* 3.1.13,15 (Krueger 120–122).

93. *Dig.* 5.1.79. (Watson 1:174).

94. *Decr. Greg. IX* 2.14.5. (Richter 293).

faulter must be given an official summons[95] by three lords of fiefs who can make a recall from memory of the judgment. And if he does not appear on the date officially assigned, once the assigned day is over, the seisin [of the property in the judge's hands] should be given to the other party, who must be prepared to return to court [*d'estre a droit*], if anything should be required of him in the suit, and must give sureties to that effect.

71. On assigning of court dates by a judge.

If someone makes a complaint to a judge about some other person concerning land, the judge should assign him a court date; and if the person given the court date defaults, the plaintiff should {appear before the judge} and speak this way: "Sir, he is in default, and I request a ruling." The judge should have the officer who served the summons speak in court, and if the officer warrants having served it, the judge should have him summoned again up to three times, and when the officer had warranted serving the three summonses, the judge can rule in a judgment that the person defaulting can be officially summoned [*atermez o jugement*]; and the judge should send three officers who can testify by recall from memory. And if the person who has defaulted three times comes to the court date of which he has been officially notified, and the other party who has made the complaint can make his complaint to him and ask for reimbursement of his damages, at sixty sous for each default if he is a gentleman; and if the other party says: "I don't want to give anything"—and states the reason why—"for I never heard or learned about any summons except this one"; and if the other party says: "I don't agree, and I don't see how he can raise this defense, for the officers have warranted that they served the summons and gave him the three court dates"; and if he says: "I make a denial against you and against the officers, [to

---

95. This form of summoning, *metre terme o jugement*, implies a strictly controlled and official summons made by officers who can testify later in court that they properly summoned the person. The term appears again in the next chapter.

be proved] as it will be ruled in my case," then the judge can rule
that if he dares swear with his right hand on the saints that he
never heard the officers or heard that they had summoned him
the three times, as they had previously warranted, then he is discharged of the defaults; and thus the court date officially notified
[*li jors jugiez*] will be like a simple summons. And if he dares not
swear the oath, he must give the gentleman sixty sous for each
default; but the latter must swear it has cost him that much for
hiring his counsel and his advocates; and for each default he must
pay the judge his wager of law.[96] And thus you get sixty sous
for each default proved and admitted and judged in favor of the
gentleman [plaintiff], whether [the defaulter] is a commoner or
a gentleman, provided the defaults are before the inspection day;
for whoever defaults after the inspection day loses the seisin of the
things shown against him, when his defaults are proved.

72. On summoning your vassal and entering your lord's
faith without default.

If there is some lord before whom some person who should
be his vassal has not appeared to do his homage, the lord should
have him summoned to come do his homage, and he should have
him summoned by a sworn vassal [*home qui foi li doie*] if he has one,
and if not then by some competent honest man [*preudome soufi-
sant*]; and if he does not come to the assigned appearance, the lord
should have him summoned again; and if he does not appear the
second time, he should summon him a third time; and if he does
not come to the third appearance, the lord should have him officially summoned to an appearance {by three gentlemen or by three
competent officers who can testify to the judgment in a recall from
memory}; and if he does not appear on the officially notified day,
the lord should let the day pass, and the next day he can take the
fief into his own hands, and he can have him officially summoned
by three gentlemen or three competent officers; and the day [for

96. A "wager of law" is five sous; see *Etablissements* I:51.

the appearance] must be seven days and seven nights later; and the officers should say to him: "Sir, because you are in default for three ordinary court dates and for one official summons, our lord has taken into his own hands the fief you should by law hold from him; and he is having you officially summoned to court seven days and seven nights from now." And if he does not appear in court on the officially assigned day seven days and seven nights later, he should be given an officially assigned date fifteen days and fifteen nights later, {as validly as we have described above}. And if he does not come fifteen days and fifteen nights later, the lord should take the testimony of the officers. And if they served the summons, and they warrant it, the lord should let the day pass and assign him a court date forty days and forty nights later, as validly as we have described above. And if he does not appear on that day, the officers should give their testimony. And if they warrant it, the lord should let the day pass and assign him a court date of a year and a day later in court. And if he does not appear, the lord can rule in a judgment that he has lost the fief, when the day has legally gone by; and the lord keeps the fief. And if he appeared before the lord had taken all these steps against him, he would not lose his fief by law; but he would have lost all that the lord had received in revenues from the fief; and he would pay a penalty for his defaults.

73. On a decision given in a judgment.

If one person makes a complaint about another concerning money, and the latter appears in court, and the plaintiff says: "You owe me this much money," and the debtor says: "I have never before heard this complaint; for which reason I request an appropriate court date; and on that day I will make a proper answer, as a defendant who never did you wrong"; and if the other party says: "I am not willing for you to have another date assigned, but I want you to admit or deny your debt to me, and I will await a ruling," then the ruling should be that he must admit or deny. And if he admits, he may have a date seven days and seven nights later to repay in front of a judge, so that if there were a dispute,

one would not be believed about paying nor the other about receiving except as the judge should rule. And if he answered that
he owed him nothing, he would have a court date assigned. And
if he defaulted, he would be given an official summons, because
when personal property has been shown [*mostrees*] in one court, it
counts as if it had been shown in [another] court.[97] And if he does
not appear on the officially assigned date, and the other party says:
"Sir, he is in default, and I request a ruling, for I am quite ready
to prove my debt," the lord should have the other party officially
summoned to come and see proved the debt the other party says
he owes him. The summons must be served by a competent person [who can testify having done so]. And if he does not come to
the one or the other appearance, and the officers warrant that they
served the summons, the lord should seize enough of his property
to pay the other party without proof. And when the thing is being
seized, if he says: "You are doing me wrong, I lodge a complaint
about the other party, because I don't owe him anything," the
judge should assign him a court date on this issue. But the judge
must be quite certain about the [alleged previous] judgment; and
if on the assigned day he says: "I owe you nothing," and the other
party says: "I can show that this is a res judicata," then the officers
who served the official summonses and those [jurors] who gave
the judgments should be heard to testify. And if they testify that
it was so, the party will be [considered] paid; and the other party
will pay a penalty to the judge whose judgment he contested [*veé*].

74. On repaying damages.

If some party complained that another party had caused him
damage, and the [second] party appeared in court and denied it
and asked for a court date, he would be given it. And if he defaulted, as we have described above, the [first] party would be
given his damages, without proof, like the other party [in Chapter 73].

97. This chapter is somewhat obscure. The last two sentences of the chapter suggest that the creditor's claim is that his debt has already been litigated in
another court, and that he has won the judgment. Now he is trying to collect.

75. On wrongs and default of judgment.[98]

If it so happened that a man made a complaint about another man [saying] that he had done him wrong with respect to some real property, and the land had been shown to the court,[99] and the defendant defaulted [at the next hearing] and was proved to have defaulted, he would lose seisin, and it would be given to the [first] party, on his giving good sureties to be in court; but the latter would not thereby have won the right [*sa droiture*][100] that the other party should not have it, if he could show that he had the [better] right to it.

76. On the right of a baron to be judged by his peers.

If a baron is summoned to the king's court on a matter of real property, and he says: "I do not wish to be judged except by my peers in this matter," then the barons should be summoned, or at least three of them; and then the judge should hold a hearing with these and other knights.

77. On the privilege of a knight.

If a claim is made against a baron or other gentleman concerning his real property, and he is not yet a knight, and he says to the plaintiff: "I wish to do you no wrong, but I request a delay until I am made a knight before answering you," he will obtain a delay of a year and a day, by law [*par droit*].

98. The heading of this chapter seems to be wrong for its contents. There may be a *wrong* here, but there is no default of judgment (refusal by a judge to give a hearing). Manuscripts *F* and *L* read: "On defaulting after an inspection on land," which is a better chapter heading.

99. That is, in an inspection [*jour de veüe*]. Other customals also state that a default after an inspection day causes loss of seisin (Beaumanoir §§74, 110).

100. *Droiture* here seems to correspond to "fundamental ownership" as opposed to seisin.

78. On the age when a child need not answer when in the care of a custodian, and on proving your age.

A gentleman is not old enough to fight [101] until he is twenty-one, nor should he hold land, nor have seisin of any land he sues for, unless he has been disseised; but for a disseisin he must make an answer. And thus a gentleman or a gentlewoman, if they have children in their custodianship, cannot claim any of [the children's] rights [to land], unless [the children's] father died in seisin and possession, or it was an inheritance that came to them by law after their father's death. And if a claim was made against the custodian for something the children's father, when he died, had been peacefully seised and in possession of, even though he were holding it wrongfully, the custodian would not have to make any answer [in court]. And if it happened that the custodian gave a child his land and had him accepted as a vassal by his lord, and someone made a claim against his real property, he would not have to make an answer until he was twenty-one. And if the custodian did not want to give him his land, and said he was not old enough to hold land, and the child offered to prove he was twenty-one, he would make proof by his godfathers and his godmothers, and the priest who baptized him; and they would have to swear on the saints; and the priest would testify by the word of a priest. And if he could not obtain [the testimony of] his godfathers and godmothers, nor the priest, because they were all dead, he could make proof by honest men and women who were quite certain of his age, and would swear to it on the saints. And then when the lord [*la seignorie*] had heard all the proofs, he should accept him as a vassal [*le doit metre en sa foi*], and [place him] in seisin of his land. And if the custodian had at his own will given him his land, he should not accept the homages of [those holding] his land [as his vassals] until he was accepted as a vassal [*en la foi*] by his [own] lord.

---

101. That is, in a judicial battle.

79. On calculating [*conter*][102] your kinship and demonstrating it to your lord.[103]

If someone had held for a long time in coholdership [*parage*][104] and the person from whom he held said to him: "I no longer want you to hold from me in coholdership, unless you can calculate your kinship for me," and if the other says to him: "I will indeed show it to you," he should give him an appointment in his court to calculate the kinship; and the other party should show him the matter and calculate who were his ancestors, from generation to generation; and if they are so close in kinship that they could not marry (if one were a man and the other a woman), he will remain in his coholdership. And if the lord will not believe him, he can swear on the saints that he has honestly calculated the kinship, as far as he knows. And when he has sworn the oath, he will remain in coholdership. And if he dared not, he would have to do homage; and when he had done homage, the lord could impose on him only [the payment] of one service horse [*roncin de servise*].[105]

80. On service as a coholder.[106]

No man gives a service horse until he leaves the faith of the person to whom he gave [his faith].[107] For if the person to whom

---

102. The Old French verb *conter* could mean "count, calculate," or "tell." In this chapter I have opted for "calculate," but an expression such as "tell about" would have been possible.

103. This chapter repeats the material in *Etablissements* 1:48.

104. For *parage* 'coholdership' see *Etablissements* 1:48, and the Introduction, p. xxxiv.

105. That is, the lord could not make him pay a horse for the end of the coholdership *and* for the beginning of the fiefholdership. See the next chapter on payment of a horse.

106. This title does not seem to fit the subject, which concerns the assigning of a service horse at the end of a man's service to a lord for a fief, not as a coholder. Some manuscripts give the heading: "On giving a service horse."

107. In his notes to this chapter, de Laurière begins: "Ce chapitre est obscur." The service horse seems to have been due in some fiefs when the lord changed *and* when the vassal changed. Any new vassal will thus owe a service horse immedi-

he had given [his faith] died, he would give the horse to his successor. And if it happened that someone had brought a service horse to his lord, and the lord wanted to transfer him [as a vassal] to his son or his daughter, and the man replied: "I do not want to leave your faith, unless it is by reason of having terminated my service, when I have given you your service horse," he need not, by law, leave his faith, unless [the lord] has him declared paid up by the other person to whom he wanted to transfer him, or [that other person] makes a declaration that he will not take a service horse from him as long as the person to whom he gave it is still living.

81. On holding in coholdership without giving any service to a lord.

No man who holds in coholdership contributes anything toward a service horse, or relief, or service which the person from whom he holds in coholdership[108] gives his lord, with the exception of rightful [*loiaus*] aids.[109]

82. On holding a custodianship on the proper terms [*en bonne estance*] without doing homage to the lord.

If some man or woman has children in custodianship, and these children hold in coholdership, and the lord says to the custo-

---

ately on coming into a fief, and if his lord dies, he will owe one to the new lord. For Beaumanoir, a service horse was owed by a vassal who came to the end of his active military (although not his judicial) service: once the service horse was given, the vassal no longer owed any military or garrison service (Beaumanoir §797).

In *Etablissements* 1:80, the language is difficult because the conditional and future tenses, and a subjunctive, are used within a series of conditional clauses that are difficult to reconcile. De Laurière does so by translating "quant je vos avrai randu vostre roncin de service" as "Puisque je vous ai payé le cheval qui vous estoit dû," which is difficult to accept. I can justify my translation of each individual sentence in this chapter, but it still does not hang together well.

There is another problem of transferring a man from one lord to another in *Etablissements* 1:120.

108. In *Etablissements* 1:47 this person is referred to as an *aparageor*.

109. For aids, see *Etablissements* 1:46, 47.

dian: "I want you to do me my homage, for these children whom you have in custodianship are not related to me [*ne me sunt riens*]; and I want you enter my faith or calculate the kinship"; then the person who has the custodianship should answer: "Sir, I do not want to do the one thing or the other; for I am only a custodian, and I want to hold on the same terms as the father of these children held [the property]; and I will await a ruling"; then the ruling should be that he need neither do homage nor calculate the kinship; instead, he will hold on the same terms as the property holder [*li heritiers*] held before he died.

83. On [appeal for] false judgment or accepting the judgment as good and valid.

No gentleman can request a modification of a judgment given him, but he must appeal against it as completely false or accept it as good, except in the king's court; for there all people can request a modification of a judgment, ⟨by law and reason, and according to written law in the *Code*, De precibus Imperatori offerendis, l. Si quis et l. ultima,⟩[110] because they cannot appeal for false judgment; for they could not find anyone to give them a hearing, since the king holds from no one but from God and from himself.

84. On seeking a hearing from the king.

And for this reason it happens that, when the king is holding something belonging to his men who are asking for it, saying: "The property [*droiture*][111] {you are holding} is rightfully ours; on which matter we are ready to accept the decision of an inquiry[112] of people of the area under oath [*l'anqueste de la gent dou païs*]," the king cannot by law refuse; instead he must command his *bailli* to cause to be summoned the men of the neighboring parishes,

110. *Cod.* 1.19.5.8 (Krueger 75).
111. *Droiture* here means fundamental ownership of a property, not merely possession or seisin. Cf. the English Writ of Right (Glanvill XII, 3, p. 137).
112. Such an inquiry seems to have been relatively rare except in Normandy and England (Gruchy XCII, pp. 212–214 and Glanvill II, 11, pp. 30–31).

and the nearby knights, and the nearby enfeoffed officers, and the neighboring barons, if the dispute is a great one. And they must be made to swear to tell the truth; for if the jury [*la jurée*] recognizes that it is the king's right, it must remain his; and the other party the same, if the jury says it is rightfully theirs.

85. How to request amendment of a judgment, and on requesting it on the same day.

No man can ask for the amendment of a judgment in the king's court, except on the day when the judgment is made; ⟨for now you must appeal according to the usage of the secular court; for judgments that are not appealed are executed, according to written law in the *Code*, De advocatis diversorum judiciorum, l. prima, in fine;⟩[113] for there would be no amendment of the judgment if the day passed; and if [the petitioner] requests it of the *bailli*, in asking he should say: "Sir, it appears to me that this judgment harms me and that it is not right; and for this reason I request an amendment and that you set a date for me; and have so many good folk appear that they can say if the revision is appropriate or not ⟨by folk who can and should do this according to the law and usage in the barony⟩." The *bailli* should give him a date, and summon the king's men and those who were present at the judgment, and other honest men [*prudes homes*] who know about the law and judgments, to rule whether the judgment is correct or not. And if the judgment is correct according to their ruling, it will be executed: and if it is not, they should amend it. And if they rule that there is no amendment, the person requesting the amendment of the judgment loses his personal property, if he is a gentleman and the king's man. And if the *bailli* would not properly amend the judgment, the other could appeal to the king; and if the king and his council say that it is right and proper, he loses his personal property; but the king should find out about it from those who were at the making of the judgment. And if the judgment was not

113. *Cod.* 2.7.1 (Krueger 98).

correctly made, the king should have [the petitioner's] costs and damages reimbursed by the *bailli* who gave the judgment.

86. On appealing against your lord for false judgment.

If some gentleman hears his lord giving him an incorrect judgment, he can very well say: "This judgment is wrong, and I will no longer litigate this matter before you." And if the lord is a baron, he should appeal to the court of the king, or the court of the person from whom he held;[114] and if his lord who gave the false judgment is a lower lord, the person appealing can appear in the court of the person from whom [his own lord] holds; and he can speak in this manner: "Sir, this person has given me a false judgment, for which reason I no longer wish to hold [my fief] from him; instead, I will hold [directly] from you, who are the overlord." And if the lower lord says: "Sir, I am ready to deny it," the other man can say: "Sir, I do not want him to be able to deny it, for he gave me a false judgment in the sight and to the knowledge of myself, who owe him my faith, and I am ready to demonstrate it against him, if he wants to deny it or say it is not true, in a battle [*encontre son cors*]." And this is how you appeal against your lord for false judgment; and there can be a ruling for a battle; and if the person accusing his lord of false judgment wins the battle, he will never hold anything from him again, but will hold from the overlord; and if he is defeated, he loses his fief. ⟨And know that no judge[115] should feel injured, if there is an appeal against the sentence or the judgment he gives, either in a great dispute or in a small one, according to written law in the *Code*, De appellationibus, l. In majoribus et in minoribus negotiis,[116] etc., where this matter is discussed.⟩

114. These words imply that a baron does not always hold directly from the king.

115. Here Viollet gives *jugement* but also adds a note to suggest that it is a bad translation of the original Latin, which reads: "Nec enim iudicem oportet iniuriam sibi fieri existimare eo, quod litigator ad provocationis auxilium convolavit." I have translated here the *iudicem* of the Latin rather than the *jugement* of the Old French.

116. *Cod.* 7.62.20 (Krueger 322).

87. On a [judicial] battle between a knight and a commoner.

If it happened that a commoner [*hom costumiers*] appealed
against a knight or other gentleman who could be a knight, for
murder or treachery [*traïson*],[117] or highway robbery, or some
other serious crime for which whoever is convicted must be put
to death, the gentleman would not fight on foot, but on horse-
back, if he wanted to; but if the gentleman appealed against the
commoner, the law is that they would fight on foot, provided it
was as serious a matter as we mentioned above. And whoever lost
would be hanged.

88. On breaking out of prison.

If someone were in prison on suspicion of murder or larceny
or some other serious crime for which it was in doubt whether he
would be put to death, and he left the prison, he would be as guilty
as if he had perpetrated the crime, and as if he had admitted it;
and he would be hanged, even if he had not committed the crime.

89. On jurisdiction over clerks, and on handing over
crusaders to Holy Church.

If the king or the count, or a baron or some vassal who has
the administration of justice in his lands arrests a clerk, or a cru-
sader, or some man in religion, even though he were a layman,
he should be handed over to Holy Church, whatever crime he
had committed. And if a clerk ⟨commits an offense for which he
should be hanged or killed, and he⟩ does not have a tonsure, the
secular authority should deal with him. ⟨And if he has a tonsure
and a clerk's habit and can read, no admission and no answer he
makes can be to his detriment; for [the secular judge] is not the
judge having jurisdiction over him [*ordinaire*]; and an admission
before a judge who is not his proper judge is invalid, according to

117. For *traïson* see note 74 above.

written law in the *Decretals*, De Judiciis, c. At si clerici and c. Cum non ab homine.⟩[118]

90. On punishing heretics and unbelievers.

If someone is suspected of heresy [*bougrerie*],[119] the judge should arrest him and send him to the bishop; and if he is convicted, he should be burned; and all his personal property goes to the baron. And this is how heretics [*herite*] should be dealt with, provided their case is proved; and all their personal property goes to the baron ⟨or to the prince. And it is written in the *Decretals*, at the title "On the meanings of words," in the chapter Super quibusdam.[120] And customary law is in agreement.⟩

91. On punishing usurers.

When there is a usurer in the district of a baron, or whatever district, and it is proved against him, his personal property should go to the baron. ⟨And afterward he should be punished by Holy Church for the sin, for it is the duty of Holy Church to cleanse each sinner of his sin, according to written law in the *Decretals*, De judiciis, in capitulo Novit,[121] where there is a discussion of the king of France and the king of England.⟩[122]

---

118. *Decr. Greg. IX* 2.1.4, 10 (Richter 240, 242).

119. *Bougrerie* may refer to the particular heresy of Catharism. De Laurière points out that the word *bougre* was also used to refer to usurers and sodomites. Since the next chapter prescribes a different penalty for usurers, it is probably not that crime which is referred to here. Beaumanoir refers to heresy and sodomy in the same short paragraph and declares that these crimes are both punished by burning (Beaumanoir §833).

120. *Decr. Greg. IX* 5.40.26 (Richter 923–924). The Latin heading is *De verborum significatione*.

121. *Decr. Greg. IX* 2.1.13 (Richter 240, 242).

122. This decretal concerns the power of the church even over kings. The text was written in a case concerning Phillip II Augustus of France and John Lackland of England. It is dated 1204, the year in which Phillip took from John the province of Normandy.

92. On foreigners and suicides.

If some man who is not from the town comes to settle in a baron's castellany, and he does not accept the lord's sovereignty within a year and a day, he would be in the lord's jurisdiction [*esploitables*]; and if by chance he died, and he had not ordered that four deniers be paid to the baron, all his personal property would go to the baron.

If it happened that someone hanged himself, or drowned himself or killed himself in some other manner, all his personal property would go to the baron. And the same thing [obtains] for a woman.

93. On persons who die unconfessed.

If some man or some woman had lain sick for eight days and eight nights, and did not want to confess and died unconfessed, all his or her personal property would go to the baron. But if he [or she] died a sudden death unconfessed, the judge would get nothing, nor would the lord. And if such a thing happened in the lands of a person who had all the kinds of justice in his lands, even though he were not a baron, he would get jurisdiction. ⟨And if he [or she] had made a will, it should be observed; for there is nothing of greater importance than carrying out the wishes of the dead, according to written law in the *Code*, De sacrosanctis ecclesiis, l. Jubemus,[123] where this matter is discussed.⟩

94. On finding [buried] treasure [*fortune*].[124]

No one but the king gets a [hidden] treasure consisting of gold. And silver treasures go to the baron and those who have

123. *Cod*.1.2.14 (Krueger 13). The sentence: "For there is nothing of greater importance than carrying out the wishes of the dead" seems to refer, in fact, to *Cod*. 1.2.1 (Krueger 12), which reads: "Nihil est quod magis hominibus debetur, quam ut supremae voluntatis, postquam iam aliud velle non possunt, liber sit stilus et licitum quod iterum non redit arbitrium."

124. It is clear from the last sentence of the chapter that it is a matter of *buried* treasure.

high justice in their lands. And if it happened that a man who did not have the low justice [*vaarie*] in his lands found some lost object on the ground, it would go to the vassal who had the low justice of the land where the thing was found. And if the person who had lost it came forward, he would get it back by swearing an oath, if he was of good reputation. And if [the baron's] sworn vassal hid [some found object] from him, and he had asked him for it, he would lose his personal property; and if he said: "Sir, I did not know I was supposed to give it back to you," he could be discharged by swearing an oath [that what he said was true], and he would have to give the thing back to the baron. Treasure is [defined as such] when it is buried under the ground, and the earth has been disturbed [*en est effondrée*].

95. On vouching your warrantor [*garent*] for something stolen.

If it happened that a man bought a horse, or an ox, or some other thing, and he was of good reputation, and another man came forward and said: "This man stole this thing from me," and he was well known; and the first man did not know from whom he had bought it; then the other person would get it, if he was willing to swear with his hand on the saints, honestly, that the thing was his; and the buyer would have lost his money; and he would have to swear he did not know whom he bought it from, and that if he could find the person he had bought it from, he would bring him before the judge, if he would come, and if he wouldn't, he would raise the cry against him. And if it happened that he said: "I know very well whom I bought this thing from, and I will have my warrantor present at the assigned court date," he should be given a court date. And if he brings his warrantor to the court date, and he says this: "I am being sued for the thing you sold me," the warrantor should ask to see the thing, and it should be shown to him. And if he doesn't ask to see it before he warrants it, it is invalid. And if after the inspection he said: "I will warrant you in this matter," the defendant must be discharged from the suit and get his money back; for even if he won the disputed thing, the person suing for it would pay the warrantor for it. And thus you can go from warrantor to warrantor up to seven; and if the last of seven warrantors said: "I will warrant [your ownership] of this thing, for I raised it"; and if it is cloth, or clothing, or some other thing, he might say: "It was made in my house"; and [if] then the other party said: "I deny it: it was stolen from me," then the judge should take charge of the thing and can make a ruling calling for a battle between the two of them (or two substitutes, if each one wanted to have a substitute). And it is the warrantor who must swear the oath; and when the day of the battle comes, they should come before the saints; and the one [the warrantor] will take the other by the hand and say to him: "Listen you, the man whose hand I am holding, and you also, the judge—may God and the saints help me!—this thing that is in the judge's charge, which I have stepped forward to warrant, was mine until I sold it, when I sold it to the person vouching me as a warrantor"; and the other party should swear against him, saying: "May God and the saints help me! You have perjured yourself in this matter." And then they can be led on to the battle ground. And the appellant must attack the other party. And the loser will not lose life or limb, because they did not accuse each other in the first instance of homicide [*traïson*] or murder or of larceny; but the person who lost must pay the other one his battle costs as much as the principal suit cost him, and the lawyers for the day the battle was ruled on, but he will pay none of the other costs and will also pay a penalty of sixty sous to the judge.

96. On reimbursement of costs and expenses for a res judicata.

The custom in the secular court is that a person reimburses [his adversary's] costs and expenses for only four cases: battles that have been won, and defaults that are proved, both before and after an inspection (if it concerned costs for the assigned court date, a gentleman pays sixty sous for each default and a commoner five sous, but they must prove by their oath that it cost them that much to hire their advocates). And if it happened that a settlement [*paiz*] was made before the judge on a completed lawsuit [*chose jugiée*], and the other party came back to court and pleaded against him again for what he had lost by the judgment or in the settlement, and the first party said: "I do not wish to answer you, because I won the suit by a judgment, and I will prove it by [the testimony of] the jurors," then it should be ruled that he must name the judge and those who were at the making of the judgment, and they should be heard to testify. And if they warrant that the judgment was as he said it was, he should be reimbursed the costs and expenses he spent on the suit, ⟨as we said above, in the chapter on Novel Disseisin [125] and according to written law in the *Code*, De fructibus et litis expensis, l. Non ignoret [126] and its concordances⟩. And if it happened that somebody made a complaint to a judge that somebody had disseised him wrongfully and by force in novel disseisin, and the other party denied it, and the first party offered to prove it, and the judge had given him seisin [*ensaisiné*], the party who lost the suit would reimburse by law the other party for the costs he had incurred in the suit. And in the secular courts [a party] reimburses costs and expenses for no other suits than the four mentioned above.[127]

97. On breach of seisin and on refusing [to swear] an oath.

If a lord appealed against his vassal saying he had broken his seisin and taken away things that were in his seisin—and he names them—and if the man replies in this manner: "I shall not deny that I took them away, but I did not know they were in your seisin, and I will do whatever I should and whatever is ruled in my case," the lord can rule that he must bring back the things he took away, or their value, and then swear with his hand on the saints that he did not know about the seisin, and by this he will be discharged

125. *Etablissements* 1:69.
126. *Cod.* 7.51.4 (Krueger 317).
127. The four procedures are: (1) judicial battle, (2) defaults, (3) res judicata, and (4) novel disseisin.

of any penalty. And if he dares not swear the oath, ⟨the penalty is that he must be held guilty [*condamnez*], according to written law in the *Code*, De juramento calumpniae, l. secunda, paragrapho Si autem reus hoc sacramentum,[128] etc., et quasi per totum titulum, and in the *Code*, De judiciis, l. Properandum[129] et quasi per totam legem, where this matter is discussed. And it should be known that⟩ if the lord wishes, he loses his personal property, if he is a gentleman; and if he is a commoner, he must pay sixty sous, according to the secular courts.

98. On seizing and holding a commoner's lodging.

If a gentleman wanted to build a residence [*se voloit herbergier*] and his commoner had a piece or two of land he held from him, the lord can take them, if he wants, to build on [*por lui herbergier*], by making a fair exchange, to make either a pond, or a mill, or another dwelling.[130]

99. On land on which a gentleman must pay a tax [*heritage taillable*].

If a gentleman owned a house that had passed to him on the king's land, or in a baron's castellany, that could be taxed [*taillable*], then however it had passed to the gentleman, whether laterally or directly, or some other way, and provided that he had a residence or cottage [*estage ou ostage*] on it for himself, and provided that he occupied it personally [*taigne en sa main*], it would not be taxable; but if he had rented it or let it out to a commoner, he could not keep it from being taxed.

---

128. *Cod.* 2.58.2.7 (Krueger 119). In some editions this citation is to 2.59.2.7, since chapter 7 is divided into chapters 7 and 8 at 7.20 (=8.1) and subsequent chapters in Book 2 have a higher number. The book's title in Krueger is *De iureiurando propter calumniam dando*.

129. *Cod.* 3.1.13 (Krueger 120–122).

130. Since the lord's house is part of his personal holdings or domain, this rule exemplifies the modern words for a taking of this sort: eminent domain.

100. On foreigners.

If a gentleman had an unknown man in his lands, if he was in the gentleman's service, and he died, the gentleman would take half of his personal property. And if he died without an heir or lineage, all his property would go to the gentleman; but he would pay his debts and execute his proper bequests [*s'aumosne avenant*]. And if the unknown man had acquired property from some lower lords [*vavasors*] other than his own lord, the other lords would not by law take anything. But they would not collect their quit-rents [*cens*] or dues [*costumes*] from the [deceased's] lord; instead, he would have to give them a commoner to serve them [work the land and pay the dues].

101. On how a bastard's estate passes.

When a bastard dies without an heir by his wife, all his property passes to his lords, each one taking what is in his own fief. But he can leave his personal property in a will [*a s'aumone*]. And his wife takes her dower, but after her death it goes back to the lords.

102. On the sale of land by a bastard.

If a bastard sold his land and he had brothers or cousins or other kinsmen, they would have no right of redemption to the bastard's sold lands; nor could the bastard get theirs, except by purchasing it. And if they died without heirs or kinsmen, the holder of the justice, or the lord from whom it was held, would take it in precedence to a bastard; for a bastard cannot ask for anything, either because of belonging to a lineage, ⟨or for any other reason, because of his inferior status. And written law is in agreement in the *Code*, On establishing the heir and what person may be an heir, in the second law,[131] and the law Si pater,[132] etc., and in

131. *Cod.* 6.24.2 (Krueger 257). The second law begins "Pater tuus . . . ," and the chapter heading in Latin is *De heredibus instituendis et quae personae heredes instui non possunt.*

132. *Cod.* 6.24.4 (Krueger 257).

the *Digest*, On the status of men, in the law Vulgo concepti,[133] etc., and according to the Custom of Orléans [*Usage d'Orlenois*], in the chapter "On bastards."[134] And the custom of the area agrees).

103. On bastards and *terrage* lands [*terres a terrage*].[135]

If some gentleman had vassals who held *terrage* lands from bastards, and they paid no other dues but the *terrages*, the lord could take the lands to plough them himself, but he could not give them to anyone else.

104. On measuring lands held for quitrent [*censives*].

If a gentleman had men holding from him land owing quitrent and he thought they were paying him [too] little quitrent, he could have the lands measured. And if he found some extra [land] they were not paying quitrent for, and this land adjoined his own, he could keep the extra land he had found; and if it did not adjoin his own land, he could not keep it for himself, but he could increase the quitrent in proportion to the extra land he had found and the former quitrent. And [the vassal] would pay the defaulting quitrent for the years he had held the land; and he would pay a penalty for the first year; and he would pay his wager of law.[136] Thus he, and not his lord, would keep the land.

---

133. *Dig.* 1.5.23 (Watson 1:17). The Latin heading is *De statu hominum*.
134. *Etablissements* 2:30.
135. Viollet defines *terrage* as "mode de tenure." It appears from the commentaries to this chapter by de Laurière, the Abbé de St. Martin, and Viollet that *terrage* is another name for *champart* 'sharecropping', where a tenant works the land without a lease and delivers a portion of the yield, probably in kind, to the owner. In this chapter, the bastard appears to be an intermediary between the owner and the sharecropper, in which case the owner can oust the sharecropper provided he then works the land himself. For the general rule, see *Etablissements* 1:170.
136. The "wager of law" is a fine of five sous; see *Etablissements* 1:51.

105. On failure to pay service dues, and on seizure for lack of a vassal.

If there was a man who had neglected to pay his service dues to his lord, in gloves or spurs, or some other service given on a day certain, and he had not paid the service dues for four or five years, or more, or less, and the lord appealed against him, saying: "You have neglected your service dues toward me for such-and-such a number of years," he would pay as a penalty his wager of law.[137] But the lord could act in another manner; for when the due date had passed and [the vassal] had not paid his service dues, the lord could seize on his fief, [that is,] on the lands [held by] the knight, animals, or other property, if he had any. And he could sell them to make up for the service dues. And if the man came before the lord and said: "Sir, you have taken my property, I ask you to give it back to me by taking sureties,[138] for I am quite ready to pay the fine [*feire droit*] in your court," the lord could reply: "I do not want you to have them, because I have sold them because of a default in [paying] service dues." But if he asked his lord for them before they had been sold, and he found them in his lord's possession, or if he did not find them provided he had acted this way [*ou il ne les trovast mie por quoi il li eüst ainsinc fet*],[139] he should get them back. And then he would pay his service dues and his wager of law.

---

137. See previous note.
138. The retrieval of things seized by the giving of sureties is called *recreance* (see Beaumanoir, chapter 53). The sureties were obligated to reimburse the person releasing the property if the person retrieving the property did not bring it back to court when the suit came on. It was like bail for property rather than for the accused. In this case the lord could refuse to release the property if he had sold it already to make up for the unpaid dues owed by the vassal.
139. The manuscript tradition is extremely garbled in this short passage, and the lesson of the other manuscripts (including those of the *Coutume de Touraine-Anjou*) makes no more sense than what Viollet prints here. The passage makes more sense if the whole passage in square brackets is omitted; but six manuscripts have this wording, and there must have been some such words in an original which were misunderstood or in error.

106. On legal excuses [*essoine*] because of sickness, and on appointing your son as your attorney.[140]

If some old or feeble man, or one who is sick, wronged some person, and the latter came to complain before the judge, he should be assigned a court date. And if the other party did not come on that day, and sent word of his legal excuse [*essoine*] of sickness, the other party should wait seven days and seven nights. And if the plaintiff appeared again and said: "Sir, I request a hearing, for the person about whom I made my complaint is sick," the judge should send competent persons [to the sick man]. And they should say to him: "A party has complained against you concerning such-and-such a matter"—and they should name it—"and you have a long-lasting illness, and you are ordered to put somebody else in your place to defend your position, unless you admit [your fault]," ⟨according to written law in the *Digest*, De procuratoribus, lege Sed et hae personae,[141] and in the *Code*, De procuratoribus, l. Exigendi,[142] and in the *Decretals*, De procuratoribus, c. Non injuste,[143] where it is written that the son can replace the father. And he must take no orders from anyone but the father, when he is an accessory person, as the said law states, for⟩ the latter must put in his place his oldest son; and if he has no children, the person to whom his land will pass should appear on his behalf. And thus it is ruled by law that he shall be named as a substitute [attorney]; and what he does will be held as firm [enforceable].

---

140. An attorney could act for a party throughout the proceedings, as a substitute or agent whose actions were binding on the party. An advocate only spoke for the party subject to confirmation, and only at certain points in the proceedings.

141. *Dig.* 3.3.35 (Watson 1:90).

142. *Cod.* 2.12.12 (Krueger 104). In some editions this citation is to 2.13.12, since chapter 7 is divided into chapters 7 and 8 at 7.20 (=8.1) and subsequent chapters in Book 2 have a higher number.

143. *Decr. Greg. IX* 1.38.14 (Richter 217).

107. On a plaintiff who offends while awaiting the
court date.

If a complaint were made against somebody, whether for assault or for battery, whether on a question of money or land, or
on some other matter, and the judge assigned a court date and he
appeared on the day; and the plaintiff asked him for his property
[*droiture*], or whatever; and the other party answered: "I deny,
fine sir, that I am doing him any harm, as a person who is holding nothing he has a right to [*sa droiture*], nor do I owe him
anything; but I want him to recompense me [*face droit*] for his
offense against me, before the court date which you assigned to
me to hear his complaint, as a person who has committed a battery against me, and other wrongs, and I will give you the details"; — "Sir," says the [first] party, "I do not want to answer him,
for I have not been summoned to hear his complaint, but he is
summoned to hear mine; for this reason, I want him to answer
my complaint"; — "Sir," says the other party, "I do not want to
answer, but he should answer concerning his offenses against me
while waiting for the court date you assigned me"; even though he
has no court date assigned for his complaint, the other party must
answer before the first defendant answers him. And if he could
prove that the other party had laid hands on him in anger [*par
mal respit*] before the court date, unless it was in self-defense, he
would pay, if he was a commoner, a fine of sixty sous to the judge;
and if he were a gentleman, he would lose his personal property.
And he would pay damages to the other party for all his losses.
And for this reason a person should be careful not to commit an
offense before the court date, for he loses the right to an answer
on the day. And he pays a penalty, as has been stated above.

108. On appealing against a man for murder or treachery
[*traïson*],[144] without release and without bail, and on
detention [under identical conditions].

If one man happened to appeal against another for murder or
treachery, or for some other offense for which he risked the penalty
of loss of life or limb, the judge should hold both of them in equal
conditions of detention, so that one was not worse off than the
other. And supposing there was some rash judge who released one
of them from prison on naming of sureties, while detaining the
other, and the party who had been released on naming sureties fled
and did not appear on the day assigned for the hearing, then the
judge said to the sureties: "You are sureties that such-and-such a
man"—and he should state his name—"would appear in court on
such-and-such a day, and he had been appealed against for such-
and-such a great crime, and he has fled: and, for this reason, I want
you to be found guilty [*provez*] and sentenced to bear the same
penalty as would the person who has fled";—[Then they might
say] "Sir, we don't want this [result] at all, for if we are sureties for
our friend [relative], we are doing what we should. But we will do
what we should." [Under these circumstances] it can be ruled that
they must pay a fine of a hundred sous and one denier; and with
that they will be discharged. And this penalty is called a man's relief.[145] And for this reason, a judge should be careful not to take
sureties for [the release] of persons who appeal against each other
for crimes as great as murder or treachery, for [the sureties] can be
assessed no other penalty than what has been explained above.

144. For *traïson* see note 74 above.
145. This penalty recalls the Frankish wergeld of a hundred solidi.

109. On various offenses and various suits.[146]

If someone complains to the judge for some offense and the judgment is deadlocked [*contende*][147] on the first court date of their arguments, the judge should give them another convenient court date. And if on that day the judgment is deadlocked on their same arguments, the judge should assign another date. On that day, he should recuse himself [*se doit lever*] and call competent people who are neither on one side nor the other, and have the arguments repeated. And he should give [the parties] a hearing on the arguments they have made, and should repeat to them what they [the new judges] have judged.[148] And thus a judge cannot recuse himself, nor should he, until the judgment has been deadlocked twice before him.

110. On requesting a judicial partition by making a judgment [*droit faisant*].

If some persons had lands or vineyards that they held in common and one party came to the other and said: "Fair sir, let us divide up our vineyards—or our lands—which we hold in common," and the other party said: "I do not want to make a partition," the first party could make a complaint to the judge. And the judge should set a court date for them. And when they came to court, if the plaintiff said: "Sir, this man and I are co-owners

146. The title of this chapter does not seem apt. Some of the manuscripts bear a more appropriate title, such as: "How the court should act concerning a judgment which has been deadlocked twice" (Manuscript *E*).

147. It appears from the use of the singular later in the paragraph ("Il se doit lever" 'he should recuse himself') that the *joutise* referred to here is a single judge, rather than a panel of judges or a jury. The panel of judges, or jury (Fr. *jugeors*), is never referred to as *la joutise*. Thus the verb *contendre* presumably refers to this judge's inability to make up his mind on the arguments presented to him. In other contexts, the *joutise* is referred to by the pronoun *ele*, which is grammatically coherent even though the person referred to was more likely a male. See also *Etablissements* 2:4.

148. The double use of a plural pronoun ("si *lor* doit retraire ce qu' il avront jugié") in this sentence presumably means that the new judges' verdict is reported to the parties.

of some lands, and I want them to be partitioned; for I want to
know where my share lies"; and the other party said: "Sir, I do
not want to do this";—and the other party said: "I am ready to do
the dividing, and you choose, who have no more than I do, as I
have no more than you; and I will await a ruling"; then the judge
could rule that the party in a hurry to divide should do the dividing, and the other party should choose [which share he wanted].
And if it happened that one had more power to administer justice
in his lands than the other, and he said: "Fair sir, I do not want
us to make a partition, for I have the power to administer justice
in the land; that much I have more than you, and you have no
more than I do of anything; and the income [*rentes*] is received
into my own hands, or into those of my agent; and it may well
be that your agent has been present and has seen this. And if dues
[*costumes*] are not paid on time, I am entitled to hold the hearing,
if you do not want to be there. And because I have these advan-
tages, I do not want to partition"—if matters stood this way, he
would by law not have to partition.

III. On millers and mills.

If a person who has the high justice in his lands has a mill
and commoners domiciled on his lands, all those within the *banlieue* [149] must take their grain to be milled at his mill. And if anyone
failed to do so, after he had been summoned, the lord could rule
that he may not take his grain to any other mill. And if the lord or
his officer caught him bringing back flour from any other mill than
his own, the flour [would go] to the lord, and the man [would
owe] no other penalty. And if the miller were to cause damages [150]
to any of those bringing their grain to his mill, with respect to the
wheat he brought to the mill, and the party went to the lord and

149. An area extending some 10,000–15,000 feet from the mill. De Laurière
states that the *banlieue* of a mill in the Anjou region is a thousand revolutions of a
wheel measuring fifteen feet, or 15,000 feet. If the "foot" is the same as the standard
American foot, this means a distance of nearly three miles. *Etablissements* 4:92.
    150. The damages seem to be short weight.

said to him: "Sir, your miller has caused me damages concerning my wheat, have him pay me a penalty [*amander*]," the lord should send for the miller and say to him: "This man has lodged a complaint against you, that you caused him damages with respect to his wheat;"—and he must say his name—and if the miller says: "I deny it"; and the other party says: "I will prove it as I should," he should be ordered to repay him his damages on his oath [*o son serment*], if it is a matter of more than twelve deniers, and, if it is less, on his affirmation [*o sa foi*]. And thus you should understand that no miller has a defense against a person bringing his grain to his mill. But the latter must swear [*jurer*] or affirm [*fiancer*] that he suffered that much in damages [while his property was] in the miller's keeping [*en la garde au monnier*]. And thus those bringing their grain to that miller will get back their damages, as we said above. And if the lord did not want to have their loss made good, they would not be obliged to bring their grain to his mill until they had been paid all their damages; and the lord could not force them to by law.

112. How you should treat the coholder of a mill.

And if somebody had a co-owned mill, and it lacked a millstone or some other thing so that it could not grind, he should go to the person who had a share with him and say to him: "Our mill needs a millstone: pay up your half." And if he said: "I will not put anything in, because I cannot," then he should show him that same thing before a judge; and if he says: "I don't want to contribute anything," the other man can have the mill repaired and he will get all the profits [*la mouture*], one half and the other, until the other party has paid his share of his costs and expenses; and thus he will receive all the profits without making an accounting. And if he had the mill repaired without summoning the other party, the other party would do no more than give him his share of the money he had spent; and he will also have to prove by his oath how much he has spent in honest outlay to repair the mill. And there will be an accounting of what he has taken in profits; and if he had taken more than the repair would have cost, he would have to pay back the extra amount.

113. On the vassal's rights and the baron's rights.[151]

No vassal can have a bake-oven as rental property [*en vilenage*], where he can make his men do their baking, unless he has a town or a share of a town. But if he has a town [*bourc*] or a share in a town, he can have a bake-oven if he has the low justice. And his men must do their baking there. And if there is someone who bakes at someone else's oven, the lord could confiscate the bread he brought back from the other oven. And the man would pay no other fine. But the bread would go to the lord. And if the baker caused damage to those baking there by not baking their bread well, the lord should have them reimbursed {on their making proof. And if the lord would not have the damages made good,} they would not be obliged to bake at his oven, until he had had their damages made good.

114. On milling at the lord's mill.

If there is some baron who has vassals in his castellany, and one of the vassals has no mill, all his commoners will have their grain processed at the baron's mill, provided they are within the *banlieue*. And if they were outside, they would not go to that mill, unless they wanted to. And the baron would have their damages made good, as we have said above, on their making proof. And if one of his vassals constructed a mill in his castellany, even though there had never been one before, all his men would go to his mill. But if a vassal constructed a mill outside his castellany, his men would not take their grain there, even though they were within the *banlieue*; and the baron would not lose any of his rights.

151. The chapter heading in most of the manuscripts does not mention the baron, who is indeed not discussed in this chapter.

115. On the general jurisdiction of barons over the fiefs within their castellanies, and on doing homage and obeissance for fiefs.

If a baron has a fief in the barony of some other baron, the baron holding the fief would hold neither the high nor the low justice; but the baron in whose castellany the fief was situated would have them. And in some fiefs it happens that a vassal holds his land from some baron, and it is in another castellany than the castellany [of the baron] from whom he holds the land, and he holds his low justice from the baron in whose castellany the fief is situated. And in this way a person does two homages for one piece of land: one for the fief of land, and the other for the fief of the low justice.[152] And if someone complained to the baron about the person holding the land fief, he could entertain the suit up until the battle. But he could not preside over the battle, because he has no jurisdiction;[153] instead the suit would be from then on before the other baron in whose castellany the fief of the low justice was situated.

116. On the king's rights to a debt admitted or proved to be owed to him.

If a baron owed money to the king, the king could not by law confiscate anything [se . . . vanchier] from the baron's men, except for dues which the men owed the baron; but he could not by law take their personal property. Nor could he do this by law for any offense the baron had committed, unless the men had deserved it.[154] And thus I say that a baron cannot make confiscations for a debt his vassal owes him, nor for any offense the vassal has committed against him, except as we have explained above. And

---

152. The power to administer justice included the power to impose and collect fines. It was thus income-producing and could be classified as real property, just like land, and held from an overlord in the same way, by doing homage.

153. That is, the baron from whom the vassal held the land did not have the high justice and thus would not be able to preside over the judicial battle.

154. Presumably by aiding and abetting the baron.

thus you can see that no judge can act in a different way from the king.[155]

117. On the king's gift "to him and to his heirs born of a legal marriage."[156]

If the king had given to some man, [as a reward] for his service or of his own will some piece of real property, "to him and to his heir by his wedded wife;"[157] and if he had an heir and then died, then when the heir came of age he would be in the king's faith [*en la foi le roi*] and emancipated from his mother. And if[158] his mother wanted her dower and he answered: "Lady, you should not have any, for if my father had died without an heir, you would not have taken any [dower], but the king would have taken [the land] free and clear; for the king gave the land only 'to him and his heir which was born to him and his wedded wife.'[159] And for this reason, if I had died, you would have taken no dower with the king." And thus you can understand that a woman has no dower rights in such gifts, whether they are given by the king, or the count, or some other man.

155. In this last sentence I have ignored the word *fors*, which appears in Viollet although it is found in only six of the manuscripts. If it is retained, the last sentence must be translated: ". . . can act in a different way except for the king," but this makes no sense since the whole passage discusses uniformity of procedures and rights.

156. In this title, Viollet has added the words [*à home*], which do not appear in any of the manuscripts, claiming that they are necessary to the sense of the chapter title. I prefer to see the heading as including a formula, which is *quoted* in the title. The expression "a lui et a son hoir né de loial mariage" represents what Anglo-American lawyers call "words of purchase," which specify how the property is held and how it descends. The chapter itself is an illustration of the meaning of this formula: namely, that a gift accompanied by these words does not include any dower rights.

157. The quotation marks used in this sentence do not appear in Viollet.

158. This "if" appears to introduce a condition; but the result clause never appears grammatically, although it is suggested by the last sentence: "she has no dower rights."

159. The quotation marks used in this sentence do not appear in Viollet.

118. On gifts between a man and his wife.

A woman cannot give anything to her husband as a bequest
[*en aumone*] as long as she is healthy, for the gift would not be firm
[enforceable]; for it might be that she had not given it willingly
nor of her own will; instead, she might have given it for fear that
he would do something worse to her, or because of the great love
she had for him. And for this reason, she cannot give him any of
her real property. But before she was married, she could give him
a third of her real property, or [she could do so] at her death, or
when she was sick, provided she did not have a male heir.[160]

119. On marriage gifts.

If a gentleman was marrying off his daughter, and the father
came to the door of the church, or the mother if she had no father,
or her brother, or someone who had the power to marry her off;
and the father or one of those persons we named above came to
the church door and said: "Sir, I give you this maid and so much
of my land, to you both and the heirs which issue from you both,"
[and] if he had heirs [and then died], and the woman took another
husband and had heirs [by him], and the woman died and the
children of the second husband said to the oldest son of the first
husband: "Partition our mother's land with us," and the eldest
said: "I do not want you to take anything, for the land was given
to my father and mother 'and to the heirs which issued from them
both';[161] and I am ready to make proof of this"; and if the younger
children said that they did not believe him, then he would have to
call [as witnesses] people who had been at the marriage, at least
three good men [*preudes hommes*] {or four who}[162] could swear
with their hand on the saints that this marriage gift was given to

160. Once a woman has a male heir, she does not own her land but merely
holds it in guardianship for the child; see *Etablissements* 1:68.
    161. These quotation marks do not appear in Viollet.
    162. Viollet believes these words were added by the Compiler of the *Etab-
lissements*.

the father and mother—and he must name them—"to them and
the heirs who issued from them both,"[163] in their sight and knowledge; and thus the oldest would keep everything. And if he could
not prove it this way, a third would go to the sons of the second
husband; and the oldest would warrant them as coholders. And
if the first husband had had only daughters, and they could make
the proof we explained above, they would keep everything, and
the younger children would take nothing. And if they could not
prove it, the oldest son of the second husband would take two-
thirds, and the daughters one-third; and he would warrant them
as coholders, and swear fealty [*feroit la foi*] if it had to be sworn.

120. On the gift to your brother of an homage [*foi*] as a
coholdership, and on doing two homages for one fief.

A duke or a count or a baron or any other lord cannot give
away his vassal [*son home de foi*][164] except to his brother or sister.
To these he may give him in coholdership;[165] but he could not give
him to a stranger, unless he gave him with all the service [*obeïssance*][166] he owned in him without keeping anything back; for if
the baron gave him to one of his vassals, it would be to the man's
disadvantage, for he would have to do two homages: to the person to whom he had been given and to the baron who had his fief,
and thus [the baron] would make two homages out of one. But if
the baron gave him in such a way that the person he gave him to

163. These quotation marks do not appear in Viollet.
164. The giving of a vassal, which makes it sound as if the man was servile,
is appropriate when the land the vassal holds and the vassal who holds it are considered as a unit.
165. Since only the principal holder of a coholdership (typically the oldest
son) does homage to the overlord, the other coholders do not do homage, even
to their brother, in Touraine-Anjou. The man given to them in a partition of the
land in coholdership would then continue to do homage to the older brother, as
the person to whom the homages of all the subfiefs were apparently due.
166. The *obeïssance* appears to be something apart from the homage owed for
a fief, since the donated man would still owe his fief-service to the donor as well as
some kind of homage to the donee. For another problem connected with giving a
man, see *Etablissements* 1:80.

held him from the king (if the baron held him from the king), or from some other lord { . . . },¹⁶⁷ for thus the baron keeps none of the homage. And in this way a vassal could give a man to another vassal, provided the person to whom he gave him held him from the person from whom the [first] vassal had held him.

121. On the custodianship of a fief, and on [not] giving the custodianship of a child to a suspicious person for fear of the dangers that could arise.

If it happened that a gentleman died, both he and his wife, and they had [minor] heirs, the person who would have the remainder [*retour*]¹⁶⁸ of the father's land would get the custodianship of the land on the father's side; and the person who would have the remainder of the mother's land would get the custodianship of the land on the mother's side. But one of those persons who received the custodianship of the land, as we have explained above, would not have the custodianship of the children; instead it would go to one of the relatives on the father's side and one on the mother's side, from their lineage.¹⁶⁹ And they should be given enough of the income of the land to feed the children and support them according to the value of the land; for those who have the remainder of the land should not have the remainder *and* the custodianship [of the children]; for there would be a suspicion that they, more than some person to whom the land would not pass, might prefer the children's death rather than their survival, because of the land that would come to them [on the children's death].

167. Viollet supplies the spaced periods, implying the omission of words to the effect that "it would be permissible."

168. "Remainder" is used loosely in this chapter, since the status of the children's probable lateral heirs is determined by law and not by an instrument. The person with the remainder is the one who stands next in the lateral line to take the property if the current owner dies.

169. By lineage is meant the extended family—uncles and aunts, etc.

122. How you should discharge [*nantir*] your surety, and on suing your principal debtor before having recourse to the surety.

If someone names a man as his surety, he must protect him from all loss, and if he suffers loss for any reason whatever, [the principal debtor] is obligated to reimburse him for his loss when he provides proof of it. And if a man is a surety given to another, the latter can seize his property, if he admits he is his surety; and if he denies it, [the creditor] should not seize his property by force; but he should make a complaint to the judge and speak this way: "Sir, this man has resisted giving me his cattle [*proie*]¹⁷⁰ and his security [*gages*], and yet he was a surety to me; now give me a ruling"; ⟨for it is the creditor's [*dou deteur*]¹⁷¹ choice whether to seize property from the surety or from the principal debtor [*deteur*] according to the custom of Orléans in the baron's court; but he should sue the principal rather than the surety when the principal is present, solvent [*bien payans*], and easy to sue [*covenir*] and serve with process [*esploitier*] and petition [*souploier*], according to written law in the *Code*, De fidejussoribus, l. Non recte,¹⁷² in Authentica Praesente; which is indicated under the said law where this matter is discussed. And then⟩ they should be given a court date. And when they appear in court, and both have made an appearance, the second party should say: "Sir, see here such-and-such a man who is my surety for this other man"¹⁷³—and he should say his name—"and for so much money, or for such-and-such a thing"—and he should name it—"and he has resisted giving me his security"; and if the other party says: "I deny it, I have never resisted giving you my security; instead, I was quite ready to do my

---

170. Viollet glosses *proie* as *bétail* in his glossary.

171. Common sense shows that *deteur* here means "creditor." The other manuscripts confirm this. *Deteur* sometimes means "creditor" in Beaumanoir (§225).

172. *Cod.* 8.40.3 (Krueger 352). In some editions this citation is to 8.41.3, since chapter 10 is divided into chapters 10 and 11 at 10.14 (=11.1), and subsequent chapters in Book 8 have a higher number. The Authentic *Praesente* is *Novel* 4 c.1.2.

173. Namely, the principal debtor.

duty to you as a surety," and the other party says: "I will prove it, in any way it is ruled that I must do so"; then a ruling can be made, since he cannot deny that he was a surety, that he must swear with his hand on the saints that he did not resist giving security; and with that he will be discharged.[174] And if he did not dare swear, he would have to reimburse the other party for all his damages resulting from the resistance, on his making proof of them; and he would pay his wager of law[175] to the judge. And if it happened that he said: "I am not your surety, and I deny it, and I will do what I have to do" {and the other party said: "I will make proof}, as it is ruled I must"; it can be ruled that if he[176] will swear with his hand on the saints that he never became a surety, he will be discharged by his oath, if the other will agree to this [*se cil le viaut laisser coure*]. And if he did not dare swear the oath, he would reimburse all the other party's losses, and he would be liable for the suretyship [*tenuz en le plevine*] and would pay a fine of his law to the judge [*feroit à la joutise une amende de sa loi*].[177] And if the suit was for more than five sous, it could be ruled in a judgment that he[178] must swear that he had made the other party liable for the suretyship, as we said above, and the other party could challenge him by a wager of battle; and the battle could be fought person-to-person or by two hired champions, if they wanted a substitute. And the person losing would reimburse the other party the costs

174. By this, the writer means "found not guilty of resisting." He will remain as a surety and is not discharged from that duty.

175. The "wager of law" is five sous; see *Etablissements* 1:51.

176. The person referred to here is the defendant, who claims he is not a surety. If he will swear he is *not* a surety, he will be discharged. The plaintiff must agree to this manner of proof, as is shown by the last few words in the sentence. From the following sentences, it appears that the oath of the defendant is valid only in cases involving less than five sous.

177. The two expressions translated "pay his wager of law" (*feroit le gage de sa loi* and *feroit une amende de sa loi*) probably have the same meaning: the man has to pay the judge a fine, which is assessed at five sous (see *Etablissements* 1:51).

178. The person referred to here as "he" is the party (the plaintiff) claiming that the other is a surety; under this interpretation, the burden of proof shifts to the plaintiff when the sum involved is more than five sous. A different manuscript tradition suggests that in cases involving more than the sum of five sous, the defendant still swears that he is not a surety, but is subject to a challenge to a judicial battle.

of hiring his champion and his lawyers at the hearing; and he would pay the judge a fine of sixty sous, if he was a commoner.

123. On appealing against a person for a default, and on losing seisin after an inspection.

If some man makes a complaint about another, saying that he owes him money or that he has caused him a loss in some matter that concerns personal property, and the person complained about defaults, he should be given a court date and officially summoned by four enfeoffed officers, provided he has heard the complaint in court. And if he did not come on the officially assigned day [*au jor jugié*] and had no legal excuse for missing the previous appearance, and the other party appealed against him for the default, the other party would be given possession of what he had asked for in his complaint, for things shown and named in court are considered as dealt with by a judgment, if they are personal property. And for this reason you should be careful not to default in this way.

124. On a legal excuse [*essoigne*] of sickness, and being summoned to the sovereign's court.

The following are reasonable legal excuses: when a man is sick, or his son {or his wife} or his father, or his mother or his brothers or his uncles or his grandchildren, provided they are in danger of death; or if he went to the funeral of any of those we have named. Or if there was someone who had a court date in the baron's court and he had to go to the king's court, and he was appealed against for default in the baron's court; and he spoke in this way: "I do not want to pay a penalty, for I had a scheduled appearance in the king's court, and such-and-such an officer summoned me"—and he should give his name.—And then the officer should be heard to testify; and the baron should send somebody to hear what the officer says; for the king's judges do not make a recall from memory in the baron's court. And if the king's judge warrants that [the person] had a scheduled appearance in the king's court, he is discharged from the default. And if the officer says he never summoned him, he is liable for the default. And if he dared to swear he was never summoned to the baron's court, then he would be discharged from the default. And a reasonable legal excuse is that of water, when you have to cross by boat. But you must go to three crossing points and do your best to cross if you can find someone to ferry you. And if somebody appealed against a party for a default, and he said he had come to three places to cross in this way and he was willing to do what the court ruled, it could be ruled by law that if he dared swear by the saints that he had been at three crossing places and done his best to get across, then he would be discharged from the default.

125. How you make reimbursement for damage caused by your animal and pay a fine [*droit faisant*].

If a man was taking his animal to market or among people, and it bit or struck someone, and the injured person made a complaint to the judge, and the other party said: "Sir, I did not know the animal had this defect," he must reimburse the damages to the injured person and will pay no fine to the judge; but he must swear he did not know about the defect. And if he dared not swear, he would lose the animal and it would go to the judge. And if the animal happened to kill a man or a woman, and the judge arrested the man who had brought it and said: "Your animal has killed a man"; and the person said: "Sir, this is not my animal," then it can be ruled that he must swear on the saints that it is not his, and that he did not bring it. And thus the animal will go to the judge; and nothing further can be done. And if he said: "The animal is mine, and I brought it, but I did not know it had this defect," then it should be ruled that he must swear by the saints, as explained above, that he knew nothing of the defect; and again the animal will go to the judge; and the animal's owner would pay a man's relief,[179] that is to say a hundred sous and one denier; and with

179. For the man's relief, see *Etablissements* 1.108.

that he will be discharged. And if he were so crazy as to say that he knew about the defect in the animal, he would be hanged for his admission [*requenoissance*].

126. On a suit against the father which devolves to the heir, and on proving your debts.

If a party appeals against another party, saying his father owed him money—and he must give his name—and his father had passed from life to death, and the first party said to [the man's] son: "Since you are the heir to the land, I ask you for my debt"; and the latter said to him: "He died after making his confession, and he did not give any orders to pay anything back, and I want to be discharged";—"And I do want you to be [discharged]," says the first party, "for I am ready to prove my debt," [then] it should be ruled in a judgment that he must prove his debt by two other witnesses [*soi tierz*]; and otherwise he will get nothing.

127. On forcing an excommunicated person to make amends, and on subsequent punishment.

If a man has been excommunicated for a year and a day, and more, and the ecclesiastical judge gives an order [*mandast*] for the secular judge or the man's lord to distrain him by seizing his property or his person, ⟨for the judgments of the bishop should be sent to the provost for execution and completion, according to written law in the *Code*, under the rubric De episcopali audentia, l. Episcopale judicium[180] cum authentica ibi signata cum suis concordantiis,⟩ if necessary, yet the judge should not arrest him provided it is a matter of debt or land; but the judge should take possession of all his property except his subsistence [*son vivre*], until he has had himself absolved. And when he is absolved, he must pay nine pounds as a fine, of which sixty sous go to the secu-

180. *Cod.* 1.4.8 (Krueger 40) and Authentic *Si quis litigantium*, which is *Novel* 123 c. 21.

lar judge and six pounds to the other judge; and this fine should be transmitted by the secular judge. And if his faith was in doubt, the secular judge should arrest him and send him to the ecclesiastical judge, ⟨for Holy Church can do no more, it must depend on the help of knights and the secular arm and force, according to written law in the *Code*, De Episcopis et clericis, l. Si quis in hoc genus).[181] And when the judge had examined him, if he found he was a heretic [*bougres*], then he would have to send him back to the secular judge. ⟨And the secular judge should have him burned. And in general all excommunicated persons are heard in the secular court, as plaintiffs or as defendants. But they are not admitted to the ecclesiastical courts as plaintiffs; for an excommunicated person should not profit from his bad faith, according to written law in the *Decretals*, De judiciis, capitulo Intelleximus;[182] but he would be heard in the ecclesiastical court as a defendant, and not as a plaintiff, for all defenses are retained to excommunicated persons by law, as it is written in the *Decretals*, De exceptionibus, c. Cum inter priorem,[183] where this matter is discussed.⟩

128. On contracts in contemplation of marriage.

If some man had a minor son and the father said to one of his neighbors: "You have a daughter about my son's age; if you wanted her to be my son's [wife] when she comes of age, I would be willing, according to a contract whereby [*en itele meniere que*] you gave me a parcel of your land and I gave you ten pounds as a deposit [*erres*], whereby the deposit[184] will be mine when your daughter is of marriageable age, if she is not willing to let the marriage take place"; thus, if she did not want the marriage to take place, the other party or his heir would keep the deposit, provided there was no kinship or other reason why the marriage should

---

181. *Cod.* 1.3.10 (Krueger 19).
182. *Decr. Greg. IX* 2.1.7 (Richter 241).
183. *Decr. Greg. IX*, 2.25.5 (Richter 376).
184. The text in Viollet's edition reads *erres* 'deposit' here, but some manuscripts have *terres* 'land', which makes more sense.

not take place. And if there was some reason why Holy Church was not and should not be agreeable to the marriage, the deposit [*erres*] would go back to the person who had given it. And if they had acted in another manner, by giving promises to give to each other a penalty of a hundred pounds, or more or less, if the marriage did not take place, the penalty would not be enforceable by law.[185]

129. On gifts to the church.

If some man gave to some abbey or religious house a parcel of land, the lord in whose fief it was would not permit them to keep it if he did not want to; instead he could take it into his own possession. But the person [to whose house] the gift had been given should appear before the lord and speak in this manner; "Sir, this was given to us in charity [*en aumone*]; if it please you, we will hold it; but if it does not please you, we will relinquish possession of it, if you wish, within the proper period"; and the lord should rule that they must relinquish possession within a year and a day. And if they did not relinquish it within a year and a day, he could annex it to his own holdings; and he would never have to answer their complaint at law.

130. On warranting as coholders, and on doing service to your lord.

If some man held as a coholder from another, and the party from whom he held it was rash [*fous*] and sold his land, and the other party appeared before the lord from whom the land was held and said to him: "Sir, the man from whom I hold as a coholder is selling his land and what he has; I request that you have him summoned"; {the lord should summon him. And when they have appeared,} the first party can say to the second: "Dear friend [*biaus*

185. Viollet quotes de Laurière's opinion that the second arrangement is improper because it stipulates penalties; but de Laurière admits that the first arrangement is not much different.

amis], you are selling what you have; I do not want you to be able to sell it, I want you to keep it to warrant me as a coholder,[186] or give me enough of your portion for me to be able to perform the service"; and if the other party says: "Dear friend, I must sell what I have for my needs; but I will do what I should";[187] it can be ruled that he need not fail to sell because of his coholder, but he must give him enough of his land for him to be able to perform his service to the person whose vassal he will be, and to whom he will promise his faith [*fera la foi*]. And a ruling should be given on how much he should receive according to the size of the fief and the services to be performed, and the service [*obeïssance*] to the lord as regards the aids[188] and other things.[189]

131. On running water.

If some gentleman had a stream running through his property, and which had [always] run through it, and the person in whose land it was wanted to forbid fishing in it, he could not do so without [going to] the court of the baron in whose castellany it was, and [going to] the vassal's court.[190]

132. On a complaint in the baron's court by a king's man.

If there was a man who owed money to one of the king's Jews, and the Jew had made a complaint to the king's judge, and

186. That is, perform the service so that the minor coholder does not have to. See *Etablissements* 1:81.

187. Viollet omits the closing quotation marks here at what is clearly the end of what the second party says.

188. A kind of tax.

189. The services paid or performed depended on the size of the property, which had to provide enough income for the holder to live on as well as perform the services.

190. Viollet notes in *Etablissements* 4:128 that a fourteenth- or fifteenth-century manuscript, Paris Bibliothèque Nationale MS fr. 18922, entitled *Coustume glosée d'Anjou et Maine*, which contains this chapter, uses the word *assentement* 'consent', which causes him to print this passage in the *Coutume de Touraine-Anjou* with the words *la cort* divided *l'acort*. This reading makes more sense here: "He could not do it without the agreement [*l'acort*] of the baron," etc.

the baron in whose castellany the man [defendant] [resided] asked to have the case sent down to his court, provided he found his man as a defendant, the case would not be sent down, for the personal property of a king's Jew belongs to the king.

133. On Jews.

And in the same way if the baron had a Jew who made a complaint about the baron's men in the baron's court, and the vassal asked to have the case sent down, it would not be sent down; for all the Jew's personal property belongs to the baron. ⟨And no Jew is allowed to testify against Christians, according to written law in the *Code*, De Haereticis et Manichaeis, l. Quoniam multi judices, in the paragraph Sed his quidem,[191] where this matter is discussed.⟩

134. On knighthood.

If some man [claimed to be] a knight, and he was not a gentleman on his father's side [*de parage*], even though he was on his mother's side [*de par sa mere*], he could not by law be a knight; and the king or the baron in whose castellany this occurred could arrest him and could by law have his spurs cut off over a dung heap [*sus I femier*]; and his personal property would go to the person in whose castellany it was; for it is not the custom [*usages*] that a woman can ennoble [*franchisse*] a man. But a man ennobles a woman; for if a man of great family took as a wife the daughter of a peasant [*vilain*], their children could by law become knights, if they wanted to.

135. How you should give a service horse [*roncin de servise*] to your lord.

If someone had a man who owed him a service horse, and he summoned him and said to him: "Give me my service horse, for I

191. *Cod.* 1.5.21.2 (Krueger 59–60).

want it; and I don't want to take money in lieu," then [the man]
should bring him his horse within fourteen days, if the other party
will not give him a longer time. And he must bring the horse with
a bridle [*frain*] and a saddle, and whatever is necessary, and shoes
on all four feet. And if the lord says: "I don't want this one, for it is
too small and too weak," the other party could say: "Sir, have him
tried, as you should," and the lord can mount a squire on it, as big
a man as he should, and a hauberk tied on behind him, and chain-
mail leggings [*unes chausses de fer*], and then he can send it twelve
leagues away; and if the horse can do them in one day, and the next
day bring the squire back, the lord cannot by law refuse it. And if
it cannot do the two days' journey, the lord can refuse it by law
and the other party would have to find another which could do
the two days' journey; and if he found one capable of it, and if the
lord refused it, he would never [legally have to] furnish the lord a
horse, as long as the lord lived. But if the lord liked, he could give
it back to him within the year, provided the horse was as sound as
when he gave it to him, and the man could not refuse; and a year or
two later, the lord could ask him for his service horse, and the man
would have to bring him one, as we have explained above. And if
the lord kept the horse for more than a year and a day,[192] by law the
man would not legally have to take it back, unless he wanted to.

136. On dividing among brothers what is inherited from
[their] father and mother.

When a commoner has children, whether sons or daughters,
each takes as much as the other of the land inherited from father
or mother; and also of the personal property and the purchased
and otherwise acquired real property, if they have any; for according to the custom in the secular courts, "a commoner's purse is his
patrimony."[193] And if the commoner had married off one of his

192. In Beauvais, this period is only forty days (Beaumanoir §796).
193. De Laurière explains that this expression means that a commoner's personal property is divided equally among his children, just like his real property. He
cannot give any one of them the advantage over the others.

sons and one of his daughters, and he had as many at home who
were not married, ⟨and he died⟩ and the married ones came back
⟨to the ones who had remained at⟩ home and asked to partake in
the distribution of the estate, those who were at home could not
by law refuse to permit it; but the others would have to bring
back [to the hotchpot] [194] [*en fraresche*] what they had been given
previously, whether it was land or a house or money or other personal property. And if one of them had improved his property, by
building a house or planting vines on the land ⟨where there had
been nothing before⟩, all these improvements would not go back
to the distribution, but there would be an estimate made by honest men of the value of the land when it was given as a marriage
gift; and what he had put into it would be counted for him; and
he would participate with the others in the distribution. And if
there was some foolish one who had let his land deteriorate and
lose value, by letting the vines get overgrown or by cutting down
trees, or by letting a house fall down, or if he had sold all he had
been given, and he asked to participate in the distribution of what
his father and mother had left; and the other brothers said to him:
"We don't want you to participate in the distribution with us, unless you make up what has deteriorated in your share"; and if he
said: "I cannot make it up, but I want an estimate made by honest men of what it was worth when it was given to me, and how
much it is worth now," in this way the honest men would value
the property; and the amount of the deterioration would be taken
into account in the distribution; and he would participate with
the others in the distribution of the rest, according to how much
he would have taken; and each would take as much as the others
of the land and the personal property. And if it happened that
one of them had [previously] been given too large a share, and he
did not want to come back to the distribution of the property inherited from the father and mother, and the others said to him:
"You were given too large a share; come to the distribution with
us, and bring it all back"; then the law would require that his share

194. For the "hotchpot" see Introduction, p. xxxiii.

be evaluated by honest men; and if he had been given too much, he would have to bring it all back, except for the improvements he had made, as we said above.

137. On holding dower property in good condition, and suing on it.

A woman commoner gets as dower half of her husband's land, ⟨and half of his personal property, and she pays half his debts; but she does not contribute to his bequests [*aumosne*]⟩. And she must keep up the dower property in good condition and must pay half of all the customary dues [*costumes*]. And if anyone wronged her in respect to her dower, she could make a complaint in the king's court or the baron's court or the court of Holy Church; and it would be her choice; and the case would not be sent down to the lord in whose lands she lived.

138. On partitions where boundaries are marked by a judge, and on being your own judge.

If brothers who were commoners divided up their land, they could mark their shares with stakes or stones without going to the judge; but they could not erect boundary markers, nor should they, without the attention of a judge. And if they did put up boundary markers without a judge, they would pay a fine to the judge of sixty sous per marker. And divisions marked out without a judge are not enforceable if anyone disagrees with them; but those that are made and marked by a judge are enforceable. ⟨And no one must mark boundaries without a judge; for no one may make himself a judge, and no one may seize property from his debtor without a judge, unless his debtor hands the property over to him, of his own will; but he should appear before the judge and ask for a hearing and make his complaint. And that it is true that no one should make himself into a judge, nor seize another's property without the order and at the will of a judge, is written in the *Digest*, in the title "Of things done by force and intimidation,"

in the law beginning Extat enim decretum,[195] where this matter is
discussed.)

139. On distribution among children.

If some commoner had had two wives, the children of each
wife would take equal shares in the land coming from the father.

And if a woman had had two husbands, the children would
take equal shares of the land coming from the mother.

And if the husband and his first wife had made a purchase, the
children of the first wife alone would take half of the purchase because of their mother, and the other half would be divided among
the first and second families; {and if the husband and the second
wife had made a purchase together, the children of the second
wife would have a half because of their mother; and the other half
would be divided among the first and second families;}[196] so that
each would have as much as the others, as we said above.

140. On [lateral] inheritances with no heir.

If some man and his wife bought land together, the survivor
would keep for life the purchased {and otherwise acquired property. And if it happened that they had no heir, and the wife died
first, the man would keep the purchased property for his lifetime;}[197] and the wife would do likewise if she lived longer than
the man. And when they were both dead, the purchased property
would go as a remainder, half to the woman's family and the other
half to the man's family.[198]

195. *Dig.* 4.2.13 (Watson 1:116). The Latin title is *Quod metus causa gestum erit*.

196. The words in the curly brackets are Viollet's reconstruction, based on
two of the three manuscripts of the *Coutume de Touraine-Anjou*. This language
does not appear in any of the manuscripts of the *Etablissements*.

197. The passage in curly brackets is fairly garbled in the manuscripts and is
partly reconstructed by Viollet.

198. Since the man and his wife had bought the property together, when the
first of them died, half of the purchased property might have gone to the deceased's
heirs. The customary rule of this chapter gives the survivor a life interest in the
dead spouse's property (i.e., the surviving spouse keeps it all). After the death of

141. On the custodian of a commoner.

No commoner has custodianship of another man's child, except in one way, which I shall explain: if some man and his wife died, the person who would get the "remainder"[199] of the land could keep the children until they could walk {and talk. And when they could go off} and talk to some other of their relatives [*amis*] whom they liked, or to some stranger, they could go [into their custodianship], if they wanted, along with their lands. And the person to whom they went would have to keep up the property in good condition, and if he did not he would have to make up for it when they left him. But he would give them none of the fruits of the land for the time it had been in his care. And thus no commoner has custodianship of children, except their father or mother, as soon as the children can say to which of their relatives they would rather go.

142. On appealing for false judgment.

No commoner can give judgment, or prove it false, nor dispute [*contendre*] it. And if his lord had given him a good and honest judgment, and he asked for an amendment of the judgment, and the judgment was so good and so honest that there was no amendment [possible], he would pay the lord the fine of his law [*l'amande de sa loi*]: five sous, or six sous and six deniers, according to the custom of the castellany. And if he had said to his lord: "You have given me a false judgment," and the judgment was good and honest, he would pay sixty sous as a fine to his lord, and to each of those who had participated in the judgment, and who were gentlemen or had fiefs; {and also to the judge}[200] he would pay the fine of his law.

---

the second spouse, since they had no descendants, each spouse's nearest kinsman (or kinswoman) would take half the property, either as a lateral inheritance or as a "remainder" after a life interest.

199. For the "remainder" see note 168 above.

200. Viollet believes these words to be a mistaken amendment by the Compiler.

143. On a marriage between a poor woman and a rich man.

If some man who had much personal property took a wife who had nothing, and the man died, even though they had no issue [*hoir*] the woman would take half the personal property. And if a rich woman took a very poor husband and died, he would take half of the personal property. And thus you can understand that personal property is common property [*communal*]. And if when the rich man had taken the poor wife she had issue and the man died, and she took another husband and they had issue, and the second husband and the wife died, and the children of the first and the second husband wanted to divide the personal property among them, the children of the first husband would take half of all the personal property they could find still in existence, whether it was barrels or other vessels, or feather beds or animals or chests, which had belonged to the first husband; and the other half, because of the mother['s share in them], would be shared out among the first and second families. Thus the children of the first husband would take half the personal property; and the other half would be divided among the first and second families because of the mother, as we said above. But the fruits [*gueaignages*] of the land would be taken in common, because they had reaped the fruits together;[201] and there would be an accounting, and each one would take as much as the others. And the personal property which the mother had acquired since the death of the first husband, and with the second husband, would be divided among the first and second families; and each [child] would take as much as the others.

144. On prodigal [*fous*] children.

If some commoner had children, and some stayed home with him and were quiet and hardworking, and he also had one who was prodigal and a drinker [*taverneret*] and a dice player [*jueor de*

201. That is, the first and second families formed a kind of partnership, so that the fruits would be shared equally.

dez] who had left the area, and the father died, and the prodigal heard about it, and came back to share in the distribution with the others, he would take as much of the land and the personal property as the other brothers; and the amount that each one had as his share, he would have by law the same amount as his share, just like those who had helped with the work. And in the same way, one of the sisters, if she had gone out in service [*meschinage*] or in some other place outside, to amuse herself or do her own will,[202] she would by law have her share in the distribution with her other brothers, just like the prodigal.

145. On making improvements[203] on another's land without reimbursement.

If some gentleman or commoner had taken a wife, and had had good houses built on his wife's land or planted good vines, and his wife died without an heir, all the improvements he had made on his wife's land would go to the wife's family; and the wife's family would not reimburse him for them unless they wanted to. And this is what you gain by making improvements on another's property.

146. On the coming of age of commoners.

When he passes fifteen years, a commoner is of age to hold land, and work for a lord, and be a warrantor; but he is not of age to fight[204] until he has passed twenty-one years, unless he wants to of his own free will.

202. Viollet sees this conduct by the girl who leaves home as something more like prostitution than mere domestic service. See Viollet 4:153–156.
203. Viollet's title reads *demander*, as do certain manuscripts. But by the reading of other manuscripts, *amendement* is more in conformity with the content of the chapter, where the word *amandement* or *amendement* appears twice.
204. The fighting referred to here is as a participant in a judicial battle.

147. On giving faith as a commoner [*De foi en vilenage*].

If some commoner purchased or otherwise acquired some property that required giving homage or faith, or if he arranged to hold some or all of his property in faith or homage from his lord, in the same faith as the portion that had been purchased, each of his children would take as much of the property as the others, save the oldest, who owed the faith; and [the oldest] would take some extra, according to the size of the property, for giving the faith and for warranting the others as coholders. And the property would be divided this way ever afterward until the third time; and from then on, the oldest would take two-thirds; and the property would be distributed after the manner of gentlemen's fiefs forever afterward.

148. On avoiding tolls.

A commoner, when he avoids a road toll, pays a sixty-sou fine to the person owning the road. And the same is true when he is found with a false measure on him, whether he is a buyer or a seller.[205]

149. On avoiding the toll and being arrested outside the boundaries.

If a merchant passes a toll road without paying the toll, and the toll owner [*paagiers*] arrests him and says to him: "You are going off without paying the toll; we want you to pay your dues and pay a fine [*gaigiez l'amande*]"; and if he speaks this way: "Sir, I did not know that I should properly pay a toll here; and I will do what I should," it can be ruled that if he dares to swear on the saints that he did not know there was a toll, he may pay his wager of law[206] and pay the toll; and with that he will be discharged. And if he dares not swear, he will pay sixty sous as a fine to the toll owner.

205. This rule is found again in *Etablissements* 1:151.
206. The wager of law is five sous; see *Etablissements* 1:51.

150. On a merchant traveling by water.

If a merchant who goes by water and uses a barge [*chalant*] avoids the toll on some stretch {where he should pay it}, and is seized and arrested, he loses the barge and all its contents.

151. On false measures and false cloth [measure].

A merchant who carries a false measure and against whom it is proved pays sixty sous.[207]

152. On a judgment for false dealing in cloth.

A merchant who takes false cloth[208] to sell, and it is proved against him by merchant drapers who have affirmed that the cloth is false by their oath, the judge should have the cloth burned,[209] in the sight and to the knowledge of the merchants and other people; and the person taking it [to sell] must pay the judge a fine of sixty sous. And if it were proved that the same person who was taking it to sell had manufactured it, he would by law lose his hand, because he had acted as a falsifier and a thief.

153. On married women merchants, and on answering married women merchants [in court].

No woman has a right to an answer [to her complaint] in the secular court provided she has a husband, except for an accusation of a crime against her person; but if someone had assaulted her or slandered her [*dite folie desloial*], she would have a right to an answer without her husband; or if she was a merchant, she would have a right to an answer concerning things she had delivered from her business. ⟨Not otherwise, according to written law

---

207. This rule was already mentioned in *Etablissements* 1:148.
208. Presumably the text here refers to cloth of improper measurement.
209. The poor syntax of this sentence is imitated from the original in both the *Coutume de Touraine-Anjou* and the *Etablissements*.

in the *Digest*, De regularis juris, l. Foeminae a publicis judiciis;[210] for a woman is barred from all [public] offices.⟩

154. On calling a man dishonest [*desloial*], or the same [slander] for a woman.

If someone called another person dishonest [*faus*] or a thief or a murderer, or stinking [*pugnais*], or some other slanderous name [*autre folie desloial*], and the person thus named complained to the judge, and spoke in this way: "Sir, this person has called me a thief—or has called me a murderer—in the hearing and knowledge of myself and honest persons, and I want you to give me a hearing on this matter," [then] if the other party says: "I deny it, and I will do what I must," it can be ruled that he may swear with his hand on the saints that he did not say the slander, and this will discharge him. And if he dares not swear the oath, he must pay sixty sous as a fine to the judge, and a hundred sous and a denier to the plaintiff. And in the same way were someone to call a woman a whore, or a thief, or some other slanderous name, then if she made a complaint, she would have a hearing, as we have explained above.

155. On having your witness [*garant*] at a hearing.

If someone slandered another person, and the person made a complaint, and he did not say that it had been in his sight and knowledge, or if he did not name a witness to the suit, or one or the other of these two things, he would not have the right to an answer. But if he said it was in his sight and knowledge, and called good witnesses, he would be entitled to an answer; and the witnesses would be heard immediately, if they were in court; and if they were not, the witnesses would be summoned and they would

---

210. *Dig.* 50.17.2 (Watson 4:957). This law is not well on point. It commences: "Feminae ab omnibus officiis civilibus vel publicis remotae sunt et ideo nec judicis esse possunt. . . ." But perhaps the author states it as an authority that married women can get access to the courts only as merchants, since they cannot be public officials.

appear in court on the day assigned. And if they testified they had heard the slander, and the party denied the accusation and the testimony, then it could be ruled that he might swear on the saints that he had not said the slander the other accused him of, as the witnesses had testified; and with that he would be discharged. And if he dares not swear, he must pay a fine of sixty sous to the court and a hundred sous and a denier to the plaintiff, as we explained above.

156. On striking your lord with evil intent.

A commoner[211] who strikes his lord with evil intent, provided the lord is a gentleman, loses his hand, unless the lord had struck him first.

157. On striking a judge or a provost or an officer.

A commoner who strikes his lord's provost or an officer of his household who bears the keys pays sixty sous as a fine to the judge, and to the person assaulted whatever damages he proves.[212]

158. On breaking the lord's seisin [trespassing] and fishing in his ponds.

A commoner who breaks his lord's seisin, or who hunts game in his lord's preserve, or who fishes in his pond or his restricted area [defois] pays a fine of sixty sous. Or if he keeps a tavern without permission [sur son ban],[213] or if he keeps his oxen or cattle, or his goats, by night in [the lord's] woods of less than three years {and one month's} growth, he pays sixty sous as a fine. Or if he resists the lord or his provost, likewise he pays a fine of sixty sous.

211. For the same crime committed by a gentleman, see *Etablissements* 1:52.
212. The assaulted person might have damages in the form of medical bills or wages lost from being unable to work; but he would have to prove in court what his actual damages were before collecting from the assaulter. See Beaumanoir §841.
213. Viollet defines *ban* here as the time when the sale of wine is restricted to the suzerain.

159. On seizure [*saisine*].

If some lord said to his commoner: "I am taking possession and seisin of this property"—and named it—and did not take seisin except that way [verbally], and the commoner removed the property or interfered with it [*remuast*], he would pay his lord only his wager of law;[214] for this kind of seisin is not certain; it is only a prohibition [*veée*]. And if he took it out of his lord's seisin, after the lord had seized and taken possession of it, he would pay a fine of sixty sous.[215]

160. On sales taxes [*ventes*].

If there were parties who exchanged lands with each other, and they were not in the same fief nor held from the same lord, the lords would have the lands appraised by honest men, and according to their appraised value the lords would receive sales taxes. But if they were held from the same lord, there would be no sales tax, except in one case which we will explain: when the lord held from two barons and had men in each castellany, and two men [from different castellanies] exchanged some of his land with each other, there would be a sales tax, because two fiefs were involved, even though they were held from the same lord.

161. On redemption by the family, and on challenging sales [*ventes*] within a year and a day.

If someone purchased from another party[216] a great purchase worth a hundred pounds more or less, whether it was in pastures or vines or arable land, or houses; and the person buying it gave

214. The wager of law is five sous; see *Etablissements* 1:51.
215. The first sentence of this chapter concerns a seizure made by a lord, but only verbally. The second sentence refers to a seizure where the lord does more than merely *say* he is taking possession.
216. The terminology is confused here. There is a buyer and a seller, but no money changes hands. I have referred to the person who gives the larger parcel and ends up with the smaller parcel as the seller.

the seller a rod [*alne*] of land that was worth only ten pounds, even though the purchase was worth a hundred pounds, more or less, as we said above, and the family [of the buyer] came forward and asked to have [the smaller parcel] by paying the price in money; and the buyer said: "I do not want you to have it, for it is an exchange, for I gave a great part of my land in exchange for it," then the family would not get this kind of purchase, according to the current custom.

In all purchases that are real property, provided they are held for a year and a day without challenge, in the sight and knowledge of the family of the person from whom it was bought.[217] If some member of the family came forward, provided he was in the diocese and he came after the year and a day had passed, and asked to redeem [218] the property, he could not do so by law. But if some member of the family appeared before the year and a day were up and asked to redeem the property, he would get it, provided he had not been summoned by the court,[219] but he would have to reimburse the buyer for all the improvements he had made. And if he had been summoned to redeem it before a judge, he would not get it.

162. On offering money for a redemption before a judge, and on improvements made after the offer.

If it happened that someone purchased some property from another and one of the seller's family {came forward} and asked {to redeem} the purchase and offered the price in money that the purchase had cost, and showed the money and said: "{Take what

217. This "sentence," which appears to have no main clause, appears this way in Viollet. It should probably be linked to the next sentence.

218. Family members have a right to buy back or redeem property sold to a stranger by reimbursing the purchase price. See note 2 above.

219. This proviso suggests that a buyer could nullify the right of family members to redeem by having them summoned by a court to exercise their option, probably before the sale. Once they had declined to do so, they could no longer press their right to redeem. This interpretation is supported by the last sentence of the paragraph.

the purchase cost you, and}[220] account for all the costs, and I will pay you back for them; here is the money"; and if the buyer did not want to take the money and afterward made improvements to the property, either by planting vines or building a house or other improvements, the party who had offered him the money before a judge would not be obligated to reimburse him for the improvements he had made; instead, he would redeem the purchase by paying the money the other had laid out for it.

163. On recovering your proven costs at a redemption.

If someone bought some property from a party who had family outside the diocese,[221] and one of them came to ask to redeem the purchase after a year and a day had passed, the buyer would not be discharged from the request because of the due date; instead, the person asking for the redemption would get it, by paying the money. And if the buyer had made improvements, he would be reimbursed for them on his making an honest proof of them; and he would not give back anything he had harvested from the land, for the law would not require that you go and summon the other party outside the diocese.

164. On redemption by the lord in the absence of family.

If someone made a purchase from a person who was not related to him [*ne li tenist riens*], the lord from whom the land was held could purchase the property, if he wanted to, rather than [have] a stranger [buy it].[222]

---

220. These words are Viollet's reconstruction.
221. De Laurière claims that whereas jurisidiction follows the secular boundaries, absence follows the ecclesiastical ones. In some later law codes, the word *pais* 'area', 'district' is used.
222. Feudal redemption (purchase by the lord) was considered to take precedence over purchase by some stranger.

165. On redeeming your land without paying sales tax.

If someone made a purchase and then a person from the seller's family made a redemption, the latter would pay no sales tax to the lord, but he would reimburse it to the person from whom he had redeemed, [that is,] both the [purchase] money and the sales tax the buyer had paid to the lord.

166. On swearing to honest costs and expenses in a redemption.

If someone had purchased pastures, or vines, or arable lands, or houses, or other things that were real property; and someone from the seller's family asked to redeem them, and the buyer said: "I am willing for you to have them, by giving me what they cost me"; and the other party said: "How much did they cost?" and he replied: "Fifty pounds," or "sixty," and said that this is what they had cost, even though they had cost only twenty pounds; and the other party said: "It did not cost you that much; it cost you only twenty pounds, and that's what I am ready to pay"—and if he said: "I will not take less than sixty pounds, for it cost me that much; and I will do what I have to";[223] it will be ruled by law that the person asking to redeem must bring to court all the money the buyer says the purchase cost him. And when the money is before the judge, the latter must say: "Here is sixty pounds in money, which is what you said the purchase cost you," and then the buyer will have to swear with his hand on the saints that that was what it had cost him in an honest purchase. And if he does not dare swear and says the following: "I will take only twenty pounds, for it cost me no more than that"; and the other party says: "Now I don't want to pay you anything for it, for I offered you twenty pounds in money in front of the judge, and in a place and at a time when I was supposed to, and you wouldn't take it; instead of that you

223. This form of words meant that the person would make whatever proof a court required.

said it had cost you sixty pounds; and you have caused me damages in seeking such a large sum of money: and because you said before a judge that it had cost you that much, and you dared not swear it or prove it, as you had undertaken to do, for this reason I request to have the purchase without paying even a penny or a half penny [*sanz denier et sanz maille*], if that is what the judgment is," and then it will be ruled in a judgment that he gets the purchase without paying a penny or even a half penny. . . .[224]

167. On postponement of sales tax by a judge.

If someone makes a purchase and does not pay the sales tax within seven days and seven nights, and he has not obtained a postponement from the judge, he will pay a fine of his wager of law;[225] or if he lets a year go by without paying or obtaining a postponement from the judge, he will pay a fine of sixty sous.

168. On redemption among brothers and sisters.

Brothers or sisters or first cousins can obtain redemption from each other as they could from a stranger; for if there were three brothers, and one sold to a second, and the third brother who was neither the seller nor the buyer requested his share of the purchase after a year and a day had passed, he would not by law get a share, provided he had let a year and a day go by without challenging, if he was in the diocese. But if he appeared within a year and a day, and asked the judge for a redemption, provided he had never been summoned before a judge to make the redemption, he would pay half the money,[226] but he would get none of the fruits the other brother had harvested.

---

224. Some manuscripts add that the redeemer must be reimbursed for his costs in procuring the money; for example, MS *B*: ". . . et li autres li rendra tout le domage qu'il avra euz a porchacier l'argent." Viollet ends his chapter with dots to suggest an omission.

225. This is five sous. See *Etablissements* 1:51.

226. Since he and the buyer brother had an equal claim to the purchase, the third brother could not redeem more than a half of the property, by paying half of the purchase money.

169. On paying your dues on a day certain.

When a commoner does not pay his quitrent and dues to his lord on the day when they are due, he pays a fine of the wager of his law.[227]

170. On taking *terrage* lands[228] for cultivation by the lord.

If someone holds land in *terrage* where there are no dues other than the *terrage*, the lord can work the land himself, but he cannot by law take the land away and give it to another person. And if there were some customary dues, such as capons or other things, the lord could not take the land away from him, except in one way: if the other party had left the land fallow for seven years, then the lord could take the land back into his domain, even though there were dues. And the man would have to make up the loss of *terrages*, for as long as he had left the land fallow; and he would pay {in damages for the *terrage*} as much as honest men estimated under oath; and he would pay no other fine, except that he would lose the land. And for this reason, you must be careful not to leave *terrage* lands fallow.

171. On appealing against a man for murder or treachery [*traïson*].

If some man is appealed against for larceny, or murder, or treachery, or for some other unlawful act, he must defend himself in the castellany where he is appealed against. ⟨And the [written] law is in agreement in the *Code*, "On crime by appeal" [*De crime de demande*], in the first law,[229] in the authentic cited in the law, Qua

---

227. The "wager of law" for a gentleman is five sous; see *Etablissements* 1:51. The *Etablissements* do not state what it is for a commoner.

228. *Terrage* is another word for *champart*, or sharecropping. See the notes to *Etablissements* 1:103.

229. *Cod.* 3.15.2 (Krueger 128). The title of the chapter here translated by the Compiler as *De crime de demande* is *Ubi de criminibus agi oportet*. The Authentic cited here is *Qua in provincia*, which is *Novel* 69 c.1.

in provincia.⟩ And the other lord[230] will not have the case sent to him, {for such persons have no power to have suspects sent to them [*point de suite*][231] }.[232] {And} if another person committed an offense in the baron's court, and the judge arrested him during the commission of the crime, he would have to defend himself in the baron's court ⟨because of the arrest during the commission, as is contained in the title "On arrest in commission [*Dou fait presant*]," in the *Usage of France* [*Usage de France*] ⟩.[233]

172. On lost bees, and following them without losing sight of them, on your oath.[234]

If a man has bees and they swarm, and the person to whom they belong sees them fly off and follows them by sight, and without losing sight of them, and they alight in another place, at the dwelling of some other man, and the person on whose grounds they alight collects them before the first man arrives, and the latter says afterward: "These bees are mine," and the other party says: "I don't believe you," and the [first] party goes before the judge in whose jurisdiction this is, and says to him: "Sir, such-and-such a man has captured my bees," the lord must send for him to appear before him, and the plaintiff must say to him: "Sir, I had some bees that swarmed out of my swarm [*essemerent de mon essain*] and I followed them until I saw them light in this man's [*preudome*] land who collected them and will not give them back to me; and I

230. That is, the man's own lord in his own castellany.

231. *Suite* is explained by the heading and wording of *Etablissements* 1:45. It implies a kind of extradition. *Point de suite* can also mean that the man must be judged by the law of the place where he is on trial, and that he cannot have recourse to the law of the place where he is a resident. Thus, the law does not "follow the man"; but that is not the meaning here.

232. Viollet thinks this clause is probably an addition of the Compiler of the *Etablissements*.

233. The *Usage de France* cited here might be the *Usage d'Orlenois*, which forms the second book of the *Etablissements*. The heading of Chapter 2 of this book includes the words *en present fait*. However, Viollet points out that another book, called the *Coutumes de France*, is quoted in the *Livre de jostice et plet*, and that this might be the same work as the *Usage de France* cited here. See Viollet 1:80–81.

234. Beaumanoir gives a similar rule for lost bees in §1967.

am ready to do whatever your court rules,[235] for they are mine and I followed them by sight and without losing sight of them"; and if the other party says: "I don't believe him, and I want him to do whatever he has to do to be believed," then it may be ruled that he must swear with his hand on the saints that the bees are his, and that they left his swarm, in his sight and knowledge, without his losing sight of them, and [went] as far as the place where the other party collected them. And upon this, he can have his bees; and he must give the other party the value of the container he collected them in.[236]

173. On a woman's dower rights; on enforcing the ecclesiastical judge's orders; and on things done out of fear of your husband and by coercion.

If a man sold his land, whether he was a gentleman or a commoner, his wife, after his death, would have dower rights in the property he had sold. And after the woman's death, it would go back to the buyer as a "remainder."[237] And if the buyer had said: "I will not buy it from you unless you have your wife swear on the saints that she will never ask for any rights in it, either in dower or for any other reason; and I want you to give her something in another place in exchange as her dower; and in addition I want a writing from the bishop's or the archpriest's ecclesiastical judge";[238] and if she had thus sworn at her own will and without coercion, and had received something in exchange; and if the buyer had had a writing concerning the gift, then she could no longer ask for any rights in it. ⟨For the writing of an ecclesiastical judge is enforced and believed until the contrary is proved, accord-

---

235. This form of words indicates a willingness to provide whatever proof the court requires.

236. De Laurière explains that the payment is necessary because the owner will use the container to take the bees away.

237. For "remainder" see note 168.

238. Viollet does not indicate by closing quotation marks the end of this speech, but it would seem reasonable to end it here.

ing to written law in the *Decretals*, De probationibus, [chapter]
Post cessionem,²³⁹ where this matter is discussed. And what has
been done by force and intimidation the judge should not enforce;
instead such contracts should be counted as void, according to
written law in the *Digest*, Quod metus causa, l. prima,²⁴⁰ when the
force is proved. The law says you must prove such force and such
intimidation as contains a danger of death or bodily harm [*tor-
ment*], according to written law in the *Code*, De transactionibus, l.
Interpositas,²⁴¹ where this matter is discussed, and in the *Code*, De
hiis quae vi metusve causa gesta sunt, l. Si donationis,²⁴² and l. Si
per vim,²⁴³ and l. ultima,²⁴⁴ et per totum titulum, and in the *Digest*, in eodem titulo Quod metus causa, l. prima in principio.²⁴⁵⟩

174. On a [judicial] battle between brothers.

Two brothers do not fight with each other on matters of fiefs,
lands or personal property, but [they do] on treachery [*traïson*],
murder, or rape. And if they appeal against each other on land or
personal property in cases where a battle is proper, they can have
hired officers or others in their place.

175. On having a judicial battle fought by champions in a
murder case, on account of an obvious infirmity [of a party].

If some incapacitated [*meaigniez*] man, or another who has
passed the age of sixty years and a day, or another who was
deaf and one-eyed, or who can demonstrate some other infirmity,

---

239. *Decr. Greg. IX* 2.19.7 (Richter 308).
240. *Dig.* 4.2.1 (Watson 1:113).
241. *Cod.* 2.4.13 (Krueger 95).
242. *Cod.* 2.19.7 (Krueger 108). The citation to Book 2, chapter 19 in this and
the following two notes may be to chapter 20 in some editions, where chapter 8
commences at Krueger's chapter 7, law 20, and subsequent chapters have a higher
number.
243. *Cod.* 2.19.4 (Krueger 108).
244. *Cod.* 2.19.12 (Krueger 109).
245. *Dig.* 4.2.1. (Watson 1:113).

or either of these two things, appealed against a {younger and healthy} man, for murder, or rape, or treachery [*traïson*], or for some other offense for which whoever was defeated could receive the punishment of death, and the plaintiff wanted a substitute [champion], and the defendant said: "I don't want you to have a champion; for you are the appellant, and I am not appealing against you, and for an offense for which I would be condemned to death if I lost," the law is that he could have a champion; he would not fail to do so because of this plea.

Here ends the *Usage of Touraine and Anjou*.

BOOK 2

The Customs of the Orléans District

HERE BEGINS: ON JUSTICE, LAW, and the commandments of the law, and the order of knighthood, and on arresting offenders in the execution of the crime, and the Practice of the Châtelet in Orléans [*Usage dou Chatelet d'Orliens*] in the baron's court, and on the punishment of offenders.[1]

⟨1. [Prologue]⟩[2]

Now hear a little thing
A small thing which is new
Which I want to tell about justice.
It is right that I should undertake
{To say something so clear}
That by rights no objection can be raised.
The law will be the judgment and the lord.
The law says you should not object
To something properly done.

The title *The Customs of the Orléans District* and the numbering "Book 2" do not appear in the manuscripts of the *Etablissements* at this point, but are used here for convenience. The French title *Usage d'Orlenois* is found at various points in the manuscript and is used in the introduction and notes of the present book to refer to the part of the *Etablissements* that follows.

1. The various manuscripts of the *Etablissements* have different beginnings at this point, and that provided by Viollet from eight of the manuscripts, translated here, is representative.

2. The title "Prologue" is added by Viollet. The stanzas of the poem evidently have twelve lines each. Four lines are missing in manuscript *N*, the only manuscript of the *Etablissements* that contains the poem, and they are supplied by Viollet from other versions of the poem called *Li droiz au clerc de Voudoi*. The restored lines are printed here between curly brackets.

For where a person is recounting good material
The law says he should not be contradicted.
This would be an wicked act of retreat.

The law forbids all wickedness.
The law shows every courtesy
And teaches us to do all good things.
The law says we should lead a good life.
{The law tells us not to be envious
So as to take away another's property.
The law tells us to be kindly}
The law tells us to be silent
About what does not concern us.
The law says you should behave
In such a way as to be pleasing to all
In whose company you are.

The law says, and I am its spokesman,
That whoever is a knight
Must speak ill of no one.
The law says he should be an honest counsellor.
The law says he should be an honest judge,
So that he cannot be contradicted.
The law says that a knight's honor
Is diminished in his jurisdiction
When he does wrong for a fee.
Instead, he should choose the right
As far as is in his power, and leave the wrong;
For this is the noble thing to do.

The law says that a baron
Should give him a swift trial
If a thief is arrested in his lands;
For the sooner he is given a trial,
The sooner he will name his accomplices
When he sees his judge before him.

If it is a thief who does murder,
{Who robs people or breaks into churches,}³
He should not be put into prison.
The law says a judge rates his soul too low
Who gives him any other treatment
Than hanging without allowing him to buy his freedom.

For this reason, I want to speak at this point about justice:
Justice is a firm will that gives everyone his due. And the commandments of the law are these: to live honestly; to do harm to no one; and to give to each person his due, according to written law in the *Institutes*, De justitia et jure, at the beginning⁴ where this matter is particularly discussed.⟩

2. On arresting offenders in the execution of the crime, and proving the same.

If some judge arrests the king's man, or someone under his own jurisdiction who claims to be the king's man, in the execution [*en present fait*] of whatever crime, in his jurisdiction or his lordship, and the offender denies he was committing the crime [*nie le present*], the judge who arrested him must prove to the king's men that [the arrest] was during the commission of the crime. And the king's men will have jurisdiction before any further proceedings. And once the arrest during the commission of the crime is proved or admitted, the offender will be sent for trial to the court of those prosecuting him. And if the arrest during the commission of the crime is not adequately proved, he will remain for trial in the court in whose jurisdiction he claimed to be, according to the general custom of the barony.

---

3. This line is reestablished by Viollet with advice from Gaston Paris.
4. *Inst.* I.Ipr. 3 (Birks I=37).

3. On the king's jurisdiction of some dispute between parties who have to make a complaint against the king [*marchir au roi*].

If some judge has to make a complaint about the king, from whatever jurisdiction, whether on real property or lordship, or some other thing, the king, for the duration of the dispute, will take the matter into his own hands, and give judgments to himself and others, for the king does not derive seisin [jurisdiction] from another, but it is derived from him, according to the practice of the baron's court.

4. On requesting seisin as the nearest relative of the heir, and on making an objection and reserving rights according to the practice in the baron's court.

No one can or should ask for seisin, unless he was previously in seisin,[5] or the person on whose account he is asking for it[6] was formerly in seisin, or he was despoiled [*despoilliés*], or [the other party] was despoiled. Whoever asks for seisin of real property must ask in this way: "My father"—or my brother—or my cousin—or my relative—"died seised and vested, holding and working [the land], sowing and reaping, and holding from a lord,[7] at the time when he passed from life to death, and he died peaceably seised, without any pending suits against him, of the following property"—and he should give its name—"situated in such-and-such a place, and in such-and-such a quitrent property—or in such-and-such a fief. And as I am the closest relative and the heir on the side from which the fief came down,[8] and Guillaume is wrong-

---

5. This form of words seems to indicate an action in novel disseisin.

6. This circumlocution may mean that the person formerly in seisin has died, and that the plaintiff is the heir.

7. All these expressions have much the same meaning, which is that the deceased was in legal possession of the land.

8. A fief could pass to an heir from his father or his mother (or from relatives of either), and the side of the family from which a fief passed to him was carefully distinguished. If a holder of land died without descendants, his land would pass to the closest relative on the side from which he had inherited it.

fully holding the said property, I am requesting to be given seisin, and I will prove my kinship, if he challenges it, by doing what I should toward you,[9] as my rightful lord, or [else I am requesting] to know in a judgment whether I am to receive seisin or not." And he should reserve the right to do and say more, if he needs to. ⟨And that he has a right to make this reservation is written in the title "On appealing against a man for murder and treachery.")[10] The law says that the heir should be in possession; and it is written in the *Code*, De edicto divi Adriani tollendo, l. Quamvis quis se filium defuncti,[11] etc.⟩

And the practice of the Orléans district is that the dead man gives seisin to the living [*li morz saisist le vif*], and that he must be given seisin, unless another person comes forward who has a greater right to the property than he does.

And the lord before whom he is requesting the aforesaid property must give him a ruling, in his court, in a judgment, by his liege vassals, by those who owe him their faith, by knights, ⟨for the things that are done in the presence of noble persons and the court of the ruler [*prince*] are enforceable, according to written law in the *Code*, "On wills and how a will is executed [*ordonez*]," in lege Omnium testamentorum solempnitatem, at the beginning,[12] etc.⟩ by burghers [or] by officers.[13]

And if the judgment is argued about and not agreed upon on the first day, and the second and the third, the lord can give his own judgment, after taking honest counsel, ⟨according to written law in the *Digest*, De re judicata, l. Inter pares⟩[14] if they cannot agree.[15]

9. This form of words indicates a willingness to provide whatever proof the court requires.

10. This is *Etablissements* 2:21.

11. *Cod.* 6.33.2 (Krueger 266). The Latin heading is *De testamentis: quemadmodum testamenta ordinantur*.

12. *Cod.* 6.23.19 (Krueger 254).

13. This hierarchy of those giving the judgment seems to suggest that the courts at different levels used different categories of men as jurymen (*jugeors*). Burghers administered justice in their own towns.

14. *Dig.* 42.1.38 (Watson 4:540).

15. This paragraph seems to deal with a situation similar to that described in *Etablissements* 1:109.

And if the lord did not do this and was in default,[16] and his default was proved, the jurisdiction of the case would go to the sovereign; and the lord would lose what jurisdiction he held, ⟨according to the custom of the area and the district; which is to say the obedience [17] according to the king's statutes [*les establissemenz le roi*] as contained in the chapter [*titre*] "On appealing against your lord for default of judgment,"⟩ [18] according to the practice of the Orléans district, in the secular courts.

5. On requesting a reclamation [*recreance*].

If someone is requesting a reclamation of some property, he must supply sureties [*pleges*] for the reclamation, for there is no reclamation without sureties, according to the practice of the secular courts.[19]

6. On refusing a reclamation according to the custom in the district.

No one should permit a reclamation of something in which there is danger to life or limb,[20] nor [bail] where the penalty might be loss of life or limb [*peine de sanc*].

---

16. By this the author means default of judgment (failing to give a hearing).

17. A vassal whose immediate lord was found to have failed to give his man a hearing lost his jurisdiction over that man, who passed under the jurisdiction of the overlord. See *Etablissements* 1:8 and 1:56 and Beaumanoir, chapter 62 and §1745.

18. This is *Etablissements* 1:8.

19. If some property was seized because of an accusation of wrongdoing and pending a trial, the accused could often get it back by promising to bring it to court when the trial took place. Some assurance was required that the property *would* reappear, and this was in the form of sureties—people who undertook to make sure the property was produced. They might have to promise to pay a fine or forfeit some of their property if it were not. Sometimes a deposit of property was accepted as a security instead of sureties (Beaumanoir, Chapter 53). In Marie de France's *Lanval*, the hero is accused of a crime and freed on the promise of his sureties that he will appear for trial. One of the sureties is Gauvain (Marie de France, *Lanval*, ed. Jean Rychner, Textes Littéraires Français [Geneva: Droz, 1958], p. 55, lines 397–400).

20. For a similar caution, see Beaumanoir §§1107, 1121.

7. On requesting seisin without pleading when not in possession [*despoilliés*].

No one should plead in any court while not in seisin [*despoilliés*], but one should ask for seisin before any other thing, or be informed in a judgment that one should get it. The law says that one should have seisin, and one is not required to answer if not in possession, nor when someone else is holding the property, nor need one make a denial, or an admission, or an answer, or any defense, ⟨according to written law in the *Decretals*, De ordine cognitionum, Cum dilectus filius, etc., capitulo Super spoliatione,[21] et per totum titulum; and according to the practice of the secular court⟩.

8. On cases of high justice, without giving property back or allowing bail, and on summoning parties without delay.

There is no bail [*recreance*] in prior judgment[22] cases, nor in murder, nor treachery [*traïson*], nor rape, nor homicide of pregnant women [*encis*], nor in ambush [*agait de chemin*], nor in robbery, nor in larceny, nor in homicide, nor in broken truce, nor in arson, according to the practice in the secular courts, for the sureties could not lose life or limb.[23] ⟨And if someone is appealed against in the above cases which carry a penalty of loss of life or limb [*poine de sanc*], an attorney is appointed in vain [*por noient*][24]

21. *Decr. Greg. IX* 2.10.2,4? (In Richter, the chapter beginning Quum dilectus filius is *Decr. Greg. IX* 2.10.2, and the chapter beginning Super spoliatione is *Decr. Greg. IX* 2.10.4.)

22. That is, when the defendant claims that the matter has already been litigated and is res judicata.

23. Chapter 1:108 states that the sureties would have to pay a "man's relief" of one hundred sous and one denier as a penalty if the accused failed to appear for trial. In the present chapter it appears that in the Orléans jurisdiction the sureties of the fugitive might lose *all* their property as a penalty, although their lives were not at risk.

24. A person accused of a capital crime had to answer in person, and not through an appointed attorney. See Beaumanoir §§152, 160.

according to written law in the *Digest*, De publicis judiciis, l. pene ultima.)[25] But [the sureties] would be at the discretion of the lord, as to their real and personal property. ⟨And in the above cases you may may make peace and a settlement [*transaccion*],[26] according to written law in the *Code*, De transactionibus, l. Transigere vel pacisci,[27] where this matter is written about and discussed, except for adultery.⟩

9. On the duties of the attorney; on continuance for a legal excuse [*contremant de essoigne*]; and on decertifying an attorney and on appointing an attorney.

⟨An attorney is the name of a person who transacts and administers another's business and acts for him, on the orders of his lord, according to written law in the *Digest*, De procuratoribus, l. prima.[28]

And without the order of the lord, there is no valid [*loiaus*] attorney; instead he is invalid [*faus*], according to written law in the *Code*, De furtis et servo corrupto, l. Falsus procurator,[29] where this matter is written about and discussed. And what is done by an invalid attorney, whether a judgment or a sentence, is invalid, according to written law in the *Code*, De procuratoribus, l. Licet in principio.[30] And an attorney can do his principal[31] no harm, if he has no authorization for what he does, according to written law in the *Code*, De transactionibus, l. Transactionis placitum.[32]

---

25. *Dig.* 48.1.13 (Watson 4:796).
26. The observance of private settlements is also recommended by Pierre de Fontaines. See *Conseil*, chapters 36 and 37, at p. 133.
27. *Cod.* 2.6.18 (Krueger 96).
28. *Dig.* 3.3.1 (Watson 1:86).
29. *Cod.* 6.2.19 (Krueger 239).
30. *Cod.* 2.12.24 (Krueger 104). In some editions this citation is to 2.13.24, since chapter 7 is divided into chapters 7 and 8 at 7.20 (= 8.1) and subsequent chapters in Book 2 have a higher number.
31. That is, the person who is delegating authority to the attorney. In modern law, this person is called the "client" if the attorney is doing legal work. Another set of terms for this relationship is "principal and agent"; the older terms were "master and servant."
32. *Cod.* 2.4.7 (Krueger 97).

And an attorney should diligently observe the orders of his principal, according to written law in the *Decretals*, De rescriptis, l. Quum dilecta in Christo[33] and in the *Digest*, Mandati, lege Diligenter[34] etc.

And no attorney has any powers in addition to what his principal gives him in his orders, according to written law in the *Code*, De procuratoribus, l. Si procurator,[35] in the letter of appointment, composed by the principal, according to written law in the *Decretals*, De officio judicis delegati, capitulo Cum olim abas, versus finem,[36] where precisely this matter is written about, according to the laws we have mentioned above and their concordances.

But⟩, according to the practice in the secular court [and] in the baron's court, no attorney is accepted in the secular court except [to act] for a person with a seal [*persone autantique*],[37] for a baron, or a bishop or a chapter, or unless it is in some case for the common good of a town or village, or a university [*université*],[38] or by agreement of the parties, ⟨—and they must send their appointment letters to their adverse parties (and much better to the judge), according to written law in the *Digest*, De procuratoribus, l. Si procuratorem,[39] etc.—⟩ or unless it is [to ask] for a continuance [*contremant*], or to take an adjournment [*essoignier*] for his lord or to extend his adjournment; ⟨for it is profitable [*profiz*] and an ordinary thing to defend a person who is not present, according to written law in the *Digest*, De procuratoribus, l. Servum quoque, §Publice utile est⟩.[40] And the [request for a] continuance must come to the judge and the adverse party, ⟨as does the decertification of an attorney, when the principal wants to do this,

33. *Decr. Greg. IX* 1.3.22 (Richter 25–28).
34. *Dig.* 17.1.5 (Watson 2:480).
35. *Cod.* 2.12.10 (Krueger 104).
36. *Decr. Greg. IX*, 1.29.32 (Richter 175–177).
37. According to Viollet's note here, a *persone autantique* is one who has a *seel autantique* 'recognized seal'. Only very important persons, such as barons and bishops, fell into this category.
38. The commentators' notes indicate that this really means a university, such as the University of Paris.
39. *Dig.* 3.3.65 (Watson 1:95).
40. *Dig.* 3.3. 33.2 (Watson 1:90).

according to written law in the *Decretals*, De procuratoribus, capitulo Mandato[41] and in the *Digest*, De procuratoribus, l. Si procuratorem[42] and in the *Code*, De satisdando, l. unica,[43] where this
matter is explained, and according to the practice of the secular court. A person not being represented by an attorney must
be counted in default, according to written law in the *Digest*, De
diversis temporalibus praescriptionibus, l. prima).[44] And you can
contest the continuance, when it is not timely, and when the party
has taken several continuances after the inspection day. And if the
attorney is taking an adjournment [*essoigne*] for his lord, he must
name the legal excuse, either sickness or some other thing; and if
the excuse is reasonable, the judge should entertain it.[45] ⟨But in
connection with the adjournment the lord must do all he is supposed to do, according to written law in the *Decretals*, De procuratoribus, c. Querelam,[46] where this matter is explained.⟩ And
when he appears on the day when he has been summoned, he
must make proof of his legal excuse or impediment; for after the
inspection day he may well lose seisin or ownership, or lose the
suit, if he does not make proof of his legal excuse, according to
the practice of the secular court, if he had heard the complaint, or
someone else had heard it for him, and [witnessed] the inspection
made by the judge,[47] ⟨according to written law in the *Decretals*, Ut
lite non contestata, c. Quoniam frequenter, §In aliis⟩.[48]

10. On confirming a bail by a judgment.

A reclamation should not be refused in a judicial action [*droit
faisant*] unless there is a good reason why, or unless it is one of the

41. *Decr. Greg. IX* 1.38.13 (Richter 217).
42. *Dig.* 3.3.65 (Watson 1:95).
43. *Cod.* 2.56.unica (Krueger 118). In some editions this citation is to
2.57.unica, since chapter 7 is divided into chapters 7 and 8 at 7.20 (= 8.1) and
subsequent chapters in Book 2 have a higher number.
44. *Dig.* 44.3.1 (Watson 4:628).
45. The legal excuses are listed in *Etablissements* 1:124.
46. *Decr. Greg. IX* 1.38.2 (Richter 212).
47. See *Etablissements* 1:70 and 2:11.
48. *Decr. Greg. IX* 2.6.5.6 (Richter 264).

above-mentioned situations; and where the reclamation is confirmed by a judge, he must assign an appropriate court date to the parties and give a hearing according to all the procedures, and according to the customs of the area and the district.

11. On appealing against a man for default after the inspection day.

If anyone is in default after the inspection day, as we have said above,[49] the plaintiff should make his complaint speaking in this way: "Whereas I made a complaint against such-and-such a man before you, asking for such-and-such a piece of land situated in such-and-such a place, and in such-and-such a quitrent property — or in such-and-such a fief — which he is holding wrongfully;" — and he should repeat the complaint — "and [whereas he] has had an inspection day, and a counsel day, and a day certain on which to answer" — and he must name the day and the default — "and on that day I was in attendance, and he was totally in default, without answering, and the time of day when you can win or lose went past; therefore, if he admits the default, I have no further proof to make; and I ask to be given seisin, or ownership, or to have won the suit, or such-and-such an award, as the court shall rule, by a valid judgment that I should be given, and [I ask] that he should suffer the loss he ought to have, seeing that it is after the inspection day." And if the other party denies this in a secular court, [the plaintiff] should ask for the recall from memory [*recort*] of the court, if he can obtain it (for a recall from memory is not to be had in the secular court,[50] unless the parties agree and assent to it, except with regard to res judicata, or in a suit that is ended, or in the king's court, or in the *bailli*'s assize) or a proof by witnesses, or by a wager of battle ⟨if it is outside the king's domain [*obeïssance*] ⟩.[51] And he must name and produce immediately the witness [*garant*]

49. This is an allusion to *Etablissements* 2:9.
50. See *Etablissements* 2:33.
51. An ordinance of 1258 forbade the use of wagers of battle in courts in the king's domain. See *Etablissements* 1:3, and Beaumanoir §§1722–1723.

who saw the court date assigned and notice served on [*assigner*] the parties, and the default made; and it can be ruled that there is a wager of battle.

And if the parties had a visible injury, and they claimed it and made mention of it or reserved their rights, they could name champions to fight for them. ⟨And if it was in the king's jurisdiction, or in his lordship or his domain, [the proof] must be made by witnesses, for the king of France forbids wagers of battle by his laws.⟩ [52]

12. On appealing against a man for murder or treachery.

If someone is accusing some other person of murder or treachery [*traïson*] [53] or [in] one of the cases mentioned above, [54] where the penalty may be loss of life or limb, the accuser must make his complaint before the judge and speak in this way: "I am making this complaint against Guillaume, who on such-and-such a day and in such-and-such a place, without my having done him any wrong, and without there being any right which I had refused him before a judge, by night and treacherously, [*en traïson*] and in ambush [*agait de chemin*] . . ."—⟨he should remember, if something has been done to him, to state it in his complaint just as it happened, if he is certain of proving it; and if [the defendant] were found guilty, he would be punished, as was said above, [55] at the beginning of the king's laws; and if [the plaintiff] failed in his proof, the same way;⟩ [56]—". . . sir, and assaulted me with his sharpened weapons, and gave me blows and sword-strokes [*colées*] so that the skin broke and gave me serious wounds [*plaies mortiex*] [57] which are plainly to be seen"—and they should be shown

52. See previous note.
53. See 1:4, 108.
54. That is, in *Etablissements* 2:8.
55. This reference is probably to *Etablissements* 1:1.
56. This reference is probably to *Etablissements* 1:4. This is also the point of maximum punctuation in this translation.
57. In spite of the word *mortiex*, these wounds are not "mortal," or the charge

to the judge—"wherefore if he admits it, I ask and request that he be punished for the relevant crime, and that my damages be made up to me, and [also] my days of forced idleness, up to a sum of ten pounds; and if he denies it, I offer to prove it ⟨by an inquest; — or⟩ by witnesses" ⟨for witnesses have the same power as writings or other instruments in a trial, according to written law in the *Code*, De fide instrumentorum, l. In exercendis litibus,[58] where this matter is discussed;⟩ "in whatsoever way the court shall rule I must [make the proof]." ⟨And the judge must state the punishment that is mentioned above at the beginning of the king's laws;[59] — if the case is in the king's domain; if it is outside the king's domain,⟩ by wager of battle.[60]

13. On appealing against a man for larceny, and on naming the stolen object [*larrecin*].

If someone is accusing some other person of larceny, he ⟨must have his proofs ready, according to written law in the *Code*, De edendo, l. Qui accusare volunt[61] and⟩ he must name the stolen object, whether it is a horse, or a gown, or a deposit [*gage*] of money, and must speak in this way: "I am complaining about such-and-such a man"—and he must put four deniers on the stolen object [*chose*] in front of the judge[62]—"who has stolen such-and-such a thing from me, and, since this larceny, I have seen it in his possession"; ⟨for larceny is a crime that is not committed openly, and concerns a thing that is taken against the will of the owner [*seig-*

---

would have been homicide and the wounded person would not be bringing it. I have therefore opted to translate "serious." See also *Etablissements* 2:24.

58. *Cod.* 4.21.15 (Krueger 161).

59. See *Etablissements* 1:4.

60. It is hard to see where the last four words of this chapter come from. They do not fit with the rest of the last sentence, but rather with the words "by witnesses" a few lines earlier, and before the words "in whatsoever way the court shall rule I must."

61. *Cod.* 2.1.4 (Krueger 92).

62. See *Etablissements* 2:18 for another mention of this custom.

neur] and without his knowledge, according to written law in the *Institutes*, De obligationibus quae ex delicto. §Furtum,[63] and in the *Code*, De furtis, l. Si quis servo alieno, circa medium,[64] etc. It is the stolen object [*larrecins*] that he must say that he has seen in [the accused's] possession after the larceny.⟩ And he must prove it by witnesses ⟨and if he fails in his proof, he is to be punished by the judge, as we said above, in the beginning, if it is in the king's domain⟩[65] if the accused does not admit the crime, or has not been arrested in the act of committing it, or if he has not been found in possession [*saisiz et vestuz*]; ⟨for an admission made in court is equivalent to a res judicata, according to written law in the *Code*, De confessis, l. unica⟩.[66]

14. On being summoned by the king and declaring that you are in the jurisdiction of another lord, and on proving your assertion to the judge.

If someone is called to appear before the king[67] or his people by being given a court date or a summons, he must appear before the king on that day, to determine whether he is justiciable by the king or not, or in his domain, or his jurisdiction, or his lordship, ⟨or in order to allege his privilege,[68] according to written law in the *Digest*, De judiciis, l. Si quis ex aliena,[69] and according to the practice in the secular court⟩. And if he is not from his domain, he should speak in this way: "Sir, I have a lord in claiming whose jurisdiction I am not trying to avoid a trial, and I am domiciled in such-and-such a place, and in such-and-such a lordship, and in such-and-such a jurisdiction"—and he should give his lord's name. And if the king's judge is certain that there is a judge in that

63. Inst., 4.1.6 (Birks 43=121).
64. *Cod.* 6.2.20 (Krueger 239).
65. This reference is probably to *Etablissements* 1:4.
66. *Cod.* 7.39.unica (Krueger 320).
67. See also *Etablissements* 2:32.
68. That is, to make his claim to be under the jurisdiction of a different lord or court.
69. *Dig.* 5.1.5 (Watson 1:165).

place, with jurisdiction over the crime for which he is being prose-cuted,[70] he can be sent back to his lord, if he requests it, and if there is no good reason why not, such as being caught in the com-mission,[71] or a denial, or an admission, or an answer; for a free man who gives an answer, or a denial, without claiming he is under the jurisdiction of [some other] court, cannot raise the issue of juris-diction after the suit has been begun; ⟨for where the suit is begun, there it should be brought to an end, according to written law in the *Digest*, De judiciis, lege Ubi,[72] in the *Code*, De foro compe-tenti, lege Nemo,[73] where it is written concerning this matter that no one can refuse the court's competence once he has made a de-nial⟩. And if the judge doubts that he is under the jurisdiction of the person he has named as his lord, he should keep him under ar-rest until the lord he has claimed as his own requests that he be sent to his court, for a case is not sent down [to a lower court judge] without his request, and no one is a legal witness in his own suit. ⟨And for this reason the judge should not give him credence, ac-cording to written law in the *Code*, De testibus, lege Omnibus.⟩[74] Nor should the judge, for this very reason, believe or lend cre-dence until he is certain of the lord's orders, either by a sure mes-senger, or by a generally known officer, or by the lord's writing, or by his provost, or his mayor, ⟨according to written law in the *Code*, "On the commands of princes," in the first law[75] where this matter is discussed; for when someone claims to be under the jurisdiction of the king or the pope, he should not be believed unless a writing is seen⟩. And when the lord asks to have him sent to his court, and he adequately convinces the king's officers, the judge should send him back, as I have said above; and if he is in doubt, he should allow him to go on bail [*recroire*], if bail is appropriate, according

---

70. Some lords had only low or middle justice, so that they could not try those accused of capital crimes such as murder. See also *Etablissements* 2:21.

71. See *Etablissements* 2:2 and Beaumanoir §911.

72. *Dig.* 5.1.30 (Watson 168).

73. *Cod.* 3.13.4 (Krueger 128).

74. *Cod.* 4.20.10 (Krueger 158).

75. *Cod.* 1.15.1 (Krueger 68). The Latin headings are *De mandatis principum* and *Si quis adserat*.

to the custom of the district, by giving adequate sureties, or by giving his own promise, or his oath, if he cannot find sureties, to submit to trial before him or wherever the ruling takes him.

And the judges should go to the place itself to inquire about the jurisdiction and the lordship, on a day certain, with the parties present who are involved in the affair; for in the secular courts a judgment is not given on a pleading by one party. ⟨No suit can be ended nor a judgment given against a party who has not been heard and adequately summoned, according to written law in the *Decretals*, "On cases of possession and ownership," in the first decretal, at the end,[76] and according to written law in the *Code*, Si adversus dotem, in the first law, at the end,[77] where it is written that the provost of the province should take jurisdiction, with the adverse party present, and according to [the practice of] the barony. And if there is a disagreement about jurisdiction between the parties, the king who is the temporal sovereign takes the matter under his jurisdiction [*en sa main*]; and the king does not take jurisdiction away from anyone, but inquires honestly about his own rights and those of others, and makes rulings for himself and for others; for jurisdiction is derived from the king, the king does not derive it from others, as we said above;[78] for the king has no sovereign in temporal matters, and he holds from no one but God and himself; and you can appeal his judgment only to God, for anyone appealing would find no one who could give him a hearing.⟩

---

76. *Decr. Greg. IX* 2.12.1 (Richter 275–276). The headings in Latin are *De causa possessionis et proprietatis* and *Susceptis*.

77. *Cod.* 2.33.1 (Krueger 112). In some editions this citation is to 2.34.1, since chapter 7 is divided into chapters 7 and 8 at 7.20 (= 8.1) and subsequent chapters in Book 2 have a higher number.

78. These words seem to be a restatement of *Etablissements* 2:3.

15. On the duties of the advocate,[79] and how you should give a judgment; and on appealing to the sovereign's court for false judgment and default of judgment.[80]

When someone has good and valid and useful defenses, the advocate or spokesman should bring forward and raise at the trial his defenses and bars,[81] and all the things he thinks should and honestly may be useful to him; ⟨for what the advocate says is as definite as if the parties said it themselves, when they listen to what he says, and do not immediately contradict it, according to written law in the *Code*, "On the errors of advocates," in the first law;[82]⟩ and all the arguments to destroy the adverse party's claim; ⟨and the advocate should say these things courteously, without uttering slander with respect to words or deeds, and he must make no deals with the person for whom he is pleading, during the suit; and this is forbidden by law in the *Code*, De postulando, lege Quisquis vult esse causidicus.[83] And this is what an honest advocate must do, as the above said law states⟩. And he should speak and request the judge this way: "My bars and defenses which I have explained and raised before you in this trial, ⟨which are useful to me, I think, I do not wish to abandon without a hearing and an honest judgment in your court, for you can add to and take away from your claim

79. This heading does not seem particularly well suited to the material of the chapter. Most of the manuscripts have a different and more general heading here: "How an advocate should behave in a case." The material of this chapter is somewhat confused. Viollet separates off the portions he considers to be additions made by the Compiler; but his analysis is conjectural and may even contribute to the confusion.

80. Default of judgment means failing to give a hearing to a person seeking redress through the courts. See *Etablissements* 1:8, 1:56, and 2:4, and Beaumanoir, chapter 62 and §1745.

81. In this chapter, the author is discussing dilatory exceptions, also called "bars," which are used merely to prolong the case without going to the main issues. Beaumanoir lists these in his §237. These issues must be raised before any defense is put forward on the main issues. Once the latter (called peremptory exceptions) have been stated, the dilatory issues are precluded. On exceptions generally, see Beaumanoir, chapter 7.

82. *Cod.* 2.9.1 (Krueger 102). The Latin headings are De errore advocatorum vel libellos seu precis concipientum and Ea, quae.

83. *Cod.* 2.6.6 (Krueger 97).

up until the judgment,⟩ and I am making a reservation to do and say more, at a place and time which the court may rule," ⟨for example, peremptory bars which are permitted until the judgment or the sentence, according to written law in the *Code*, Sententiam rescindi non posse, lege Peremptorias exceptiones;⟩[84] "so that I do not commit a wrong to the plaintiff nor to the judge; wherefore I request you, as a judge, to give me a ruling, as to whether you should give it[85] to me or not." He should say this as a request, and in asking for a ruling. And the judge should cause a ruling to be given to him in a judgment, and have his defenses and bars judged by those who can and should do so, according to the practice of the area, and give an honest judgment on the matters raised before him, according to the practice of the secular courts. And no one should refuse a hearing in his court to those in his jurisdiction; instead he should give them a hearing, according to the custom of the district.

16. On judging honestly your men's cases; on petitioning in the king's court; and on appealing immediately without delay.

When the parties are ready for [*colées en*] judgment,[86] the provost or the judge should have the parties retire and then call competent [*soufisanz*] men who are not parties. And the judge should repeat what the parties went to court over, for the one and the other party, and hand over the pleadings [*paroles*] to the jurors. ⟨And they must give an honest judgment on the actions[87] of the men, and must not judge on the face of things [*selonc la face*], but they must give an honest judgment, and must keep God be-

---

84. *Cod.* 7.50.2 (Krueger 317). See also Beaumanoir §248.

85. It is hard to say what "it" is here. It is probably a judgment or hearing, or possibly the granting of the advocate's request to make reservations.

86. It is clear that the word *jugement* here means not the final judgment and decision, but the next phase of the trial, namely the consideration by the jurors of the pleadings and proofs.

87. Some manuscripts read *filz* and others *faiz* here. I have chosen to translate *faiz* 'actions' rather than *filz* 'sons'.

fore their eyes; for a judgment is an awesome [*espovantables*] thing according to written law in the *Code*, De judiciis, l. Rem non novam, §Scituri.[88] Nor should they remember love, or hate, or gift or promise, when it comes to the judgment.⟩ And when the judgment is completed without disagreement, and they are of one mind, the judge should announce [*retraire*] his judgment to the parties. But before he gives the judgment, if he wants, and he sees that it is a good and honest thing to do, he should tell the parties to make peace, and he should do his honest best toward peace; ⟨for every honest judge [*joutise*], and all arbitrators [*juges*], should break up suits and disputes [*noises*] and bring legal actions [*quereles*] to an honest conclusion, according to written law in the *Digest*, Si certum petetur, lege Quidam existimaverunt).[89] And if they cannot come to an agreement as to a peace, the judge should call the parties and, in their presence, give and render his judgment, as it has been established; for the judge should not make the judgment, according to the practice of the secular courts.[90] And he should speak in this way: "As you began this suit and declared it ready for judgment on such-and-such complaints and such-and-such defenses,[91] asking for a judgment"—and he should repeat them—"these honest men [*preudes homes*], who are present, give you this honest ruling, by law and in a judgment, that the arguments that you have set forth do not require a postponement of the answer, and that you must answer the complaint." And if the suit is on real property, or personal property, or defamation or

88. *Cod.* 3.1.14.2 (Krueger 122). According to Viollet, many manuscripts of the *Etablissements* read Sicut(i) rather than Scituri. The word *scituri* does not appear at the beginning of a sentence in Krueger 3.1.14, where a sentence containing the word *scituri* begins: "Sic etenim attendentes . . ." The words apparently translated in the *Etablissements* about judgment being an awesome thing appear in this sentence: ". . . cum etiam ipsis magis quam partibus terribile iudicium est . . ."

89. *Dig.* 12.1.21 (Watson 1:361).

90. The judgment is given by the jurors.

91. These answers are evidently of a procedural nature (also called dilatory exceptions) which the defendant has put forward in an effort to delay having to answer the complaint. The judgment a few lines later declares these defenses invalid, so that the defendant must answer on the main issues. The suit has not proceeded very far at this point, not even to the point of the *litis contestatio* or *plet entamé*.

some other thing, [the judge] should speak in this way: "We declare him not guilty [*nos l'asolons*]" or "We condemn him according to the charge that this party made against him, by the honest
hearing [*jugement*] we have provided, in a judgment,"

⟨Which must be given to all
And must not be sold.⟩[92]

And if either of the parties feels aggrieved by a judgment that
has been given to them wrongfully and a grievance that is obvious, he should immediately and without delay appeal to the overlord, or the king's court where honest judgments are made, ⟨or in
the court of the person from whom he holds his land, by stages,
as we have said in the chapter "How you should appeal a judgment without delay."⟩[93] And he must appeal without delay, for
cases judged in the baron's court and not immediately appealed
are held to be enforceable [*estables*] according to the practice of
the secular courts, and according to written law in the *Code*, "On
advocates and various judges," in the first law,[94] where this matter
is specifically discussed. And he should speak this way: "I ask to
have this judgment amended," as we have said above, in the chapter "On asking for an amendment of a judgment,"[95] if he can get
an amendment, and if his request for an amendment of judgment
cannot be heard, he must reserve his right to prove the judgment
false;⟩ and he should say right away: "This judgment is not good
or honest, but it is false and wicked; and I appeal against it to the
sovereign, and I want to know who made this judgment"[96]—and
he must name the court to which he is appealing, that is to say
the next higher one—"and I will prove it to be what I say it is be-

92. These octosyllabic lines rhyme in the Old French version.
93. See *Etablissements* 1:85.
94. *Cod.* 2.7.1 (Krueger 98). The Latin headings are *De advocatis et diversorum
judiciorum* and *Si patronum*.
95. This refers to *Etablissements* 1:85.
96. If a wager of battle were to follow, it would be important to know who
had to fight. See *Conseil* 22:16–17 and Beaumanoir §§1753–1755.

fore the sovereign," ⟨or: "as the ruling shall be made," according to the king's laws. And if he fails to make a proof, he is to be punished, according to the custom of the area and the district, as is said above at the beginning of the king's laws.[97] And if the lord is convicted of false judgment, he loses the homage [*l'obeïssance*] of the other party, according to the practice of the secular court⟩.

And if the judgment was given in the court of the provost or the *bailli* or the king, he must petition for amendment of judgment; ⟨for in the king's court a petition must be made, and not an appeal; for an appeal includes a charge of evil and wickedness [*felonie et iniquité*], according to written law in the *Code*, "On offering prayers to the prince," and the law Si quis adversus,[98] et lege Instrumentorum[99] and in the *Code*, De sententiis praefectorum praetorio, lege unica,[100] and in the *Digest*, De minoribus, lege Praefecti,[101] where this matter is discussed:⟩ for you must petition the king to review the judgment or have it reviewed; and if it is against the law, then he should have it annulled; and if it is not against the law, then he should have it executed and confirmed by the custom of the area. ⟨And he cannot forbid this to the parties according to the king's law, as we have said above.[102] And if it is outside the king's domain, and it comes into the king's court because of higher jurisdiction [*resort*] or on appeal for default of judgment or false judgment, or refusal of reclamation,[103] or for wrong or aggrievement, or for refusing the judgment of his court, [the appellant] must say that the judgment is false; otherwise his appeal would not be entertained, according to the practice of the secular court, if he was not[104] appealing against his lord

---

97. This refers to *Etablissements* 1.7.

98. *Cod.* 1.19.5 (Krueger 75). The Latin chapter heading is *De precibus imperatori offerendis et de quibus rebus supplicare liceat vel non.*

99. *Cod.* 1.19.8 (Krueger 75).

100. *Cod.* 7.42.unica (Krueger 314).

101. *Dig.* 4.4.17 (Watson 1:131).

102. This probably refers to *Etablissements* 1:85.

103. For reclamations, see *Etablissements* 2:6, 8 and Beaumanoir, chapter 53.

104. Viollet prints "s'il n'apeloit" 'if he was *not* appealing', but many of the manuscripts read "s'il apeloit" 'if he *was* appealing', which makes more sense here.

in the above-mentioned cases;[105] and the overlord would have the proceedings in his court recalled from memory, while giving the hearing; and it must be proved by witnesses, as is said above in the king's law.[106] And the person found to be in the wrong must pay a fine according to the custom of the area and the district.⟩

17. On bad reputation, and the duties of the judge, and on punishing offenders.

If someone gets a bad reputation because of a [hue and] cry or by repute, the judge should arrest him, and inquire about his actions and his lifestyle and where he lives. And if [the judge] finds through an inquest that he is guilty of an action for which the punishment is loss of life or limb, he should not condemn him to death, where nobody is accusing him, or when he has not been caught in the act, or by any information, or when he has not accepted to submit to an inquest. But if he will not submit to an inquest, then the judge can and should banish him from the kingdom, ⟨according to whether he is guilty of the offense, and according to the results of the inquest he has made in his official capacity; for the duties of the provost and any honest judge include cleaning up his province and his jurisdiction over evil men and evil women, according to written law in the *Digest*, "On receivers," in the first law,[107] and in the *Digest*, De officio praesidis, lege Illicitas [108] et lege Praeses provinciae [109] et lege Congruit,[110] etc. And as we have said above, in the chapter "On punishing suspicious persons"⟩.[111] And

105. The first part of this sentence appears confused. If there had been a judgment in a lower court, the appellant would have to declare the judgment to be false; but if the appeal was for default of judgment, it would be because there had been no judgment or even a hearing in the lower court, and ipso facto no judgment to declare false.

106. This refers to *Etablissements* 1:3.

107. *Dig.* 47.16.1 (Watson 4:789). The Latin headings are De receptatoribus and *Pessimum genus*. See also Beaumanoir §14.

108. *Dig.* 1.18.6 (Watson 1:35).

109. *Dig.* 1.18.7 (Watson 1:35).

110. *Dig.* 1.18.13 (Watson 1:36).

111. See *Etablissements* 1:38.

if, after the banishment, he was found in the district, he would be liable to be hanged, according to the practice of the secular courts.

But if he submitted to the inquest, and the inquest found that he was guilty, the judge should condemn him to death, if it was one of the cases we have described above;[112] ⟨for every judge should always inquire and learn how he should and can punish offenders, for an offender should never remain unpunished, so that others do not take an example from their misdoings, according to written law in the *Digest*, Ad legem Aquiliam, lege Ita vulneratus, circa medium;[113] for the wicked refrain from doing evil for fear of punishment; and the good in order to have the love of God, according to written law in the *Digest*, De justitia et jure, lege prima, at the first response⟩.[114]

18. On claiming something that has been stolen, and on doing business wisely and without suspicion.

If somebody is looking for [*siut*] something that has been stolen from him, and he claims [*entierce*][115] it as having been stolen, he must place four deniers on the object[116] [*chose*], as we said above,[117] by the custom of the Orléans district, and must say this to the judge: "Sir, this thing has been stolen from me, and I am ready to swear orally, and with my hand on the saints, that I never did anything to lose possession of it"; and [if] the person in

---

112. This refers to *Etablissements* 2:8.

113. *Dig*. 9.2.51 (Watson 1:292). The Latin *circa medium* warns the reader that the relevent part of the law referred to is halfway through the text. The words that the writer of the *Etablissements* appears to be referring to here are in fact more than three-quarters of the way through *Dig*. 9.2.51.2. The words refer to the punishment of offenders, rather than the value of the punishment as a deterrent: ". . . neque impunita maleficia esse oporteat . . . ," which Watson translates: "Misdeeds should not escape unpunished."

114. *Dig*. 1.1.1.1 (Watson 1:1).

115. The whole procedure of *entiercement* as described in 2:13 and 2:18 is compared by Viollet to a Germanic or Scandinavian custom, where a person entering a house to seek a stolen object placed a sum of money on the threshold as an eventual indemnity. Viollet 1:223–224.

116. This implies that the object itself is in court.

117. See *Etablissements* 2:13.

whose possession the thing is found says that he bought it from an honest and trustworthy man [*preudome*], according to his belief, and he dares to swear it on the saints, then he will be out of suspicion and out of danger; but he will lose his chattel, unless he can find his warrantor. [118]

And if he vouches a warrantor, he gets a court date on which to produce him, according to the terms of the charter,[119] on an appropriate day.[120] And if the warrantor testifies that he sold him the property, he [in his turn] will remain before the judge, unless he finds *his* warrantor; and the other party will be freed from suspicion.[121]

And if he can produce no warrantor, he must swear what I mentioned above, and also swear that if he can find his warrantor, or catch sight of him, he will arrest him if he can, or raise the cry, or inform the judge. And he will lose his chattel, once the plaintiff has proved it was his, unless the merchant had bought it at the Easter fair. And if he had bought it there, he would be reimbursed his money, according to the custom of the Orléans district: and he will be free from suspicion, if he is a man who customarily buys such things, and is of good repute, ⟨according to written law in the *Code*, at the beginning of the sixth book, at the title "On thieves and corrupted slaves," lege Incivilem rem,[122] and in the other law Civile,[123] where this matter is specially discussed. And he must not say he has bought it from an unknown person; but they[124] must do business wisely, so that they do not fall into [accusations of] crime from false suspicion [*mauvaise soupeçon*], as the above-

118. The warrantor is the person who can substantiate his claim to ownership (in this case, the person who sold the thing to him). See *Etablissements* 1:95.

119. This probably refers to a city charter, such as that of Orléans.

120. Appropriate because the warrantor might, because of his status, be entitled to fifteen days' notice. See Beaumanoir §1046.

121. On warrantors of warrantors, see *Etablissements* 1:95.

122. *Cod.* 6.2.2 (Krueger 238). The Latin heading is *De furtis et de servo currupto.*

123. *Cod.* 6.2.5 (Krueger 238).

124. This plural pronoun probably refers to those who customarily buy such things, that is, merchants.

mentioned law says at the end,[125] for suspicion should be alien to all honest men⟩.

19. How you should seek your lord and enter into his faith [*foi*], without delay, and give him your obedience [*obeïssance*] as liege.

When a man should hold his property in fief from a lord, he should seek out his lord within forty days. And if he does not do so within forty days, the lord can and should seize [*assener*] his fief, and whatever he found there would be his, without restitution;[126] and [the new vassal] should do his duty toward his lord with respect to the relief. And when someone wants to enter the faith of his lord, he must seek him out, as we have said above, and he should speak in this way: "Sir, I am petitioning you as my lord to place me in your faith and homage, respecting such-and-such a property situated in your fief, and which I have purchased"— and he should give the name of the seller. And the [seller] who is in the lord's faith must be present, to give seisin to the other party and to disseise himself into the lord's hand, if it is a question of a purchase. Or if it is a question of lateral or direct inheritance, he should name [his predecessor]. And with joined hands he should speak in this way: "Sir, I am becoming your man, and I promise you faith [*feauté*] and loyalty [*loiauté*] from this day forward, against all mortal men, paying the fees that the fief owes, and giving you the relief[127] due to a lord"—and he should state the nature of the transfer: in custodianship,[128] by lateral or direct descent, or by purchase. And the lord should immediately reply:

125. This refers to *Cod.* 6.2.2 (Krueger 238), which states: "Curate igitur cautius negotiari, ne non tantum in damnum huiusmodi, sed etiam in criminis suspicionem incidatis." 'Take care, therefore, to deal cautiously, that you not only not fall into any kind of harm, but also not fall into suspicion of a crime'.

126. That is, the lord seizing the fief can take the fruits without having to restore them later to the vassal when he does homage.

127. That is, the fee due from a person inheriting or purchasing a fief.

128. That is, as a custodian of a minor child who has inherited the property but who will not administer it until coming of age. See Beaumanoir, chapter 15.

"And I accept and take you as my man, and kiss you in the name of faith, reserving my rights and those of others, according to the practice in the Orléans district." And the lord can take the harvest for the year and the income,[129] unless he is making an accommodation. And it is the same for a relief for quitrent property [*relevoisons*]. But there is no quitrent relief [*relevoisons*][130] for custodianship, nor should anyone pay it for quitrent property, nor for dower property nor for property in coholdership.

And no one is entitled to a counsel day for a [transfer in] coholdership, nor an inspection day, according to the practice of the Orléans district, except for one situation;[131] for when a person is entering into ownership as a custodian, he must assure the parties[132] that when the children come of age, the person who has the custodianship will satisfy them[133] [*fera traire* for *taire*][134] at his own cost and expense, and will protect from loss those from

129. This is the normal relief: one year's yield of the property.

130. The word *relevoisons* may be used wrongly here. De Laurière states that *relevoisons* relief is paid to the lord for quitrent property. But in the present chapter, it is stated that there is no custodianship (bail) of quitrent property (*en vilenage n'a point de bail*). Thus it does not make sense to say that no one pays quitrent relief for custodianship property. Perhaps the writer should have written here the word *rachat*, used above for relief of a fief. Or perhaps the writer meant that when a custodian takes over a fief for a minor, or a widow takes her dower, or coholders inherit from an ancestor, the inheritance may include some quitrent property, on which they pay no relief, just as they pay no relief on fiefs that they take at the same time.

131. It is hard to see how what follows explains the "one case" mentioned here.

132. The parties are probably the overlords who will be paid the relief when the children come of age.

133. Is the antecedent of the word "them" the parties or the underage children? It is hard to decide on the basis of the grammar alone. If it is the parties, then the custodian is promising to pay them when the children come of age; if it is the children, the custodian may be promising to indemnify the parties against suits by the children after the latter come of age.

134. An explanation of this rather obscure and perhaps corrupt passage might be that underage children could not be sued, and the overlord had to wait for their relief until the age of majority. But the custodian also had the duty of handing over the fief free of encumbrances when the child came of age. Therefore, the custodian would promise to satisfy, or *faire taire* 'cause to be silent', the lord by paying the child's relief when he came of age. The manuscript tradition of this passage is somewhat murky, indicating that the scribes had trouble understanding it. In Beauvais, the problem was stated a different way, even if the result was the same: the heir paid no relief, but the custodian did. See Beaumanoir, chapter 15.

whom quitrent property is held.[135] Custodianship is in respect to a fief, but in villeinage [quitrent property] there is no custodianship, according to the practice in the Orléans district.

20. How you should ask for bail for your vassals, and on an inquest when the case is under the king's jurisdiction.

If some judge arrests in the king's domain [*obeïssance*] the king's man, whether he is a townsman or a commoner, or a man who claims to be the king's, the king's officials [*gent*] should send a message to the judge in this way: "We require you to hand over [*rendez*] or release on bail [*recreez*] such-and-such a man who claims to be the king's man, whom you have arrested or had arrested, or whom you are detaining wrongfully"—there would be no bail unless he said "wrongfully," according to the practice in the barony—"or appear before us on such-and-such a day." And he should be given an appropriate court date, according to what the king's judge sees should be done, the [importance of] the person he has arrested, the propriety [*honeste*] of the judge, and whether he holds directly from the king. And on the assigned day, he must appear or send a representative, or give an adequate response as to why he need not do it [release the accused]. And if he has a good reason—that the prisoner was arrested in the act, as we said above,[136] or some other reason that persuades the judge—he should be listened to. And if he does not give a good reason, or he will not give him up, or have him given up or released on bail, the king's judge must force him to do so by detaining his men or his property, without giving it back or allowing a reclamation, until they obtain custody of the [arrested person] who is, or who says he is, the king's man. ⟨And when they have him in their custody, the king will give a ruling for himself or another, as we have said above, for the king does not take jurisdiction away from another;

---

135. That is, he will pay the *relevoison* for quitrent property, as he will the relief for the fief, to the overlords.

136. This refers to *Etablissements* 2:2 and also 2:14.

rather, it is derived from him.)[137] And he must pay a fine for refusing the release on bail of the king's men, for the king has seisin
and possession [of jurisdiction]; for whoever refuses bail to [the
king's] people must reimburse them [*rant quite*] and pay a fine for
the refused bail, according to the custom of the area and the district. And the king's officers will hold an inquest as to his jurisdiction [*droit*] by good and honest people, and by good proofs, if he
wants to produce them. And if he is within his rights, the case will
be sent back down to him for trial on what is found in the court,
according to an honestly conducted inquest. ⟨And this is how you
proceed in all disputes where you have to go against the king;⟩
whether in a dispute, or concerning a lateral inheritance, or personal property, or real property or something dependent on such,
or jurisdiction, or lordship, ⟨for the king holds from no one but
God and himself; and you cannot appeal his judgments except to
God, as we said above, according to the king's law).[138]

And no judge of the king should sue concerning his jurisdiction [*droit*], nor his real property, nor his lordship, except in his
court; and the king cannot lose through his lower officers [*foible
sergent*], ⟨but you can lose to him, and win nothing from him; but
the *bailli* who is above the officers should oversee them and let
the king know about the judgments [*droiz*], according to written
law in the *Code*, in the title "On the king's advocates," in the law
Fisci advocatus.[139] And he must be careful not to take away the
king's rights, nor harm his interests, where it concerns real property or some other great matter, for no officer can cause the king's
loss, nor give away his rights [*droiture*], but [only] guard them
diligently according to the law in the *Digest*, "On the duties of
Caesar's attorney," in the first law;[140] nor should he do anything
against the law, according to written law in the *Code*, De precibus

137. See *Etablissements* 2:3 and 2:14.
138. *Etablissements* 1:83, 2:3, and 2.14.
139. *Cod.* 2.8.3 (Krueger 102). In some editions this citation is to 2.9.3, since
chapter 7 is divided into chapters 7 and 8 at 7.20 (= 8.1), and subsequent chapters
in Book 2 have a higher number.
140. *Dig.* 1.19.1 (Watson 1:37).

imperatori offerendis, l. Nec dampnosa fisco,⟩[141] etc. But he can work to his advantage and make an inquiry concerning his rights, according to the practice of the secular court and of the king's household, which is enforceable when it is a matter of ownership or jurisdiction or lordship.

21. On appealing against a man for murder or treachery [*traïson*]; on giving an immediate answer; and on making a reservation to proceed in the baron's court, without defaulting.

If one person appeals against another for treachery or murder or rape or one of the cases mentioned above,[142] where there is capital punishment [*poine de sanc*] or danger of losing life or limb, the accused must answer right away without delay and without a counsel day; for nobody is entitled to a counsel day for such offenses,[143] according to the practice of the Orléans district; but there is such an entitlement for all other offenses, according to the content of the charter.[144] And against the other's appeal he must make the appropriate defense according to the practice of the barony. And if the day passed without his making an answer [*s'an meïst en plait*], he could suffer great loss from the default. And if he was from a different jurisdiction, he should say what I have explained above.[145] And he must make a reservation ⟨which is called [in Canon Law] a *protestacion*. And that a reservation is valid is written in the *Decretals*, De hiis quae vi metusve causa fiunt, in the first chapter which begins Perlatum,[146] where is given

141. *Cod.* 1.19.3 (Krueger 75).
142. This refers to *Etablissements* 2:8.
143. See also *Etablissements* 2:38.
144. This probably refers to the charter of the city of Orléans.
145. This refers to *Etablissements* 2:14.
146. *Decr. Greg. IX* 1.40.1 (Richter 218–219). This decretal tells the story but also instructs the Bishop of Huesca and the Abbot of St. Mary's in Saragossa to hold an inquest as to whether the woman entered the convent of her own will or not. What the woman did was to propose a kind of condition or even make a threat that if she was forced to enter a convent, she would leave it at the first opportunity. This is not, strictly speaking, a reservation or a *protestacion*. Reservations were

the story of the noble lady who made a *protestacion* [by virtue of which] she would leave her convent, if she was forced into it by her husband, and this was valid). And he should speak in this way: "If my lord happened not to have the appropriate jurisdiction in that place, I offer to raise my defenses either here or in whatever court the ruling may say, as I should, and where I should." And he should give his lord's name, and [the lord] should have somebody in court, during the hearing [*droit faisant*], to ask to have his case sent down, as we have said above.[147] And thus [the appellee] could avoid the default, ⟨and the judge should keep both parties in equally harsh imprisonment,⟩[148] until the judge had taken jurisdiction of him, and his lord had asked to have him sent down; for if he falsely claimed to belong to some lord, or if his lord did not have the proper jurisdiction in his lands, that could do him great harm, unless he had made the reservation, as I said above. ⟨And lower vassals do not have that kind of jurisdiction; it is barons who have it, as we have said above, at the end of the chapter "On vassals' jurisdiction."⟩[149]

22. On the king's rights; on holding a man in prison for his admitted and proven debt; on abandoning your property, according to the custom of the Orléans district; and on authorizing a sale for your debt.

My lord the king has the general jurisdiction [*est en saisine et en possession*], with respect of debts to him that are admitted and proven, to arrest persons and seize both personal and real property, according to the practice of the secular court; and no man is imprisoned for debt except to the king, ⟨according to written law in the *Decretals*, De solutionibus, c. Odoardus,[150] cum suis concor-

---

appropriate during preliminary pleadings, and up to the *litis contestatio* or *plet entamé*; see *Etablissements* 2:15.

147. This refers to *Etablissements* 1:44, 2:14.
148. See *Etablissements* 1:108.
149. The reference is to *Etablissements* 1:34.
150. *Decr. Greg. IX* 3.23.3 (Richter 532).

dantiis; and in the *Code*, Si adversus fiscum, lege tertia).[151] But he must swear [*faire la loi du païs*] that he will pay as soon as he can, and swear on the saints that he has not the wherewithal to pay the whole or the part; and that as soon as he has more wealth, he will pay;[152] and he must swear he will sell his land within forty days, if he has any; and if he did not, the creditor [*deteres*] could sell it, and he would have the sale authorized according to the practice of the secular court.[153]

23. On the king's commands.

When my lord the king orders his *bailli* to give a hearing to some plaintiff, he gives the order in this form: "We order you that you give a good and speedy trial to the bearer of this writing, according to the custom of the area and the district," ⟨for the king's intention is not to abolish anyone's jurisdiction, nor to go against the custom of the area and the district. And [written] law is in agreement in the *Code*, De inofficioso testamento, l. Si quando talis, in principio;[154] for where the written law is not used, you should fall back on the custom of the place and the area; and custom is superior to written law [*costume passe droit*],[155] and is upheld by [written] law. And that this is true is written in the *Digest*, De legibus et senatus-consultis et longa consuetudine, l. De quibus causis,[156] where this matter is explained, and in the *Code*, Quae sit longa consuetudo, in the first law, and in the second and in the third[157] where this matter is discussed⟩. But the *bailli* can make an

151. *Cod.* 2.36.3 (Krueger 112). In some editions this citation is to 2.37.3, since chapter 7 is divided into chapters 7 and 8 at 7.20 (= 8.1), and subsequent chapters in Book 2 have a higher number. See Beaumanoir §696. Louis IX had promulgated an ordinance to that effect in 1256.

152. This part of the sentence translates more or less a part of the cited title of the *Decretals*, which might have been cited more appropriately here, as de Laurière points out.

153. See Beaumanoir §1593.

154. *Cod.* 3.28.35 (Krueger 135).

155. This principle, in Latin *Consuetudo superat legum*, expresses the spirit of customary law. It was proclaimed by Philip the Bold in 1274 and 1277.

156. *Dig.* 1.3.32 (Watson 1:13).

157. *Cod.* 8.52.1–3 (Krueger 362). In some editions this citation is to 8.53.1–3,

inquiry, in order to learn the king's rights, and give back owner-ship according to the king's special order,[158] when he is certain through good and valid proofs that somebody [else] has the right to the property; ⟨for the king gives rulings to himself and others, as we have said above,[159] and according to the practice of the bar-ony⟩.

24. On fines in the court of high justice for spilling blood or causing bruises.

If someone makes a complaint about another that he has caused him loss of blood or a bruise that is visible and shown to the judge,[160] the party shown to be in the wrong and to have given the blow, where he is proved guilty by witnesses, must pay sixty sous to the judge, and fifteen sous to the plaintiff if he wants to demand them, and he must pay for the plaintiff's lost days of work and his damages and must have [the plaintiff's] wound healed.[161] But [the judge] must look at where the blood came from, and if there is a serious wound [*plaie mortiex*],[162] he must pay the fine mentioned above, according to the practice of the Orléans district; for townsmen and commoners pay no more than sixty sous as a fine, whatever offense they have committed, except for larceny, or rape, or murder, or treachery [*traïson*]; or unless there is some loss of limb, such as foot or hand, nose or ear, or eye, according to the provisions of the charter, as it is said above.

---

since chapter 10 is divided into chapters 10 and 11 at 10.14 (= 11.1), and subsequent chapters in Book 8 have a higher number. The Latin headings are *Praeses provinciae*, *Consuetudinis*, and *Leges quoque*.

158. The words "and give back ownership according to the king's special order" do not appear in any of the manuscripts except *N*.

159. This refers to *Etablissements* 2:3.

160. See also *Etablissements* 2:12, 35.

161. See Beaumanoir §841.

162. In spite of the mord *mortiex*, these wounds are not "mortal," or the charge would have been homicide and the wounded person would not be bringing it. I have therefore opted to translate "serious." See also *Etablissements* 2:12.

25. On fines for words where no blows are struck.[163]

If someone says to another insulting [*vilainnes*] words, with no blows and no blood, the plaintiff receives five sous, if he proves it was done to him, and five sous [are paid] to the judge.[164] But a woman pays only a half fine of three sous.

26. On gifts by man and wife.

What a father and mother do for their children during the marriage is firm [*estable*]. And if [a father] marries off his son (or his daughter), he gets free and clear what [his] father and mother give him, without bringing it back,[165] ⟨unless he participates in a direct inheritance⟩. And the father or mother may not, after the death of the spouse, give more to one of their children than the other, except by the consent of the children, and have it be enforceable according to the practice of the Orléans district.

And the first gets the real property and the later ones get the personal property, according to the general custom.[166]

---

163. See also *Etablissements* 1:154.

164. For fines for insults, see Beaumanoir §844. For the situation in the Midi, see Jean-Marie Carbasse, "Consulats méridionaux et justice criminelle au moyen âge" (Diss., Montpellier, Faculté de Droit et des Sciences Economiques, 1974), pp. 254–261. Carbasse notes that the fines are very small, that there are always civil damages in addition to the fine, and that women (for example, at Castelnau and Labessières, p. 258) are fined half as much as men for insults.

165. The "bringing back" refers to what might happen after the death of a parent: a child who had already received a portion of the patrimony could elect to keep that portion and renounce any share in the inheritance on the parent's death, or to "bring it back" into the parent's estate, which would then be divided among the children. The customs were different in different areas: evidently in Orléans the remaining brothers and sisters could not force the married sibling to bring back his or her property and share it with the others. See Introduction, p. xxxiii; *Etablissements* 1:136; Beaumanoir §§479, 482, 1972.

166. This last paragraph appears only in manuscript N. It contradicts the usual rule; see *Etablissements* 1:10.

27. On being in default and resisting an officer.

If someone is summoned by the provost, and he does not appear on the assigned day, the provost gets five sous for the default; and if the man wants to swear that he did not know about the summons, and did not hear it, he can be discharged [from the fine]. And the same thing with a summons by ban [*la bannie*]. And if he resists the confiscation of his property [*esceut son gaje*] by the officer, he pays sixty sous for his resistance,[167] if it is proved. And if he wants to swear and claim that he did not resist, he will be discharged against the officer's testimony, according to the practice of the Orléans district. But if it is proved by witnesses, he must pay the fine.

28. On being a judge in your own suit.

If someone makes a complaint in the king's court, concerning his lord and a debt his lord owes him, or a promise or a contract he had made, the lord will not have the case sent down to his own court; ⟨for no one should be a judge nor give a judgment in his own suit, according to written law in the *Code*, Ne quis in sua causa judicet, lege unica,[168] in rubro et in nigro, where this matter is discussed⟩. But if he made a complaint against his lord concerning a fief, or real property, or some other thing that should be held from his lord, the lord would have the case sent down and would have jurisdiction [*obeïssance*] during the trial [*droit faisant*]; ⟨for in a judgment three things are necessary: a judge, a plaintiff, and a defendant; and, in such a case, the lord would be a party; and for this reason the court would not be disinterested [*igauz*], for a judgment should not limp [*clochier*], according to the [written]

---

167. The term *rescourre* (here *escourre*) suggests a kind of rescue, or taking back by force that which has been seized. If the seizure was by an authorized agent, then to resist the seizure constituted an offense. The word is also used in the reflexive to mean "resist arrest." See Beaumanoir §876.

168. *Cod.* 3.5.unica (Krueger 125).

law in the *Decretals*, in the title "On exceptions," in the chapter Cum inter priorem[169] and the practice of the secular court).

29. On giving a guaranteed peace [*asseürement*].

If someone gives to a plaintiff a guaranteed peace in the king's court, and, after the guarantee, breaks the truce or the guaranteed peace, and he is summoned to appear before the king's officers, he must answer in their court, even though he may be a resident in another lordship, and even though his lord has the high justice in his lands. And he must stay there for the trial because the guaranteed peace was made in the king's court, and by his officers, according to the practice of the barony, even though he was not arrested in the commission of the breach; for the king is the sovereign; and therefore his court should be over all [*souveraine*].

30. On seizing your fief for default of a vassal, and on disavowing your lord.[170]

If some gentleman seizes his fief for default of a vassal, or for nonpayment of the relief or the service horse, or for some other thing, acting within his rights, and the man who is holding the land admits holding it from him, the lord will give him back his property, or give a reclamation, and send him a message, and assign him an appropriate court date, within fifteen days or not, according to the practice in the Orléans district between vassals, and he will give him a trial and a judgment according to the custom of the district. And if he claims before a judge not to hold his land from him, and claims to hold from another, [the first lord] cannot and must not seize the fief; instead, the jurisdiction of the case goes to the lord from whom the man claims to hold; but if [the first lord] has a right to the fief, he can and should sue him.[171]

---

169. *Decr. Greg. IX* 2.25.5 (Richter 376). The Latin heading is *De exceptionibus*.
170. That is, claiming to hold your fief from someone else.
171. See Beaumanoir, chapter 45.

And if he can show that the man has made a false claim to hold the
land from someone [else], and that the land should be held from
him and that it was never held except from him and his ancestors,
⟨and that [the defendant] has made a new claim to hold it from
someone, for the king has forbidden such claims,⟩ he will lose the
land, if he is proved guilty ⟨of having made a false claim and had
it proved against him. And for this reason vassals and gentlemen
should be careful not to claim to hold from a lord other than their
rightful lord; for a loss such as forfeiting your land could come of
it, according to the practice of the barony; and it is a mortal sin to
disavow your rightful lord; for you lose your soul and your land.
And⟩ a ruling may be given for a wager of battle, ⟨if it is outside
the king's domain;⟩ for [the holder of] a fief can be pitted against
[the holder of] a subfief, ⟨according to the practice of the secular
court; and if it is in the king's domain [the matter is settled] by an
inquest, according to the king's law⟩.[172]

31. On bastards and strangers; on appealing against a man as
your serf; on forbidding persons to change the lord they
claim to hold from; and on being free.

If some alien [*aubain*] [173] or bastard dies without heirs or lineage, the king is his heir, or the lord in whose lands he dies, if he
dies in the castle itself [*ou cuer de son chastel*]. And no bastard or
alien can validly and enforceably make anyone except the king his
lord in his domain, or in somebody else's lordship or in his own
jurisdiction, according to the practice of the Orléans and Sologne
districts.[174] And the same is true of foreigners [*avolé*].

And if anyone claims to be the king's man, the king has him
under his protection [*en sa garde*] until the opposite is proved;[175]
⟨for you should believe that everyone is what he says he is, until

172. See *Etablissements* 1:3.
173. An *aubain* is a nonnaturalized foreigner.
174. The referent of the possessive adjectives in this sentence is not clear.
175. See *Etablissements* 2:2.

the opposite is proved, according to written law in the *Decretals*, De presumptionibus, in the last Decretal,[176] and De scrutinio, in the first Decretal,[177] and in the *Digest*, De re militari l. Non omnes, §A barbaris).[178] If somebody is claiming [another party] is a serf, he should make his claim in this way: "Sir, I am asking for Guillaume, for he is my man in body and head [*de cors et de chief*]; for my father died with him in his possession, as his serf, and under his jurisdiction, in suits, and inheritances, and with respect to personal property or personal crimes, and concerning real property, and I, since the death of my father, have had him in my jurisdiction as my serf; wherefore if he admits what I say, I request you to hand him over to me as my serf; and if he denies it, I offer to prove it, in any way I should according to the ruling of the court." Then the claim will be heard in court. The person asked for should ask for a counsel day and must be given it according to the practice of the barony; and on the day he is to answer he must put forward all his valid defenses; ⟨and then the judge should explain to the plaintiff the penalties according to the king's law; for if he proves what he claims, he will get him as his serf, and if he fails in his proof, his fine will be at the discretion of the court; and he must accept [the possibility of] this penalty before doing anything else;[179] and the defendant⟩ should speak in the following way: "Sir, I am the king's man, and I claim to be such, and I hold from him my personal property and my other property, wherefore I request that you give me back my property or permit me a reclamation of it, in this hearing [*droit faisant*] before you." It should be given to him, according to the practice of the barony.[180] And he can speak in the following way: "Sir, my mother was the king's free woman and

176. *Decr. Greg. IX* 2.23.16 (Richter 358–359). The Latin heading is *Dudum archidiacono*. This citation is to the last sentence of the title.

177. *Decr. Greg. IX* 1.12.c. unic (Richter 123–124). The Latin heading is *Ex parte tua*.

178. *Dig*. 49.16.5.6 (Watson 4:895).

179. See *Etablissements* 1:4.

180. A man did not have to plead while not in possession of what he claimed was his property. See *Etablissements* 2:7 and Beaumanoir §1413.

no one shares [the children of a serf] with the king [*nus ne part au roi*] [181] except [the abbeys of] Sainte Croix and Saint Aignien, according to the practice of the Orléans and Sologne districts, whose general [law] and custom I wish to prevail, according to which I should follow the status of my mother." ⟨And the law is in agreement: at it is written in the *Code*, De rei vindicatione l. Partum ancillae, [182] where this matter is discussed.⟩ "And since the death of my mother we have been in the king's jurisdiction for ten years, twenty years, thirty years, and more"—[he should state the number of years] if he is sure of making his proof, otherwise not—"in the sight and knowledge of [the people of] the area; for which reason we wish to continue to claim the king as our lord, if the ruling says so." ⟨The law and the practice of the barony is that a period of ten years, when a serf is held by some one other than his [true] master, or especially when he is free, legalizes the situation [*vaut*]; for freedom cannot be broken [*brisiée*], according to written law in the *Digest*, De regulis juris, l. Libertas, [183] where this matter is discussed word for word. And for this reason my lord the king generally upholds [*deffant*] claims to belong to new lords when they are admitted or honestly proved. And he sues [184] no one but bastards and strangers. And no bastard can swear fealty. And nothing that you do to a bastard can cause loss to the prince in respect to losing his jurisdiction, nor the rights he has over his person, according

181. Viollet explains that *nus ne part au roi* is a maxim that expresses a general legal truth. If a king's serf married the serf of another lord, the offspring would *all* belong to the king, for the king shares with no one. However, the author of the *Etablissements* notes that an exception exists for serfs belonging to the abbeys of Ste. Croix and St. Aignien. As explained later in the chapter, in these cases offspring *were* divided, with the deceased father's owner receiving the first pick.

182. *Cod.* 3.32.7 (Krueger 138).

183. *Dig.* 50.17.106. (Watson 4:963). Viollet gives this citation as 50.17.104. *Dig.* 50.17.104 reads: "Libertas inaestimabilis est," which Watson translates: "Liberty is a thing beyond price." The Latin word *inaestimabilis* would be better translated into Old French as "prisiee" rather than "brisiee" as Viollet has it. According to Viollet, all manuscripts except one (*N*, which reads *passee*) read *brisiee*. In addition, four manuscripts (*B*, *C*, *D*, and *T*) omit the *ne*, producing a contre-sens. Further down in this same paragraph, the word "prisiee" appears again, and one of the manuscripts also reads "brisiee" for this occurrence of the word.

184. That is, he maintains his right to retain lordship and jurisdiction over such persons.

to the practice of the Orléans district and the custom of Sologne.⟩
And if he can prove that he is the son of the king's free woman or
free man, he will remain in the king's jurisdiction, unless he is a
man or woman of Sainte Croix or Saint Aignien. And when partitions [of a serf's children] are made, the father's lord should get the
first child, according to the practice of Sologne. ⟨And if another
party sues him, he will remain the king's man, if he can prove a
ten-year tenure; for the law is in agreement in the *Decretals*, "On
the homage of a serf," in the chapter Dilectus filius,[185] in the sight
and knowledge of the other party, and he remained peacefully in
the king's jurisdiction; for no one shares [the children of a serf]
with the king except Sainte Croix and Saint Aigniens, as we said
above.⟩ And if it happened that the person appealed against as a
serf was a minor, he would give no answer until he was of age,
and he would keep seisin and possession of the property of which
his father was seised and vested when he passed from life to death.
And he must give good sureties to keep the property in good condition and to go back to the lord as his serf, if he proved he was
his serf [*hom de cors*], when he came of age, if his lord wanted to
appeal against him, ⟨according to written law in the *Code*, De Car-
boniano edicto, lege prima,[186] where this matter is discussed word
for word⟩. And if somebody is appealed against for being a serf
before the officers of Sologne, the king's men must not plead their
suit on servitude before [the officers]; for the latter cannot and
must not take cognizance of a suit in which real property may be
lost; ⟨and it is a case for great and benevolent leniency that can be
heard [*prisiée*] only in a noble court [*en franchise*], and which they
cannot take cognizance of; instead the *bailli* or the provost should
take cognizance. And it is written thus in the *Code*, in the title De
pedaneis judicibus, in the second law which begins Placet nobis,[187]
at the end, where this matter is discussed⟩. And this is the privilege of the king's men or those who claim to be the king's men in

185. *Decr. Greg. IX* 1.18.8 (Richter 143). The Latin heading is *De servis non or-
dinandis*, of which *De hommage de serf* is a very inexact translation.
186. *Cod.* 6.17.1 (Krueger 249).
187. *Cod.* 3.3.2 (Krueger 124).

Sologne, according to the practice in the baron's court: that they are not required to answer or to plead before them [in the officers' courts], according to the practice of the secular court.

And if some baron or some vassal who has the jurisdiction in his lands summons or causes to be summoned the king's man, the king's man is required neither to appear before them nor to go to their court date, unless he is a resident in their castle itself, or holds property from them. He is not in their jurisdiction for his personal acts, nor for his personal property, nor for his legal affairs [*choses*]. Nor have they power to arrest, nor jurisdiction or lordship over, the king's man, unless he is caught in the commission of a crime. ⟨And if he denies [being caught in commission], the king's officers have cognizance and jurisdiction, as we said above at the beginning of the *Usage d'Orlenois*, in the title "On arresting offenders in the commission of a crime,"⟩[188] where this matter is discussed, and according to the practice and custom of the secular court, in the baron's court.⟩

32. On asking to have a case sent down when it concerns those in your jurisdiction, in court [*droit faisant*]; on enforcing the sovereign's rulings [*fait*]; and on runaway serfs.

If some person complains about another in the king's court or before his officers concerning the ownership of real property or a fief or quitrent lands, and the parties have proceeded to an answer[189] without claiming to be in the jurisdiction of another person or court, and they are [in fact] in the jurisdiction of some baron or vassal, and this lord appears in the court and asks to have the case sent down, and it concerns real property that should be held from him, he will not lose his power to administer justice [*l'obeïssance*] nor his jurisdiction, when the king's judge is con-

188. *Etablissements* 2:2.
189. The giving of an answer to a complaint was a decisive step. It precluded the later raising of preliminary issues such as lack of jurisdiction or the recusing of judges. See *Etablissements* 2:14, and Beaumanoir §239.

vinced that he should have the case sent down;[190] and the case will be sent down in the position in which the defendant finds himself in the king's court, and according to the steps [*esplois*] taken in the king's court and the proceedings in the suit; and he will give them a trial according to the custom of the district, and according to the proceedings in word and deed in the higher court. And if the king's officers found some defendant in the baron's court, or in the court of some other lord who had jurisdiction in his lands, they could have the case removed to their court, if it was a matter of which the king should have jurisdiction, even though the parties had proceeded to a denial and defense; but the steps and proceedings in the suit carried out in the baron's court would not be taken into account in the king's court; instead, the defenses would be raised de novo; and they would be given a trial according to the custom of the area and the district; for it is not appropriate that the acts of a lower lord [*joutisable*] be taken into account in the sovereign's court. And this is the rule according to the practice of the barony, in the secular court.

And if the case is on personal property, or an inheritance, or something dependent on personal property, or a personal suit, and [the parties] have proceeded as far as an answer or denial, in the king's court, the lord would not have the case sent down; instead, they would remain there for their suit, unless they had claimed to be in the jurisdiction of some other lord before an answer was made; for a free man can in such a case make anyone he likes his judge, when [the person] knows he has jurisdiction in his lands; ⟨and a free man can abjure what is done in his name, according to written law in the *Code*, De pactis, l. Si quis in conscribendo,[191] where this matter is discussed⟩. And if he is a serf [*sers ne home de cors*] he can make no one his judge except his lord; ⟨for a serf is not a legal person and he may not be condemned, unless it is at

---

190. The jurisdiction of a lord over suits concerning land held from him is thus upheld; in other kinds of suits (for example, on personal property) there is no such right; see below in this chapter. In Beauvais, once an answer had been given in the count's court, no case of any sort was sent down; see Beaumanoir §§256, 308.

191. *Cod.* 2.3.29 (Krueger 94).

the will of his lord, according to the practice of the barony, and according to written law in the *Code*, "On judgments," in the third book, l. Servus in judicio,[192] where this matter is precisely discussed. And a serf, when he flees from his lord, commits a larceny of himself; and the flight of a serf can in no way harm his lord, according to written law in the *Code*, De servis fugitivis, in the first law,[193] where this matter is discussed, and according to the practice of the barony⟩.

No vassal or gentleman can free his serf in any way without the agreement of the baron or the overlord, according to the practice of the secular court.[194]

33. On the jurisdiction of a vassal[195] without recall from memory [*recort*].[196]

⟨No vassal's court includes a recall from memory [of prior proceedings]; but you can ask for the recall from memory of knights and townsmen who are at the trial, and require an adequate recall from the knights, not from the vassals [themselves]; but a person need not accept a recall from memory unless he wants, especially in the vassals' courts; for the [use of the recall] is reserved to the high justice courts; for no court uses recall, except the king's or the barons' courts, as we said above in the chapter

192. *Cod.* 3.1.6 (Krueger 120). The Latin heading is *De iuduciis*.

193. *Cod.* 6.1.1 (Krueger 237). The Latin heading is *Servum fugitivem*.

194. See also Beaumanoir §§1437, 1446.

195. In this chapter, and in general throughout the *Etablissements*, the word *vavaseur* has been translated "vassal." For this chapter it is important to distinguish a baron from a vassal. A "baron" is a vassal who holds directly (or nearly directly) from the king. He is a high nobleman, with jurisdiction over capital crimes (high justice). What is here called a "vassal" is a lower nobleman, who holds from a baron and has no jurisdiction over capital crimes, except larceny, but does have jurisdiction over other areas of the law (low justice).

196. In an oral culture such as that of thirteenth-century France, where written records were still rare, it was nevertheless necessary sometimes to remember things exactly. When persons were deemed competent to remember what they had seen (typically contracts, pleadings, judgments, payments, etc.), they could be called into court later to tell what they had seen and heard. This process is called *recort*, which I have systematically translated as "recall from memory." Notice that this word does *not* mean a "written record."

[*titre*] "On default after the inspection day."[197] And⟩ no vassal has [jurisdiction over] proceedings for murder, or rape, or larceny, or treachery [*traïson*] or treasure trove, or taking by force,[198] or forbidden weapons [*espée privée*],[199] or strangers, [neither] by common law [nor] by an act of procedure [*par esploit*];[200] for such jurisdiction belongs to the baron. And a vassal has only low justice, according to the practice in the secular courts. ⟨No vassal may release a man or woman thief, without the consent of his baron, as is stated above in the title "On releasing thieves," in the *Usage de Touraine*;[201] instead, the baron takes cognizance; nor can [a vassal] hold an inquest that belongs to so high a jurisdiction;⟩ and he cannot erect a pillory [*joutise*] or a gibbet [*fourches*] unless the case comes to him already decided.[202] And if by chance the gibbet falls down, he cannot put it back up, without the consent of the baron or the overlord; ⟨nor can he make a man leave his castellany, or banish anyone; and if he does so, he loses his jurisdiction; for the vassal has no jurisdiction over this, as is stated above, in the *Usage de Touraine*, in the title "On the jurisdiction of a vassal,"⟩[203] [and] in the *Usage d'Orlenois*, in the title "On appealing against a man for murder and treachery, and on making a reservation,"[204] at the end, according to the practice of the secular court⟩.

Generally no one holds as a baron, unless he holds part of a barony after a partition or a distribution [*fraraige*], or unless he holds it as a gift from the king, holding back nothing except superior jurisdiction [*resort*]. And a person who has a market, and a castellany, and a toll road, and guard duties at the lord's castle,

197. *Establissements* 2:11.
198. In Beaumanoir this is called simply *force*. See Beaumanoir §956.
199. Viollet speculates that *espée privée* means the use of forbidden weapons.
200. The meaning of *par esploit* is obscure here. Perhaps it means that a vassal cannot obtain jurisdiction over these crimes just by letting the suit commence in his court. A higher court *could* sometimes get jurisdiction by allowing a case to proceed without the knowledge of the lower lord, who could have requested to have the case sent down. See Beaumanoir §§308, 309.
201. *Establissements* 1:43.
202. *Establissements* 1:42.
203. *Establissements* 1:34.
204. *Establissements* 2:21.

holds as a baron, correctly speaking. And their court includes a recall from memory of cases judged, and of suits brought to closure,
and various other things, according to the practice of the secular
court. And [such men] must be adequately summoned as barons,
generally by trustworthy [*certain*] officers, because of their barony; otherwise, they would not be required to answer, unless they
wanted to do so, according to the practice of the Orléans region.

34. On a sentence given in mercy, and on executing a
judgment.

If someone is appealed against as a serf, as is explained
above,[205] or for murder,[206] or for some other offense for which
the punishment is loss of life or limb, and proofs are advanced
against him, and the judge is of the opinion that the facts are adequately proved, and the defendant has raised in court the defense
that he committed the act in self-defense, and this contention is
adequately proved,[207] and the proofs on one side and the other are
perfectly equal; or if the person accused of being a serf has proved
himself to be in a condition of freedom, or some other presump-
tions that should be favorable to him, as was said above,[208] and
the proofs are perfectly equal on the one side and the other, the
law says that the sentence and the judgment be given to the person who is accused and appealed against as a serf rather than to the
other party. And the same thing [applies] for the person accused
of murder, ⟨according to written law in the *Decretals*, in the title
De probationibus, in the decretal which begins: Ex litteris tuis,[209]
where it is written that if the proofs are perfectly equal on one side
and the other, the decision should be given for [the man's] free-

205. *Etablissements* 2:31.
206. *Etablissements* 2:12, 21.
207. By this, the author may mean no more than that two witnesses have
given identical testimony concerning the matter.
208. *Etablissements* 2:31.
209. *Decr. Greg. IX* 2.19.3 (Richter 307).

dom or to the party who is accused rather than to the accuser, for the law is readier to forgive than to condemn to death, as is written in the said decretal word for word; and the practice of the area is in agreement.[210] And this is how any honest judge should have judgment given; for the actions of vassals [*les filz des homes*][211] should be honestly [*loiaument*] judged, if those who are accused and those who are the accusers do not prove anything. And the judge hands over the inquest and the proofs to the jurors. And the law says in the *Decretals*, in the title De officio judicis delegati, in the good decretal Prudentiam, in the second response,[212] where this matter is precisely discussed, that a judgment should be executed which is confirmed by several sentences. And the tested custom of the area and the practice of the secular court are in agreement).

35. On appealing against a man for treachery [*traïson*] or a broken truce, and on stating your legal reasons [for having a hired champion].

And when someone appeals against some person for murder, or a broken truce, or larceny, or treachery, ⟨or the cases mentioned above in the title "On high justice"⟩[213] and in the title "On appealing against a man for murder and treachery,"⟩[214] he should state how the treachery came about, or if it is a case of a broken truce; and he should show blood, or a wound, or a cut, or a bruise; for treachery is not committed by words; but a visible sign [*fet aparissant*][215] must be shown to the judge. And according to the pleadings, a wager of battle may be ruled; and in cases of murder, actual

210. See also Beaumanoir §1205.
211. See also the chapter heading for *Etablissements* 2:16. Should the word *filz* 'sons' be read as *faiz* 'actions'? It has seemed so to me.
212. *Decr. Greg. IX* 1.29.21 (Richter 164–166). The citation is to a part of the decretal which immediately precedes the portion marked "§1."
213. *Etablissements* 2:8.
214. *Etablissements* 2:12, but see also 1:4, 5, 169 and 2:21.
215. For the *fet aparissant* see Beaumanoir §1674. In Beaumanoir, the term *fet aparent* refers to an act which would be justification for starting a private war, or a *casus belli*. In Gruchy, the *loy aparissant* is a criminal case for which the punishment could be death or dismemberment (Gruchy 162).

observation and certain knowledge need not be alleged.[216] And if someone accuses another person before a judge of treachery, he must speak in this way: "When I was on such-and-such a day in such-and-such a place without doing harm to anyone, and having denied no one any right, and without having any reason to be on my guard against anyone, Guillaume appeared before me as before a person who was in a truce with him, and under a guaranteed peace[217] made by such-and-such a judge on such-and-such a day; and he struck me, like a treacherous person, so that my skin broke and blood came out; wherefore, if he admits it, I require that he be punished appropriately according to his action; and he caused me to bleed and have a wound"—for blood is a witness, according to the practice of the secular court—and it was shown to a judge. "And if he denies it, I offer to prove it and affirm it [*l'averer*] on the battlefield, or as this court rules I should do so, as a man who has his legal excuse [for having a champion]." And if the legal excuse is visible, he should make the reservation. If he does not claim a visible impediment, the battle must be person to person, according to the practice of the secular court. ⟨And the other party must immediately respond to this accusation by a denial and the proper defenses, as we have said above, in the title "On appealing against a man for murder and treachery."⟩[218] And if it is in the king's domain, there must be an inquest; for by his law the king forbids wagers of battle in his domain.⟩[219]

36. On the jurisdiction of all judges, and on cases of high justice.

If a man commits a murder or a homicide or some other offense for which the penalty is loss of life and property and land,

---

216. The Old French text reads: "Et ne convient pas que on mete en murtre le voir et le savoir." One of the elements of murder was that it was done in secret. There were therefore no eyewitnesses nor anyone with certain knowledge. For "le voir et le savoir," see Beaumanoir §1234.

217. For guaranteed peace [*asseurement*] see *Etablissements* 1:31, 41 and 2:29.

218. *Etablissements* 2:12.

219. See *Etablissements* 1:4, 30, 122 and 2:12.

in some jurisdiction, and the lord [of the jurisdiction] has all the power to administer justice in his lands—both high and low justice—and the murderer has property in some other castellany or some other jurisdiction, the lord will, as a result of the murder or the homicide, get the personal and real property that are in his jurisdiction, even though [the murderer] is not domiciled in his district. And in general all lords who have the high justice in their lands will get the things that are in their jurisdictions, and in their lordships; ⟨for murderers and homicides cannot be extradited [*n'ont point de suite*],[220] according to the practice of the secular court and according to the law in the *Code*, "On where a crime can be prosecuted," in the first law,[221] and in the authentic designated [*seigniée*] Qua in provincia.[222] And the custom is in agreement. And it is in the discretion of the lords whether to hold the lands as their own domain or to ravage them, that is to say to cut [*estreper*] the vines, and demolish the houses, and ring-bark[223] the trees and plough the pastures, according to the practice of different areas. And this jurisdiction and practice belongs to gentlemen, according to the practice of the secular court⟩. And this is how you should punish murderers, and homicides, and highway robbers, and robbers of churches, and arsonists, and counterfeiters ⟨and various other offenders, as we have explained above in the *Usage d'Orlenois*, "On cases of high justice,"⟩[224] where this matter is discussed word for word. And who has high justice and who has low justice is explained in the *Old Digest*,[225] in the title "On the juris-

---

220. See also *Etablissements* 1:45, 171.

221. *Cod.* 3.15.1 (Krueger 128). The Latin headings are *Ubi de criminalibus agi oportet* and *Questiones*.

222. This Authentic Qua in provincia is *Novel* 69 c.1, and is referred to by *Cod.* 3.15.2 (Krueger 511).

223. Trees can be killed by cutting a ring of bark from all round the trunk. This means the lord does not have to take the trouble of cutting the tree down in order to destroy it. See *Etablissements* 1:28 and note.

224. *Etablissements* 2.8. See also *Etablissements* 1:27, 32.

225. The *Old Digest* was a name given to the first of three volumes into which the *Digest* was commonly divided. The other two volumes were the *Infortiatum* and the *New Digest*. The divisions came after *Dig.* 24.2 and at the end of title 38.

diction of all judges," in the law Imperium.[226] And the practice of
the area and the district is in agreement).

37. On executing judgment in cases where fault is admitted
and judged, and on abandoning one's possessions.

When someone admits in court that he owes a certain sum
of money to some person, and, as a result of this admission, the
debtor has given a writing by the provost or some other regular
[*ordinaire*] judge, and he defaults on the payment on the due date;
and [the creditor] appears as a plaintiff before the judge for the en-
forcement of his writing, by the making of a payment, the judge
should order [the debtor] to pay, ⟨and he should force him to do
so by seizing his property in order to make the payment. And it is
part of the duties of the provost and all judges to enforce payment,
according to written law in the *Code*, de executione rei judicatae,
in the second law,[227] at the end, and in the *Code* in another place,
De transactionibus, l. Si causa cognita,[228] in fine, and in the *Digest*, De re judicata, l. A divo Pio,⟩[229] unless he tries to allege payment or forgiveness [of the debt] or an extension of the due date.
And then, he must be heard by the judge; and he must be given
an appropriate court date, according to the practice of the secular
court, in order to prove his allegation. And if he fails in his proof,
the judge should distrain him by the seizure of his property, ⟨as is
said above⟩.

And if someone were in such a position that he had neither
personal property nor chattels with which he could pay the debt
that was admitted and judged, he would have to swear on the
saints that he had nothing with which to pay in full or in part,
and that he would pay as soon as he was in a better financial position. ⟨And he must abandon his property by an oath. And the
law is in agreement in the *Decretals*, De solutionibus, in the decre-

226. *Dig.* 2.1.3 (Watson 1:40).
227. *Cod.* 7.53.2 (Krueger 318).
228. *Cod.* 2.4.32 (Krueger 96).
229. *Dig.* 42.1.15 (Watson 4:537).

tal Odoardus clericus;[230] and as we have explained above, in the *Usage d'Orlenois*, in the title "On the king's rights,")[231] where this matter is discussed word for word.)[232]

38. On a mounted expedition under arms made on another's property; and on disavowing your lord.

When someone makes a complaint in court against some person who has come into his jurisdiction [*a son droit*] or onto his fief, or into his lordship, by force and wrongfully, in a place where he held nothing from [the plaintiff] in fief or in domain, and in a place where he had no rights of seizure [*prise*] or sovereignty, or to punish offenders, or jurisdiction {he should speak in this way: "I am complaining about G[uillaume] who by force and wrongfully, and by force of arms, entered my fief and lordship,}[233] which fief and lordship I hold from the king, person to person, along with my other fiefs, for which I am in the king's faith and homage, and I am his liegeman, and he is taking away or causing to be taken away my personal property"—and he should name it—"wherefore I request that the place should be reseised completely [to me] and my damages made good, up to the value of one hundred pounds"—and in his complaint he should name the place, and the date of the armed incursion. "And if [the other party] admits that he came as I have described, I request you as my sovereign to make my losses good [*amander*]. And if he denies it, I offer to demonstrate it ⟨by inquest or by witnesses,⟩ as the court shall rule I should, ⟨according to the king's law").[234] And once the complaint has been heard in court, the defendant must immediately make the denial or defense that he should against the complaint; for in cases of force, or armed excursions, or personal crimes, no one gets a counsel day,

230. *Decr. Greg. IX* 3.23.3 (Richter 532).
231. *Etablissements* 2:22.
232. Note that in this chapter there is no mention of forcing a debtor to sell his real property in order to repay a debt. For a different law, see Beaumanoir §1593.
233. Viollet supplies the words between curly brackets by conjecture. These words, although plausible in this context, are not found in any of the manuscripts.
234. *Etablissements* 1:3, 6. That is, without a wager of battle.

⟨according to the king's laws which are written above, at the beginning,⟩[235] unless a gift or endowment [*franchise*] of the king or the tested custom of the district gives it to him. And if he came wrongly, as I said, into the place whose overlord is the king, he must pay the fine according to the custom of the area and the district. And the fine is sixty pounds if he is a baron or a knight or a gentleman. But no one protects [*garantist*] [those who come with him],[236] according to the practice of the Orléans region, unless he is a baron or a knight or holds as a baron.[237]

⟨And if he wrongfully claims not to hold the fief from his liege lord, and he is found guilty, he loses his fief, as we said above in the *Usage d'Orlenois* in the title "On seizing your fief for default of a vassal, and on disavowing your lord,"[238] where this matter is discussed word for word. And practice and the general, tested, and ancient custom, and the common law, are in agreement; for by his laws our lord the king forbids arms and excursions, and claiming to hold your land from a new lord, and [private] wars.[239]

Here end the laws of the good king of France.⟩

235. Viollet notes that the law referred to here is not to be identified in the *Etablissements*. He speculates that an ordinance may have been appended at the end of the manuscript, since one of the manuscripts reads "written below."

236. When the leader of the *chevauchee* paid a fine, it indemnified (or protected) all those who went with him. See Beaumanoir § 880.

237. For the definition of a baron, see *Etablissements* 2:33.

238. *Etablissements* 2:30. See also Beaumanoir, chapter 45.

239. Both Louis IX and Phillip III may have issued ordinances against the bearing of arms, private wars, and disavowals. It is unclear which might be meant here. See Viollet 4:322–323.

Bibliography

EDITIONS OF THE *ETABLISSEMENTS DE SAINT LOUIS*

Etablissements de Saint Louis, ed. Charles Du Cange. In his edition of Join-ville, Jean, sire de, *Histoire de S. Louis par Jean, Sire de Joinville*. Paris: Sébastien Mabre-Cramoisy, 1668. Cited as Du Cange.

Les Etablissements de Saint Louis, ed. Paul Viollet. 4 vols. Société de l'Histoire de France. Paris: Renouard, 1881–86. Text cited as *Etab-lissements*; notes by Viollet cited as Viollet.

Les Etablissements de saint Louis, roi de France, suivant le texte original, et rendus dans le langage actuel, avec des notes, ed. Abbé de Saint-Martin. Paris: Nyon l'aîné, 1786. Cited as Saint-Martin.

Les Etablissements de saint Louis, in *Ordonnances des rois de France de la troi-sième race*, ed. Eusèbe de Laurière, et al. 21 vols. Paris: Imprimerie Royale, 1723–1849. 1:1–291. Volume 1 is cited as de Laurière.

FRENCH CUSTOMAL COMPILATIONS (CUSTOMARIES)

Beaumanoir, Philippe de. *Coutumes de Beauvaisis*, ed. Am[édée] Salmon. 2 vols. 1899–1900. Paris: Picard, 1970. Cited as Beaumanoir.

Coutumes de Lorris, ed. Ad. Tardif. Recueil de textes pour servir à l'en-seignement de l'histoire du droit. Paris: Picard, 1885. Cited as *Cou-tumes de Lorris*.

Coutumiers de Normandie: Textes critiques publiés avec notes et éclaircisse-ments, ed. Ernest-Joseph Tardif. 2 vols. [Tome I.] Premiere partie: *Le très ancien coutumier de Normandie: Texte Latin*. Rouen: Cagniard, 1881. Deuxième partie: *Le très ancien coutumier de Normandie: Textes français et normand*. Rouen: Lestringant; Paris: Picard, 1903. Tome II. *La Summa de legibus Normannie in curia laicali*. Rouen: Lestrin-gant; Paris: Picard, 1896.

d'Ableiges, Jacques. *Le grand coutumier de France*, ed. Ed. Laboulaye and R. Dareste. Paris: Durand and Pedone-Lauriel, libraires, 1868.

L'ancien coutumier de Champagne (XIIIe siècle), ed. Paulette Portejoie. Poi-tiers: Oudin, 1956.

L'ancienne coutume de Normandie, ed. William Laurence de Gruchy. St. Helier, Jersey, British Channel Islands: Charles le Feuvre, 1881. Cited as Gruchy.

La très ancienne coutume de Bretagne, ed. Marcel Planiol. Bibliothèque Bretonne Armoricaine, 2. Rennes: Plihon et Hervé, 1896.

Le conseil de Pierre de Fontaines, ou traité de l'ancienne jurisprudence française, ed. M. A. J. Marnier. Paris: Durand, libraire and Joubert, libraire, 1846. Cited as Fontaines.

Li livre Roisin, coutumier lillois de la fin du XIIIe siècle, ed. Raymond Monier. Paris: Domat-Montchrestien; Lille: Raoust, 1932.

Li livres de Jostice et de Plet, ed. Rapetti, [Pierre-Nicolas], glossary by P. Chabaille. Collection de documents inédits sur l'histoire de France publié par les soins du Ministre de l'Instruction publique. Première série, Histoire politique, 81. Paris: Firmin Didot, 1850.

OTHER WORKS

Akehurst, F. R. P. "Murder by Stealth: *Traïson* in Old French Literature." In *Studies in Honor of Hans-Erich Keller: Medieval French and Occitan Literature and Romance Linguistics*, ed. Rupert T. Pickens. Kalamazoo: Western Michigan University, 1993. Pp. 459–473.

Baldwin, John W. "The Intellectual Preparation for the Canon of 1215 Against Ordeals." *Speculum* 36 (1961): 613–636.

Bongert, Yvonne. *Recherches sur les cours laïques du Xe au XIIIe siècle*. Paris: Picard, 1949.

Bracton, Henry de. *De legibus et consuetudinibus Angliae*, ed. George E. Woodbine. 4 vols. Yale Historical Publications, Manuscripts and Edited Texts 3. New Haven, CT: Yale University Press; London: Milford for Oxford University Press, 1915–42. English version: *On the Laws and Customs of England*, translated, with revisions and notes, by Samuel E. Thorne. 4 vols. Cambridge, MA: Belknap Press, 1968–77.

Buisson, Ludwig. *König Ludwig IX., der Heilige, und das Recht. Studie zur Gestaltung der Lebensordnung Frankreichs im hohen Mittelalter*. Freiburg: Verlag Herder, 1954.

Carbasse, Jean-Marie. *Bibliographie des coutumes méridionales (Catalogue des textes édités)*. Recueil de Mémoires et Travaux, publié par la Société d'Histoire du Droit et des Institutions des Anciens Pays de Droit Ecrit, 10. Montpellier, France: Faculté de Droit et des Sciences Economiques, 1979. Pp. 1–89.

———. "Consulats méridionaux et justice criminelle au moyen âge." Diss., Montpellier: Faculté de Droit, 1974.

Gaudemet, Jean. "L'influence des droits savants (romain et canonique) sur les textes de droit coutumier en occident avant le XVIe siècle." *Actes del III Congresso internacional de derecho canónico, Pamplona 1976: La norma en el derecho canónico, 1.* Pamplona, 1979. Pp. 165–194.

Les Olim ou registre des arrêts rendus par la cour du roi, sous les règnes de Saint Louis, de Philippe le Hardi, de Philippe le Bel, de Louis le Hutin et de Philippe le Long, ed. le comte Beugnot. 4 vols. Paris: Imprimerie Royale, 1839–44. Cited as *Olim.*

Marie de France. *Lanval,* ed. Jean Rychner. Textes Littéraires Français. Geneva: Droz, 1958.

Montesquieu, Charles-Louis de Secondat, baron de. *Oeuvres complètes.* 2 vols. Bibliothèque de la Pléïade. Paris: Gallimard, 1951.

Ragueau, François, and Eusèbe-Jacques de Laurière, eds. *Glossaire du droit françois.* New ed. Niort: Favre, 1882.

Ranulf de Glanvil(le) (supposed author). *The Treatise on the Laws and Customs of the Realm of England Commonly Called Glanvill,* ed. and trans. G. D. G. Hall. Medieval Texts. London: Nelson, 1965. Cited as Glanvill.

Sutherland, D. W. *The Assize of Novel Diseisin.* Oxford: Oxford University Press, 1973.

Tanon, L. *L'ordre du procès civil au XIVe siècle au Châtelet de Paris.* Paris: Larose et Forcel, 1886.

Tardif, Adolphe. *La procédure civile et criminelle au XIIIe et XIVe siècles ou procédure de transition.* Paris: Picard, 1885.

Teulet, Alexandre, Joseph de Laborde, Elie Berger, and H. F. Laborde, eds. *Layettes du trésor des Chartes.* 5 vols. Paris: Plon, 1863–1909.

List of Topics

This list by no means exhausts the topics treated in the *Etablissements*. Numbers following each entry refer to the book and chapter numbers where the topics are to be found.

Advocate — **Book 1**: 69, 71, 96; **Book 2**: 15, 16, 20.

Attorney — **Book 1**: 106; **Book 2**: 8, 9, 20.

Banishment — **Book 1**: 28, 34; **Book 2**: 17, 33.

Bastards — **Book 1**: 101–103; **Book 2**: 31.

Champions — **Book 1**: 30, 95, 122, 174, 175; **Book 2**: 11, 35.

Church-state problems — **Book 1**: 93, 127, 129; **Book 2**: none.

Civil procedure — **Book 1**: 1, 28, 29, 31, 44, 45, 47, 49, 53, 59, 60, 62, 69, 70–72, 74, 76, 77, 84, 85, 87, 88, 90–92, 95, 96, 107–110, 123–125, 126, 135, 142, 155, 174, 175; **Book 2**: 2–25, 27–38.

Coholdership — **Book 1**: 10, 24, 25, 46–48, 79–82, 119, 120, 130, 147; **Book 2**: 19.

Commoners — **Book 1**: 25, 65, 69, 71, 85, 87, 96–100, 107, 111, 114, 122, 136, 137–139, 141, 142, 144–148, 156–159, 169, 173; **Book 2**: 20, 24.

Contract — **Book 1**: 128; **Book 2**: 28.

Counsel day — **Book 1**: none; **Book 2**: 11, 19, 21, 31, 38.

Crime — **Book 1**: 5, 27–29, 31–33, 35–37, 39, 40, 42, 44, 45, 54, 55, 62, 87–91, 108, 148, 153, 156, 157, 171, 174; **Book 2**: 2, 8, 12–14, 18, 21, 24, 31, 34, 36, 38.

Custodianship — **Book 1**: 19, 55, 56, 68, 78, 82, 121, 141; **Book 2**: 19.

Debt — **Book 1**: 10, 17, 73, 100, 116, 122, 126, 127, 137, 138; **Book 2**: 22, 28, 37.

Default — **Book 1**: 70–75, 96, 104, 105, 123, 124; **Book 2**: 9, 11, 21, 27, 33, 37.

Default of judgment — **Book 1**: 8, 44, 56, 61, 75; **Book 2**: 4, 15, 16.

Disavowal — **Book 1**: none; **Book 2**: 21, 30, 38.

Distribution of real property — **Book 1**: 10–12, 15, 139, 144; **Book 2**: 26, 33.

Dower | Book 1: 13, 15, 16, 18, 20–22, 101, 117, 137, 173; Book 2: 19.

False judgment | Book 1: 83, 86, 142; Book 2: 15, 16.

Feudal law (see also Disavowal) | Book 1: 82, 92; Book 2: 19, 31.

Fines | Book 1: 6, 7, 9, 59, 65, 107, 108, 113, 122, 125, 127, 138, 142, 149, 152, 154, 155, 157–159, 167, 169, 170; Book 2: 16, 20, 24, 25, 27, 31, 38.

Fraud | Book 1: 166; Book 2: none.

Gifts | Book 1: 10, 11, 13, 20, 26, 68, 117–120, 129, 136, 173; Book 2: 16, 26, 33, 38.

Guaranteed peace | Book 1: 31, 41; Book 2: 29, 35.

High justice | Book 1: 5, 27, 33, 44, 94, 111, 115; Book 2: 8, 24, 29, 33, 35, 36.

Horse (see also Service horse) | Book 1: 32, 35, 58, 67, 87, 95; Book 2: 13.

Hotchpot | Book 1: 136; Book 2: none.

In flagrante | Book 1: 171; Book 2: 2, 13, 14, 17, 20, 29, 31.

Inheritance | Book 1: 23, 24, 78, 117, 147; Book 2: 19, 26, 31, 32.

Inquest | Book 1: none; Book 2: 12, 17, 20, 30, 33–35, 38.

Inspections | Book 1: 50, 60, 70, 71, 95, 96, 123; Book 2: 9, 11, 19, 33.

Insults | Book 1: 154; Book 2: 25.

Intimidation, fear | Book 1: 138, 173; Book 2: none.

Jews | Book 1: 132, 133; Book 2: none.

Judgment | Book 1: 1, 4, 5, 7, 8, 18, 19, 30, 43, 50, 60, 67, 69, 70–73, 83, 85, 96, 109, 110, 122, 123, 126, 127, 142, 152, 166; Book 2: 1, 3, 4, 7–11, 14–16, 20, 28, 30, 32, 34, 37.

Judicial battle | Book 1: 3, 4–9, 30, 42, 49, 86, 87, 95, 96, 115, 122, 174, 175; Book 2: 11, 12, 30, 35.

Jurisdiction | Book 1: 4, 5, 20, 26, 27, 31, 34, 38, 42–44, 47, 60, 62, 65, 89, 115, 127, 132, 137, 138, 171, 172; Book 2: 2–4, 11, 14–17, 20–23, 28, 30–33, 36, 38.

Knights | Book 1: 21, 65, 76, 77, 84, 87, 105, 127, 134; Book 2: 1, 4, 33, 38.

Lateral inheritance | Book 1: 22–24, 99, 140; Book 2: 19, 20.

Legal age | Book 1: 19, 78, 117, 128, 146; Book 2: 19, 31.

Legal excuse | Book 1: 28, 106, 123, 124; Book 2: 9, 35.

Lord's prerogative | Book 1: 93, 94, 97, 100, 101, 104, 105, 111, 113, 114, 131, 135, 156–158, 159, 164, 170; Book 2: none.

Low justice	**Book 1**: 33, 42, 45, 69, 94, 113, 115; **Book 2**: 33, 36.
Merchants	**Book 1**: 149, 150–152, 153; **Book 2**: 18.
Novel disseisin	**Book 1**: 69, 96; **Book 2**: none.
Oaths (swearing)	**Book 1**: 1, 24, 29–31, 42, 43, 50, 57, 58, 67, 69, 78, 79, 84, 94–96, 97, 111, 112, 119, 122, 124, 125, 149, 152, 154, 155, 166, 170, 172, 173; **Book 2**: 14, 18, 22, 27, 31, 37.
"Official summons"	**Book 1**: 70–73, 123; **Book 2**: none.
Otherwise acquired real property	**Book 1**: 10, 16, 136, 140, 147; **Book 2**: none.
Partnership	**Book 1**: 112; **Book 2**: None.
Penalties	**Book 1**: 125, 127; **Book 2**: 6, 8, 12, 31, 36.
Personal property	**Book 1**: 10, 17, 28, 42, 51, 54, 57, 58, 67, 85, 90–94, 97, 100, 101, 107, 116, 123, 132–134, 136, 137, 143, 144, 174; **Book 2**: 5, 8, 16, 18, 20, 22, 26, 27, 31, 32, 36–38.
Police powers	**Book 1**: 38, 92, 125; **Book 2**: none
Private war	**Book 1**: 52, 53; **Book 2**: 38.
Proof	**Book 1**: 1–6, 8, 14, 30, 31, 37, 41–43, 48, 49, 54–56, 61, 65, 71, 75, 78, 90, 91, 96, 107, 111, 112, 116, 119, 126, 142, 151, 152, 157, 163, 166, 173; **Book 2**: 2, 4, 9, 11–14, 16, 18, 20, 22–25, 27, 30, 31, 34, 35, 37.
Quitrent	**Book 1**: 69, 100, 104, 169; **Book 2**: 4, 11, 19, 32.
Ravaging property	**Book 1**: 28; **Book 2**: 36.
Real property/land	**Book 1**: 10, 19, 21, 22, 24, 25, 68, 75, 110, 117, 119, 121, 136, 145, 147, 160–170; **Book 2**: 3, 4, 7, 8, 16, 19, 20, 22, 23, 26, 28, 30–32, 36, 38.
Recall from memory	**Book 1**: 44, 70, 71, 124; **Book 2**: 11, 16, 33.
Reclamation/bail	**Book 1**: 108; **Book 2**: 5, 6, 8, 10, 14, 16, 20, 30, 31.
Redemption	**Book 1**: 10, 16, 102, 161–166, 168; **Book 2**: none.
Relief	**Book 1**: 24, 66, 81; **Book 2**: 19, 30.
Remainders	**Book 1**: 18, 19, 121, 140, 141, 173; **Book 2**: none.
Removal	**Book 1**: 44, 60, 61, 132, 133, 137; **Book 2**: 2, 14, 20, 21, 28, 32.
Res judicata	**Book 1**: 44, 73, 96; **Book 2**: 11, 13.
Resisting (arrest, seizure, etc.)	**Book 1**: 54, 122, 158; **Book 2**: 27.
Self-defense	**Book 1**: 30, 107; **Book 2**: 34.
Serfs	**Book 1**: 6, 8; **Book 2**: 31, 32, 34.

Service (feudal)	**Book 1**: 57, 59, 65–67, 69, 80, 81, 100, 105, 117, 120, 130; **Book 2**: none.
Service horse	**Book 1**: 48, 79–81, 135; **Book 2**: 30.
Sureties	**Book 1**: 29, 69, 70, 75, 105, 108, 122; **Book 2**: 5, 8, 14, 31.
Taxes	**Book 1**: 63, 64, 99, 160, 165, 167; **Book 2**: none.
Terrage	**Book 1**: 103, 170; **Book 2**: none.
Vouching a warrantor	**Book 1**: 95, 146, 55; **Book 2**: 18.
Wager of law	**Book 1**: 51, 71, 104, 105, 122, 149, 159, 167, 169; **Book 2**: none.
Wills	**Book 1**: 16, 93, 101; **Book 2**: 4.
Witnesses	**Book 1**: 1–4, 6, 8, 9, 119, 126, 155; **Book 2**: 11–14, 16, 24, 27, 35, 38.
Women	**Book 1**: 11, 12, 35, 67, 68, 78, 119, 153; **Book 2**: 8, 17, 25, 31, 33.
Writing	**Book 1**: 3, 6, 173; **Book 2**: 12, 14, 23, 37.

Index

The translator gratefully acknowledges the help of University of Michigan students John R. Durant, Sarah Grace Heller, Michelle Reichert, Jean-Luc Roche, and Ellen Wormwood in the compiling of this index.

Accomplices, 27
Accusation, accused, xxiv, xxv, xxvii, 13, 25, 40, 97, 99, 126, 136, 139, 141, 156–158
Accuser, 124
Adjournment, xxiv, 121
Administration of justice, xxvi, 29, 30
Admission, xxv, 7, 48, 119, 126, 127, 142, 150, 160
Advocate, xxiii, 46, 48, 63, 128, 129, 132, 140
Agency, agent, xxiii, xxviii, xxxi
Aid, feudal, 32
Alibi, xxv
Amendment, 132, 133
Anjou, province, 3, 15
Answer, xxv, 10, 13, 123, 127, 131, 139
Appeal, xxiii, xxvi–xxviii, 11, 13, 14, 24, 25, 35, 55, 56–58, 70, 82, 83, 93, 105, 108, 109, 117–119, 123–125, 128–130, 132, 133, 140, 141, 151, 155–157
Appellant, xxiii, 62, 109
Appellee, 14, 142
Arbitrators, 131
Archpriest, 107
Arms, bearing, 38, 39
Army, 41, 42
Arrest, 29, 31, 38, 40, 96, 106, 127, 139, 142, 152
Arson, xxx, 12, 119, 159

Assault, 69, 124
Attorney, xxiii, xxiv, 119–122, 140; decertification, 121
Authentic, 105

Bail, xxiv, xxx, xlii, 70, 118, 119, 122, 127, 139, 140
Bailli, xxviii, 13, 123, 133, 140, 143, 151
Bake oven, 74
Bakehouse keepers, 41
Baldwin, John W., xxxvii, n. 14
Ban, 146
Banish, banishment, 23, 135
Banlieue, 74
Bar, peremptory, 130
Baron, xxviii, 3, 12, 23, 25, 26, 29, 31–34, 36, 39, 40, 42, 51, 56–61, 64, 74, 75, 78, 79, 88, 100, 106, 113, 121, 141, 152–156, 162
Barony, 22, 115
Bastards, xxviii, 65
Battery, 69
Battle, 25, 29, 62, 148, 157, 158
Beaumanoir, Philippe de, xxii, xxvi, xxviii, xxix, xxxi, xxxv, xxxvi, xxxviii, xliii
Bees, xliii, 106, 107
Bequests, 65
Bishop, 59, 84, 107, 121
Brittany, province, xxii

Brother(s), 17, 21
Burning, as punishment, 26, 28, 59, 85
Buyer, xxxiii

Carbasse, Jean-Marie, xxxvi
Castellany, 20, 26, 29, 31, 36, 40–42,
60, 64, 74, 75, 87, 88, 93, 100, 105
Castle, 38, 42
Cavalcade, 37
Champagne, province, xxii
Champion, 25, 81, 108, 109, 124
Charitable gifts, 16
Charter, 136, 141, 144
Châtelet, xxii, xxvii, xxxviii, xxxix, xli,
xliv
Chesé, 17, 21
Church, xxviii, 23, 24, 26, 27, 58
Church door, 17, 20, 77
City dwellers, xxviii
Claim, 51, 135, 148–152, 158
Clerk, xxv, xxviii, 58
Code, 8–10, 23, 24, 27–29, 37, 46, 55–
57, 60, 63–65, 68, 80, 84, 85, 88, 105,
108, 117, 120–122, 125–133, 136, 140,
143, 146, 150, 151, 153, 154, 160
Coercion, 107
Coholdership, xxxiv, 16, 17, 21, 22, 32,
33, 53, 54, 78, 86, 87, 96, 138
Command, 25
Common law, 155, 162
Commoners, xxviii, xxx, xxxi, xxxiii,
xxxv, xxxvii, 21, 41, 42, 45, 48, 58,
64, 65, 69, 72, 89, 92–94, 99, 100,
107
Commonly known. See Notorious
Compiler, xxi, xxxviii, xxxix, xl, xlii,
xliv
Complaint, xxiv, xxv, 3, 7, 8, 10, 11, 13,
20, 31, 39, 40, 47, 50, 51, 80, 82, 87,
91, 98, 116, 122–124, 131, 144, 146,
161
Conduct, xxiii
Confession, 60
Confiscation, xxxi, 4
Consent, 145, 155
Conspirators, xxviii

Continuance, xxiv, 10, 11, 120–122
Contracts, xxiii, xxvii–xxix, 85, 108,
146
Corpus iuris canonici, xxviii, xl
Corpus iuris civile, xl
Costs, 45, 46, 62, 63, 73
Counsel, 48, 117
Counsel day, 123, 138, 141, 149
Counterfeit, xxx, 26, 159
Court, xxii, xxiv, xxvi, xxvii, xxxi, xliii,
10, 13, 44, 46, 50, 51, 57, 82, 83, 98,
99, 101, 103, 115, 117, 119, 123, 125–
127, 129–131, 140–142, 146, 147, 149,
151–154, 156, 160, 161; bailli's, 13;
baron's, 3, 29, 34, 80, 82, 83, 87, 88,
91, 106, 113, 115, 116, 121, 132; ecclesiastical, xxviii, 20, 85, 91; king's, 13,
20, 29, 34, 36, 37, 39, 40, 51, 55–57,
82, 91, 129, 130, 132, 133; provost's,
10; secular, 3, 4, 10, 11, 13, 24, 25,
44, 56, 62–64, 89, 97, 118, 119, 121–
123, 126, 128, 130–133, 141–143, 148,
152–154, 157–160; sovereign's, 82
Court date, 7–9, 32, 34, 39, 47, 48–50,
61, 68, 69, 71, 80, 82, 99, 123, 124,
126, 136, 139, 152
Cousins, 21
Coutume d'Orléans, 80
Coutume de Touraine-Anjou, xxvii,
xxxvii–xxxix, xli, xliii
Coutumes de Beauvaisis, xxii, xliii
Creditor, 143, 160
Crime, xxiii, xxvii, xxviii, xxx, xxxi, 4,
24, 40, 97, 106, 113, 115, 125–127, 136,
149, 152, 161; serious, xxix; capital,
xxxvi, xxxvii, 12
Criminal justice, xxii
Crusaders, xxviii, 58
Custodian, custodianship, xxii, xxv,
xxxv, 19, 37, 44, 52, 54, 55, 79, 93,
137–139
Custom, customary law, xxx, xxxvi–
xxxviii, 3, 8, 10, 11, 13–15, 37, 44, 88,
89, 91, 93, 101, 105, 113, 115, 118, 123,
128, 130, 133, 135, 136, 140, 142, 143,
145, 147, 150, 153, 159, 162

Customaries, xxviii, xxix, xxxii, xxxiv, xliii, xliv
Customary dues, 41

Damages, 19, 45, 46, 50, 72, 73, 81, 99, 144, 161
Daughter(s), 16, 17, 43
De Laurière, Eusèbe, xli
Deadlocked judgment, 71
Death, 107, 108, 116; penalty, xxix, xxx, xxxvii, 24, 109
Debtor, 49, 80, 91
Debts, xxxv, 16, 18, 50, 75, 84, 87
Decretals of Gregory IX, xl, 3, 12, 27, 46, 59, 68, 85, 108, 119, 121, 122, 128, 141, 142, 147, 149, 151, 156, 157, 160
Defamation, slander, 97, 98, 129, 131
Default, xxiii, 31, 40, 46–51, 62, 67, 82, 83, 122–124, 141, 142, 146, 147, 155
Default of judgment, xxvi, 14, 31, 51, 118, 129, 133
Defendant, xxiii, xxiv, xxv, xxvii, 3, 8–11, 13, 46, 51, 61, 109, 124, 146, 148, 153, 156, 161
Defense, xxiv, xxv, 8, 10, 11, 24, 37, 119, 129–131, 142, 149, 156
Deflowering, 37, 38
Delay, xxiii, xxiv, 51
Denial, xxv, 47, 80, 81, 98, 99, 115, 119, 127, 153, 158
Detention, 70
Digest, 8, 46, 66, 68, 91, 98, 108, 120–122, 126, 127, 131, 133, 135, 143, 150, 159, 160
Dilatory exception, xxiv, xxv
Direct inheritances, 21
Disavowing, xxix, 147, 148, 162
Dispute, private, xxiii
Disseise, 45, 46, 51
Distribution, xxxiv, 16, 17, 21, 22, 90, 92, 96
Divorce, xxviii
Dower, xxxiv, xxxv, 18–21, 65, 76, 91, 107
Drawing (form of punishment), 23
Drowning, 60

Du Cange, Charles, xli
Dues, 65, 67, 72
Dying unconfessed, 60

Emancipation, 76
England, 59
Etablissements de Saint Louis, xxi, xxii, xxiv, xxv, xxvi–xliv; editions of, xxii
Excommunication, 85
Execution of judgment, xxv, xxvi, xxxvi, 7
Expeditions, mounted, 41, 42
Expenses, 46, 62, 63, 73

Faith, xxix, 21, 44, 57, 96, 137, 150, 161
False judgment, xxvi, 55, 57, 93, 132
Father, 15–18
Feud, xxiv
Fief, xxviii, xxix, xxxii–xxxiv, 15, 16, 18, 21, 22, 32–37, 39, 42–44, 47, 49, 57, 65, 67, 75, 78, 79, 86, 87, 93, 96, 97, 100, 123, 137, 139, 146–148, 152, 161, 162
Fine, penalty, xxviii, xxxi, xxxv, 11–14, 29, 30, 35, 36, 39, 41, 42, 49, 50, 62, 64, 66, 69, 70, 73, 74, 82, 83, 85, 86, 91, 93, 96, 98–100, 105, 118, 119, 124, 140, 144, 146, 149, 158, 162
Fontaines, Pierre de, xxii
Foreigners, 59, 65
Forfeit, xxxi, xxxvi, xxxvii, 19, 23, 148
France, xxii, xxxvi, 3, 4, 7, 59, 124
Freedom, xxiii, xxviii, xxxii, 148, 150, 151, 156

Gentleman, nobleman, xxviii, xxx–xxxiii, xxxv, xxxvii, 3, 15, 16, 20, 21, 29, 32, 35–37, 41, 44, 47, 48, 51, 52, 55–58, 62, 64–66, 69, 77, 79, 88, 89, 107, 148, 154, 159
Gentlewoman, lady, 18, 19, 39, 42, 43, 52, 142
Gifts, xxxii, xxxiii, 15, 20, 77, 78, 86, 107, 131
Godfather, godmother, 52
Gold, 60

Good reputation, xxix
Grain, 72, 73
Grandparents, 20, 21
Guarantee, 147, 158, 162
Guaranteed peace, xxix, 25, 28, 29, 147
Guardian, guardianship, xxxv, 19, 20, 37

Hanging, 23, 25–27, 37, 58, 60, 84, 115
Hearing, 34, 36–38, 55, 71, 72, 129, 130, 132, 142, 143, 149
Heir, xxxiv, 17–19, 44, 65, 76–79, 84, 85, 92, 116, 117, 148
Heresy, heretics, xxviii, 59, 85
Holy church, 86
Homage, xxxii, xxxiv, 21, 22, 33, 48, 52–55, 75, 78, 79, 96, 133, 137, 151, 161
Homicide, xxx, 22, 28
Horse, 39. *See also* Service horse
Hotchpot, xxxiii, xxxiv, 90

Income (annual), 17, 72
Inheritance, xxxii, xxxiii, xxxv, xliii, 20, 52, 140, 145, 149
Inquest, xxxvii, 135, 140, 148, 158, 161
Inquiry, 34
Inspection day, 39, 40, 48, 122, 123
Institutes, 115, 126
Intimidation, 108

Jews, xxviii, 87, 88
Jostice et plet, Li livre de, xxx, xxxix–xli
Judge, xxiii–xxvi, xxx, xxxvii, xliii, 3, 4, 8, 12, 24, 25, 28, 39, 40, 45–49, 57–59, 61–63, 68–72, 76, 80–85, 91, 93, 97–99, 101–103, 106, 108, 113, 115, 116, 121, 122, 124–132, 135, 136, 139, 142, 144–146, 149, 152, 153, 156–158, 160; baron's, 39; ecclesiastical, 84, 85, 107; king's, 39, 42, 82, 87, 126
Judgment, xxiv–xxvi, xlii, xliii, 4, 9, 12, 13, 19, 20, 25, 30, 34, 38, 40, 44, 46–50, 55–57, 63, 71, 81, 82, 84, 97, 116, 117, 119, 120, 122, 123, 128–133, 140, 147, 154, 156, 157; affirmation of, 13; amendment of, 56; reversal of, 13

Judicial battle, judicial combat, wager of battle, xxii, xxv, xxvi, xxxi, xxxvii, xxxviii, 10–14, 25, 29, 33, 34, 52, 57, 58, 81, 95, 108, 123–125, 148, 158
Judicial order, 23
Jurisdiction, xxiv, xxvi, xxviii, xxx, xxxi, xliii, 3, 12, 22, 25, 26, 29, 30, 32, 39, 42, 58, 60, 75, 106, 113, 115, 116, 118, 126–128, 130, 139–143, 146, 148–155, 158–160; king's, 124
Jurors, jury, xxvi, xxxvii, 50, 56, 63, 130, 157
Justice, 26, 30, 31, 144, 152, 155, 158, 159; high, xxix–xxxi, 12, 61, 72, 75; low, xxxi, 61, 74, 75

Killing, 24, 27, 29
King, xxiv, xxvii, xxviii, xxx, xxxii, xxxviii, 7, 9, 13, 22, 36, 42, 56, 58–60, 64, 75, 76, 87, 88, 115, 116, 118, 124, 126, 128, 133, 139, 140, 142, 161, 162
King's domain, 126
King's law, 40, 124, 125, 133, 148, 149, 161
Kinship, 21, 33, 52, 55
Knight, knighthood, 3, 20, 42, 51, 56, 58, 67, 113, 114, 117

Lady. *See* Gentlewoman
Land, xxiii, xxvii, xxviii, xxxii, xxxiv, xxxv, xliii, 26, 31, 44, 47, 51, 52, 64, 65, 67–69, 71, 72, 75–77, 79, 84–87, 90, 92–95, 100–103, 105, 107, 108, 132, 147, 148, 152, 158
Larceny, 12, 29, 31, 58, 62, 105, 119, 125, 126, 144, 155
Lateral inheritances, xxxii, xxxiv, 20, 21, 92
Law: canon, xxviii, xxxix, xl, 141; procedural, xxiii, xxxvi; roman, xxxix, xl; substantive, xxiii, xxxvi, 63
Laymen, 58
Legal excuse, *essoigne*, xliii, 23, 68, 82, 83, 120, 122
Lèse-majesté, xxx
Life interest, 17
Lineage, 37, 65

Livestock, 26, 41

Loire river, xxii

Lord(s), xxiii, xxix–xxxi, xxxiv, 14, 15, 21, 22, 26, 29–31, 33, 34, 36, 37, 39, 40, 43–50, 52–54, 57, 60, 63, 65, 67, 72, 73, 78, 79, 87–89, 91, 93, 95, 96, 99, 100, 102, 103, 105, 106, 115–117, 120, 122, 124, 126–128, 133, 140–142, 146–148, 150, 151, 153, 154, 159, 160, 162; lord's will (discretion), 13, 14, 120

Loss, of life and limb, xxvi, 12, 26, 28, 118, 119, 124, 141, 144, 156; of property, xxvi

Louis IX, king of France. See Saint Louis

Lying, 27, 38

Maine, province, xxxix

Man's relief, 83

Manuscripts, xxxix, xl

Marketplace, 23, 31

Marriage, xxviii, xxxiv, 16–18, 20, 33, 43, 44, 76, 77, 85–86, 89, 90, 94, 97

Measures, standard, false, 29, 30, 37, 97

Memory, recall from. See Recall from memory

Merchant, xxviii, xxxi, 97

Mill, miller, 41, 64, 72–74

Millstone, 73

Minor children, xxiv, xxxv, 19, 85, 139

Money, 69

Montesquieu, Charles Louis de Secondat, baron de, xxi, xliv

Mother, 17, 18, 20

Murder, xxiii, xxx, xxxvii, 11, 22, 31, 58, 62, 70, 98, 105, 108, 109, 115, 117, 119, 124, 141, 144, 155–159

Murderer, 26, 27, 31, 40

Negligence, 19

New Digest, 11

Nobleman. See Gentleman

Normandy, province, xxii

Notorious (commonly known), 12

Novel disseisin, xxx, 63

Oath. See Swearing

Offense, xxiv, xxx, xxxv, xxxvi, 75, 109, 141, 144, 156, 159

Officers, xxiv, xxvii, xxviii, xxx, xxxvii, 38, 41, 82, 83, 99, 108, 117, 127, 139, 140, 146, 151

Official status, xxii

Ordeal, xxxvii

Ordinances, royal, xxxviii

Orléans district, xxii, 117, 135, 136, 138, 141, 142, 144–148, 150, 151, 156, 162

Ownership, xxiii, 123, 128, 138, 144

Panel of residents, xxvii

Paris, xxvii, xxxviii, 7

Partition, xxxiv, 15, 18, 20, 71, 72, 89, 91

Party, xxiii, xxv, xxvi, xxvii, 7, 8, 12, 39, 80, 81, 83–87, 98–100, 103, 107, 116, 121, 128–130, 132, 137, 138, 142, 144, 146, 151, 152, 156

Peace. See Guaranteed peace

Penalty. See Fine

Persons, law of, xxx, xxxi

Plaintiff, xxiii–xxv, xxvii, 7–9, 11, 13, 49, 51, 71, 85, 98, 99, 106, 109, 123, 124, 130, 136, 142, 144, 145–147, 161

Plead, pleadings, xxvi, 33, 130, 152

Pond, 19, 37, 64

Pope, 127

Possession, 100, 119, 126

Postponement, 11, 131

Practice, 11, 13, 113, 131, 132, 138, 139, 141, 143–152, 154–160, 162

Principal, 120, 121

Procedure, xxvii, xxxviii, xliii, 7, 10, 13, 14, 30

Proceeding, 9, 13, 115, 153, 154

Prologue, xli, 3–4

Proof, xxiii, xxvi, xxxvii, xxxviii, 8–15, 37, 46, 50, 107, 115, 118, 122–126, 132, 133, 136, 140, 142, 144–146, 148, 150, 151, 157, 160; irrational, xxxvii

Property, xxiii, xxxii, 4, 15, 20, 23, 28, 45, 55, 67, 69, 84, 100, 107, 118, 119, 136, 137–139, 142, 144, 146, 147, 149, 151, 152, 158–161; personal, xxiii,

Property (*continued*)
xxxv, xxxvi, xxxvii, 16, 18, 23, 29,
36–39, 44, 50, 56, 59–61, 64, 65, 69,
75, 80, 82, 88–91, 94, 95, 108, 120,
131, 140, 142, 145, 149, 152, 153, 159,
160, 161; purchased or otherwise
acquired, xxxii, 89, 92; real, xxxii–
xxxvi, xxxvii, 7, 10, 15, 16, 18, 51, 52,
76, 77, 87, 90, 93, 95, 96, 101–103,
116, 120, 131, 140, 142, 145, 146, 149,
151, 152, 159
Prosecute, xxx
Provost, xxviii, 7–10, 27, 42, 84, 99,
127, 128, 130, 133, 146, 151, 160
Punish, punishment, xxiii, xxiv, 4, 10,
11, 14, 29, 84, 109, 113, 125, 126, 133,
135, 141, 156, 158, 159
Purchased real property, 18
Pursuit, 31

Quitrent property (villeinage), xxviii,
xxxii, xxxv, 65, 66, 105, 116, 123, 138,
139, 152

Rape, rapist, xxx, xxxvii, 12, 22, 37,
108, 109, 119, 141, 144, 155
Rapetti, Pierre-Nicolas, xl
Ravaging of property, xxxvi, 23
Recall from memory, xxvii, 31, 82, 123,
154, 156
Reclamation, xlii, 118, 122, 133
Redemption, xxxiii, xxxiv, 15, 18,
100–103, 107
Redhanded, being caught, 106, 113,
115, 126, 127, 139, 152
Reimbursement, 36, 40, 46, 47, 57, 62,
63
Relief, 21, 43, 70
Remainder, remainderman, 19, 20, 79,
92, 93
Rental property, xxviii, 74
Res judicata, xxiv, 31, 50, 119, 123, 126
Restitution, 137
Robbery, xxxvi, 23, 58, 119
Ruling, 50, 55, 81, 117, 124, 128, 130,
131, 142, 144, 149, 150, 152, 157

Saint Louis, xxv, xxx, xxxviii, 3
Saint Martin, abbé de, xli
Sales tax, 41, 100, 103
Seal, 121
Security, 43, 80, 81
Seisin, 46, 48, 51, 52, 63, 99, 100, 116,
117, 119, 122, 123, 128, 137, 140, 151
Seize, seizure, 84, 91, 100, 137, 142, 147,
160–162
Self-defense, xxv, 69, 135
Seller, xxxiv
Sending down to a lower court, 30, 31,
39, 40, 127
Sentence, 29, 120, 156, 157
Serf, serfdom, xxiii, xxv, xxviii, xxxii,
13, 14, 148, 149–151, 154
Serious (capital) crimes, xxiv, 12, 29
Service, 42, 86, 87
Service horse, xxxvi, 33, 53, 54, 88, 89,
147
Settlement, 63, 120
Siblings, 16, 20
Sisters, 17
Sologne, province, 148
Sovereign, 28, 29, 31, 147, 161
Spurs, 67
Squire, 39
Status, xxiii, xxviii, xxxii, 148–150
Strangers, xxxi, xxxiii
Suicide, 60
Suit, lawsuit, xxix, xxxi, 7, 11, 13, 14,
20, 75, 81, 84, 98, 123, 127, 129, 131,
140, 146, 147, 149–151, 153, 156
Summon, xxiv, xxvii, xliii, 23, 24, 32,
37, 38, 41, 47–51, 55, 56, 72, 73, 82,
83, 86, 88, 101, 122, 126, 146, 147,
152, 156
Sureties, xxix, xxx, 24, 45–47, 51, 67,
70, 80, 81, 118, 120, 128
Suspicion, 24, 30
Swearing, oath, xxx, xxxvii, xxxviii, 8,
9, 11, 24, 25, 29, 30, 36, 38, 39, 48, 52,
53, 55, 61–64, 73, 77, 78, 81, 83, 97,
98, 103, 105–107, 128, 135, 136, 143,
146, 160

Tax, 64

Tax-free status, 41
Terrage lands, 66, 105
Testify, 47, 50, 82, 88, 89
Testimony, xxvi, 9, 10, 12, 14, 49, 52,
    63, 99, 136, 146; false, 14
Theft, xxvii, 26, 27
Thieves, 26, 27, 29–31, 40, 98, 114, 115
Threats, 28
Tolls, 31, 35, 41, 96
Touraine-Anjou, xxii, xxxiv, xxxvi, 15
Treachery, xxx, 12, 25, 26, 37, 58, 70,
    105, 108, 109, 117, 119, 124, 141, 144,
    155, 157, 158
Treasure, buried, 60
Trees (fruit-bearing), 19, 23
Trial, xxiii–xxv, xxvii, xxix, xxx, xxxvii,
    xliii, and passim
Trial, civil, xxiii, xxiv
Truce, 25, 29, 119, 147, 157, 158
Tunis, 3

Usage d'Orlenois, xxvii, xxxvi, xxxviii,
    xl, xli, xliii, 66, 152, 155, 159, 161, 162
Usage de France, 106
Usage de Touraine, 109, 155
Usurers, 59

Vassal, lower lord, xxiii, 22, 26, 29, 31,
    33, 34, 36, 37, 41, 42, 48, 52, 57, 58,
    61, 63, 65, 67, 74, 75, 78, 79, 87, 117,
    137, 142, 147, 148, 152, 154, 155, 157,
    162
Villeinage, xxxii, xxxv

Vines, 19, 23, 25, 71, 90, 100
Viollet, Paul, xxxviii, xxxix–xlii
Virgins, virginity, 17, 18, 37

Wager of battle. See Judicial battle
Wager of law, 35, 48, 67, 81, 96, 100,
    105
War, 36, 37
War, private, xxviii, xxix
Warrantor, xxvii, 16, 17, 61, 62, 95, 96,
    136
Wheat, 72, 73
Widows, xxviii, xxxiv, xxxv, 17, 43
Wife, 15, 17, 20, 21, 37, 39, 76, 77, 79,
    82, 85, 88, 92, 94, 95
Will, 18, 60, 117
Witness, xxiii, xxv, xxvi, xxix, xxxvii,
    8–14, 84, 98, 99, 123, 124, 126, 127,
    144, 146, 158, 161; bias, xxv; chal-
    lenge to, 8, 9, 11, 14; false, 10, 14;
    interrogation of, xxv
Women, xxv, xxviii, xxxi, 16–23, 26–
    27, 35, 37, 41–43, 76, 77, 88, 91, 92,
    94, 97, 98, 107, 142, 145, 149, 151;
    pregnant, 22, 119
Wood (forest), 19, 36
Wounds, 24
Writings, xxv, xxvii, xxxi, xxxviii, 10,
    13, 107, 125, 127
Written law, 8–12, 23, 24, 27–29, 37,
    80, 84, 85, 88, 97, 108, 115, 117, 119–
    122, 125–132, 135, 136, 140, 142, 143,
    146, 150, 151, 153–157, 161